European Monographs in Social Psychology

Explanations, accounts, and illusions

European Monographs in Social Psychology

Executive Editors:
P. RICHARD EISER and KLAUS R. SCHERER
Sponsored by the European Association of Experimental Social Psychology

This series, first published by Academic Press (who will continue to distribute the numbered volumes), appeared under the joint imprint of Cambridge University Press and the Maison des Sciences de l'Homme in 1985 as an amalgamation of the Academic Press series and the European Studies in Social Psychology, published by Cambridge and the Maison in collaboration with the Laboratoire Européen de Psychologie Sociale of the Maison.

The original aims of the two series still very much apply today: to provide a forum for the best European research in different fields of social psychology and to foster the interchange of ideas between different developments and different traditions. The Executive Editors also expect that it will have an important role to play as a European forum for international work.

Other titles in this series:

Unemployment by Peter Kelvin and Joanna E. Jarrett
National characteristics by Dean Peabody
Experiencing emotion by Klaus R. Scherer, Harald G. Wallbott and Angela B. Summerfield
Levels of explanation in social psychology by Willem Doise
Understanding attitudes to the European Community: a social-psychological study in four member states by Miles Hewstone
Arguing and thinking: a rhetorical approach to social psychology by Michael Billig
Non-verbal communication in depression by Heiner Ellgring
Social representation of intelligence by Gabriel Mugny and Felice Carugati
Speech and reasoning in everyday life by Uli Windisch
Account episodes. The management or escalation of conflict by Peter Schönbach
The ecology of the self: relocation and self-concept change by Stefan E. Hormuth
Situation cognition and coherence in personality: An individual-centred approach by Barbara Krahé

SUPPLEMENTARY VOLUMES

Talking politics: a psychological framing for views from youth in Britain by Kum-Kum Bhavnani

Explanations, accounts, and illusions

A critical analysis

John McClure
Department of Psychology, Victoria University of Wellington

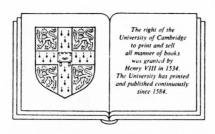

The right of the
University of Cambridge
to print and sell
all manner of books
was granted by
Henry VIII in 1534.
The University has printed
and published continuously
since 1584.

CAMBRIDGE UNIVERSITY PRESS
Cambridge
New York   Port Chester
Melbourne   Sydney

EDITIONS DE LA MAISON DES SCIENCES DE L'HOMME
Paris

Published by the Press Syndicate of the University of Cambridge
The Pitt Building, Trumpington Street, Cambridge CB2 1RP
40 West 20th Street, New York, NY 10011, USA
10 Stamford Road, Oakleigh, Melbourne 3166, Australia
and Editions de la Maison des Sciences de l'Homme
54 Boulevard Raspail, 75270 Paris Cedex 06

First published 1991

British Library cataloguing in publication data
McClure, John
Explanations, accounts, and illusions: a critical
analysis. – (European monographs in social psychology).
1. Man. Social behaviour. Explanation. Psychological
aspects
I. Title   II. Series
302.

Library of Congress cataloguing in publication data applied for

ISBN 0 521 38532 6 hardback
ISBN 27351 0386 2 hardback (France only)

Transferred to digital printing 2002

Contents

      The information-processing versus motivation dispute   102
      Illusory attributions and locus of control   105
      Misattribution therapy   112
      Helplessness: taught and sometimes learned   113
      The shaping of intention   121
      Seeing through illusions   122

8   **Phenomenological, cognitive, and linguistic therapies**   124
      Phenomenological paradigms   124
      Cognitive and linguistic therapies   131
      Social cognition and psychopathology   143

9   **Discounting and dialectics: contradictions in explanations**   144
      The discounting principle   144
      Research on discounting   146
      Extremity and moderation   149
      Models and analogies: from science to magic   157
      The economy of discounting   163

10 **Conclusion**   164

      References   167
      Index of names   183
      Index of subjects   187

Acknowledgements

Some of the material in this book is adapted from previously published articles. Chapter 4 includes material adapted from the article 'Telling more than we can know: the positivist analysis of verbal reports and mental processes', published in the *Journal for the Theory of Social Behaviour* in 1983, by Basil Blackwell; chapter 5 includes material adapted from the article 'On necessity and commonsense: A discussion of central axioms in new approaches to lay explanation', published in the *European Journal of Social Psychology* in 1984, by Wiley; chapter 6 includes material adapted from the same article, and material adapted from 'Explanations, discourse, and attributions: a response to Michael', published in *New Ideas in Psychology* in 1989, by Pergamon Press; chapter 7 includes material adapted from 'The social parameter of "learned" helplessness: its recognition and implications', published in the *Journal of Personality and Social Psychology* in 1985, by the American Psychological Association.

I am very grateful to Dick Eiser for his help and encouragement in completing the book and to Marion Smith for her ready editorial assistance to me from the other end of the earth. I especially wish to thank colleagues and friends who have read and commented on sections of the book in the present or some earlier form. These include Bob Abelson, Garth Fletcher, Denis Hilton, the late Jos Jaspars, Barry Kirkwood, Mansur Lalljee, Diane Mackie, and Jonathan Potter. I also wish to thank Mick Billig and Ed Sampson for their encouragement of my interests and inquiry. Finally, I am most grateful to Jenny McClure for her generous support and her many valuable comments on the manuscript.

1 Introduction

Explanations for behaviour

Recent years have seen substantial claims emerging in the field of social cognition. First and foremost, claims are made concerning people's understanding of their mental processes and their actions. Nisbett and Wilson (1977) conclude in a classic paper on this issue that 'one has no more certain knowledge of the workings of one's own mind than would an outsider with intimate knowledge of one's history and of the stimuli present at the time the cognitive process occurred' (p. 257). This claim implies a significant discovery: the finding that people do not know the workings of their own minds. And does this assertion reflect an empirical finding, or is it merely opinion? The authors claim that it is an empirical finding, certified by evidence: 'The evidence indicates it may be quite misleading for social scientists to ask their subjects about the influences on their evaluations, choices or behaviour. The relevant research indicates that such reports, as well as predictions, may have little value except for whatever utility they may have in the study of verbal explanations per se' (p. 247). Scientific investigations, according to this view, show that people's explanations of their actions have little value for understanding their behaviour (Wilson, 1985).

In these and similar assertions, researchers in social cognition claim to have solved major questions about human consciousness and action. The most notable thinkers of Western philosophy and psychology have wrangled and are wrangling still with the issues of consciousness, explanations of behaviour and, in particular, self-explanations (e.g., Davidson, 1963; MacIntyre, 1971; C. Taylor, 1964). Many of the claims in social psychology favour schools of thought which explain mental processes and action in deterministic terms, and place a low value on introspection and the role of intention in action. The field of social cognition, in which these claims are made, is riding on the crest of psychology's cognitive wave (Carroll and Payne, 1976), and is at the forefront of developments in mainstream social psychology.

There have been critical reactions to the sorts of claims cited above. The

1

assertion that people lack any special access to the causes of their actions is strongly criticized by authors who argue for a phenomenological view of human action as purposive and intentional (e.g., Buss, 1978; deCharms, 1968; Locke and Pennington, 1982; Shotter, 1981a, b, 1984). In countering the claims made in social cognition, this alternative position is frequently argued in axiomatic or conceptual terms. DeCharms and Shea's (1976) and Shotter's (1984) case for intention rests heavily on re-labelling people 'Persons' and behaviour 'actions'. In their theory of self-explanations, deCharms and Shea write that 'The new approach is based on the concept of a Person as an agent in the world', and that 'the distinguishing characteristic of an action is that it is done by a *Person* who has an Intention' (p. 259). Buss (1978) also attempts at one point to save intentions from dissolution at the hands of science by his use of particular definitions. He contests claims that people's self-explanations are valueless on the basis of the distinction between reasons and causes. People never give causes for their own behaviour, he suggests, but only reasons. Research in social cognition only explains people's reference to causes, and therefore does not explain the giving of reasons. Similar arguments are posed by Shotter (1981a, b, 1984) and Locke and Pennington (1982).

Whatever their validity and significance, these arguments tend to carry the issue back to philosophy. In challenging the claim that research shows that introspective access does not assist self-explanation, critics arguing for a more phenomenological perspective have not provided a close examination of the evidence and inferences that underlie the argument. These critics frequently do not tackle the argument on empirical territory, although there are interesting exceptions (e.g., Gergen, 1980, 1982). Empirical counter-arguments, however, are provided by authors who consider the issue in terms of models and research in cognitive psychology, rather than from a specifically phenomenological stance (Bargh, 1984; Ericsson and Simon, 1980; Gavanski and Hoffman, 1987; Morris, 1981). In this book, an attempt is made to discuss the research and theory on these issues in both conceptual and empirical terms. In addition to discussing the more polarized positivist and phenomenological views on the issues, and various positions between these extremes, the argument considers and advocates a critical perspective which takes into account both intentional and deterministic factors in people's action and cognition. The discussion also examines several recent developments in social cognition relating to cognition and self-explanation, particularly the concepts of self-schemata, person memory and action identification. Equal consideration is given to recent developments in alternative paradigms, in particular discourse analysis.

Cognitive distortions and illusions

Research in social cognition connects with broader concerns in the human sciences on a second issue, the source of people's cognitive biases and illusions about their behaviour. The illusory nature of cognitions and self-perceptions is also a central concern of critical theories, which are concerned with explaining the illusions and ideologies which they consider to characterize and inhibit much human thinking (Billig, 1982; Habermas, 1970; Sampson, 1983). Researchers in social cognition claim to explain cognitive and perceptual illusions and to do so in terms of non-motivational factors, such as errors in information-processing (e.g. Nisbett and Ross, 1980). The discussion here reviews research in social cognition dealing with illusions and self-misattributions, and suggests that certain cases of illusions may be interpreted in terms of a critical perspective that takes account of both motivational and contextual factors.

The issue of illusions and cognitive biases leads into abnormal and clinical psychology. It is often claimed that attributions and related cognitions play a significant part in several major disorders and in therapeutic change. Research on locus of control focuses on the effect of people's perceptions of uncontrollable causes for their actions and outcomes, and several authors link attributions to the occurrence of depression and helplessness (e.g., Abramson, Seligman and Teasdale, 1978). Other clinicians have manipulated attributions as a form of therapy for anxiety disorders. Laing (1961/1971) claimed that the internalization of interpersonal attributions is a factor in the etiology of schizophrenia. These applications have frequently been couched in terms of either behavioural (or positivist) models, in the case of locus of control, helplessness and misattribution therapy, or phenomenological models, in the case of Laing's account of schizophrenia. The behavioural accounts emphasize deterministic causes while the phenomenological models argue for an intentional dimension to people's actions and perceptions in this context. The discussion here attempts to achieve a degree of synthesis of key aspects of these two approaches in terms of a perspective that incorporates cognitive, motivational and social factors. It is suggested that this approach has valuable implications for therapy that are largely precluded by the assumptions of the alternative approaches. The discussion links these ideas to therapies that focus on cognitive and linguistic processes relating to psychopathology and therapeutic change.

The book proceeds according to the following plan. Chapter 2 outlines the main features of three dominant paradigms in the explanation of behaviour: these are referred to as the positivist, phenomenological and critical approaches. Each paradigm provides an account of intentions, reasons, causes and self-perceptions. It is argued in this chapter that positivist explanations fail to capture important aspects of cognition and action relating to intention, but that phenomenological stances commit the opposite fallacy of treating people's behaviour as wholly intentional, and self-awareness as necessarily accurate. The chapter argues for a more sceptical stance to self-knowledge, as espoused by critical explanations. The chapter serves as a reference point for the basic axioms of these three approaches that emerge in several parts of the book.

Following the argument supporting a critical perspective in chapter 2, chapter 3 describes critical accounts of illusory perceptions, particularly the issue of how those perceptions are induced and how they are eliminated. Starting from Fromm's (1970) synthesis of common features of ideological and psychodynamic accounts of illusions, the discussion then reviews changes in critical theories made by the Frankfurt School. The discussion then moves to Habermas's (e.g., 1970) linguistic formulation of cognitive distortions, and his discussion of the interests underlying different forms of scientific inquiry. This section is followed by specific examples of contemporary critical perspectives in social psychology, focusing particularly on ideology (e.g., Broughton, 1986), intergroup relations (Billig, 1976) and theories of justice and equity (Sampson, 1975, 1983).

Chapters 4, 5 and 6 deal with theories and research focusing on self-perception and explanations of actions. The chapters focus both on models in social cognition and on theories drawing on alternative theoretical roots. These theories include models which arrive at similar conclusions to the corresponding viewpoints in general psychological theory (chapter 2). But the conclusions are reached, at least apparently, on the basis of empirical research. This evidence and the inferences that researchers make are examined in some detail. Chapter 4 discusses the way in which action, cognition and self-awareness are dealt with by contemporary models in social cognition. The chapter begins with D. J. Bem's (1972) and Nisbett and Wilson's (1977) argument in favour of a fairly positivist stance, and proceeds to discussions of self-schemata, person memory, and Vallacher and Wegner's (e.g., 1987) theory of action identification. Chapter 5 reviews the way in which the same issues are dealt with in alternative paradigms such as phenomenology and hermeneutics (e.g., Gergen, 1982; Shotter, 1984). Chapter 6 examines arguments favouring models that capture the functional nature of explanations, especially self-presentational factors, and various functions that characterize common discourse (Michael, 1989; Potter and Wetherell, 1987).

Chapters 7 and 8 broaden the discussion to applications in abnormal psychology, and show how the issues and assumptions seen in social cognition apply to the abnormal domain. These chapters clarify the practical significance to many observations made in earlier chapters. Chapter 7 deals particularly with cognitive biases in relation to attribution, locus of control, attribution therapy and most extensively, learned helplessness. Chapter 8 first examines Laing's and Rogers' phenomenological accounts of psychopathology and therapy. It then considers cognitive models that focus on the beliefs and thinking of the client (e.g., Meichenbaum, 1977) and linguistic therapies that focus on the discourse on the client and therapist (e.g., Labov and Fanshel, 1977).

Chapter 9 turns to theory and research dealing with conflict and contradictions in cognitions, focusing particularly on the concept of discounting. Whereas discounting notions suggest that people discount alternative or contradictory explanations, other concepts, such as dialectical models, suggest that people's cognition may incorporate opposing causal forces that reflect opposing causes in the external world. The discussion deals with a number of theoretical perspectives and analogies that could replace the analogy between people's thinking and scientific inference.

The various themes in the book are drawn together in the conclusion (chapter 10), providing a basis for future research and theory.

2 Paradigms of explanation

The previous chapter cited claims that research in social psychology resolves important issues concerning the significance of consciousness and people's explanation of their actions. This chapter provides some background to these issues. The chapter defines the disputed issues concerning explanations of behaviour, and outlines major theories dealing with these issues. This survey is shaped around three paradigms which have been dominant in the explanation of cognition and behaviour: the positivist, phenomenological and critical. Each of these paradigms articulates a particular theory of the causes of behaviour, and employs methods of explanation that reflect that theory. In psychological theory there are, of course, many shades of opinion that fall somewhere in between these three positions. But the point of this chapter is to present the major contrasting stances, and to give a clear picture of the different ways the central questions are tackled.

In social psychology, conclusions about these issues are ascribed to experimental evidence (an ascription evaluated in later chapters), but arguments concerning these three stances in general psychology draw on many different factors, including metaphysical assumptions as well as empirical developments. This chapter evaluates these various assumptions and findings. By clarifying the major assumptions, arguments and methodological issues that characterize the main approaches, the chapter also serves as a form of reference point for later chapters. Many of the issues dealt with in this chapter recur where the same issues are dealt with in social cognition and applied contexts. This review begins with the positivist approach which has exercised a particularly strong influence in psychology.

Positivist explanations

Descartes's (1596–1650) systematization of the interests and categories of philosophy, which then included psychology, articulated a dualism of being and knowledge, ontology and epistemology, causality and method. Humans, wrote Descartes, are made up of two fundamentally different kinds of substance. The body is extended or spatial substance and, as a material object, functions as a machine. Animals, and a small number of human behaviours which were later called reflexes, are also automata, and operate in response to deterministic forces. By contrast, the soul and mind are a form of unextended or non-spatial substance, and operate at the enterprise of the will.

The advance of causal explanations

Descartes's demarcation of these categories was followed by repeated attempts either to expand the domain of spatial substance to include all human behaviour, or on the other hand to differentiate humanity from beast and machine, thereby preserving the will and intention. The drift of most British, French, and later Russian and American philosophy has entailed the consuming of intention with material substance and mechanical explanation. This development can be portrayed in terms of the four types of cause that make up explanations: material causes (physical substance or matter), efficient causes ('mechanical' propulsion), formal causes (structure or pattern in substance) and final causes (teleological or purposive propulsion) (see e.g., Rychlak, 1968). In the seventeenth century Bacon proposed that all events were explicable in terms of material and efficient causes, and that science must only include concepts from those two categories of cause (Rychlak, 1977). This injunction was accepted by the British empiricists and associationists, who applied it to the realm of psychology.

The compass of Locke's (1632–1704) analysis spatialized consciousness so that it was seen as a conglomerate of associated elements. The mind can be analysed, Locke wrote, into discrete items or units known then as ideas. The structure of a person's mind derives from the way these ideas are associated by their simultaneous or successive occurrence. This spatialized and mechanized conception of mind was harnessed to an empiricist epistemology. The contents of the mind, by this account, arrive not from internal sources, but rather from the environment. Introspection, then, reveals material that derives from people's sensory impressions of their environment.

In the following century, Hume (1711–76) was to argue that there can be no sensations of an abstract object or intangible substance, thus removing the grounds underlying Descartes's distinction between extended and unextended substance. This argument enabled Hume to carry empiricist and associationist ideas to the kernel of Descartes's voluntarism, the consciousness of self. In Hume's account, one's consciousness of self derives from sense impressions of oneself, that is, from perceptions of oneself doing something. Intention is thus displaced by self-perception. The empiricist epistemology of this 'physical of the mental' (Neu, 1977) entailed that introspection revealed, not intentions or thoughts, but a scene rather like a bucketful of reflecting glass which the environment filled up while passing.

In France, Descartes's homeland, the modification of Descartes's heritage was to take a different form. In fact Descartes himself, even while defending the idea of non-extended substance, had by his demarcation of categories and choice of terminology set the tone for a materialistic and spatialized model of psychology. Examples are his reference to the mental dimension as a kind of 'substance', and his locating the meeting-point of soul and body at the pineal gland. So, unlike the British, whose associationism spatialized and mechanized mind but nonetheless retained a mental analysis, the French turned mind into matter. La Mettrie (1709–50), when ill with fever, became aware that his mental capacities were affected by the fever as much as his body. He inferred that thought must be the result of the mechanical action of the brain and nervous system (Neu, 1977). Subsequently, La Mettrie formed a mechanistic account of mind and a materialistic philosophy. The study of mind, he said, was to be a natural science. The new metaphysic acquired a kind of authoritative symbolic status after the French Revolution, when the new religion of nature occupied French cathedrals, usurping supernature.

This alliance of materialist and naturalist philosophy in France obtained a systematic formulation in Comte's (1798–1867) work. Writing in the light or perhaps the shadows of the triumphs of natural science, Comte called for the application of the same type of science to the study of humans. Linking the history of science to an hierarchy of disciplines extending from physics to sociology, he argued that the scientific spirit had been gradually applied through this hierarchy and was slowly approaching those disciplines studying humanity. Comte's historical analysis portrayed a progression from the theological through the metaphysical to the positive spirit, a development accompanied by the retraction of explanations in final causes, such as intentions. In applying the spanners of Newtonian mechanics to Descartes's intentional realm, Comte's positivism specified two methodological requirements. He postulated, first, that science uses extraspective observations, such as observations of behaviour, and that introspection is not acceptable. His second stipulation was that science is built entirely on observations or facts (Giddens, 1976).

The combined influence of Comte's positivism and Darwin's evolutionary account underlay the emergence of the theory that consciousness is epiphenomenal. Spencer and Huxley argued that humans are conscious automata and that consciousness is no more than the heat given off the wires (Jaynes, 1976). Positivism and the new religion of nature reached a zenith in the 1920s, when the self-ordained theocracy of the Vienna Circle set about replacing all metaphysics of the past with the first systematic metaphysic for science. This company of scholars in Vienna was bound together in a common enterprise: a scientific philosophy entailing the abolition of metaphysics (Stevens, 1939). The declaration by the Circle which is most relevant to the issues considered here was the injunction that the language of physics must be used in all sciences. The human sciences are seen as an extension of physics; Carnap (1937) stipulated that psychology is a branch of physics.

Similar conclusions or premises were being voiced in the context of psychological research. Russian psychology operationalized the French materialism in Pavlov's paradigm of conditioned reflexes and Bechterev's call for objectivism. Wundt's element-seeking introspection, problematic enough in his homeland Germany, was a most unfitting garment to button around America's pragmatism. In 1913 Watson declared America's independence in a new identity, behaviourism: 'Psychology as the behaviourist views it is a purely objective branch of natural science' (Watson, 1913, p. 158).

Behaviourism emerged as the primary vehicle for a positivist psychology. Later Skinner (1938) was to differentiate Watson's model of 'classical' conditioning from operant learning. In the latter framework, a behaviour is emitted, rather than elicited, and its re-occurrence is determined by its consequences. Operant models proved a more powerful form of behaviourism for explaining a range of human behaviour. In Skinner's account, all human behaviour is determined: 'As a determinist, I must assume that the organism is simply mediating the relationships between the forces acting upon it and its own output, and these are the kinds of relationships I'm anxious to formulate' (cited in Evans, 1968, p. 23). Skinner argues that intentions and the experience of purpose are a by-product, or description, of contingencies:

> In human behaviour, a 'felt intention' or 'sense of purpose' which precedes behaviour is sometimes proposed as a current surrogate for future events...But men behave because of operant reinforcement even though they cannot 'state their purpose' – and when they can, they may simply be describing their behaviour and the contingencies responsible for its strength. Self-knowledge is at best a by-product of contingencies; it is not a cause of the behaviour generated by them. Even if we could discover a spider's felt intention or sense of purpose, we could not offer it as a cause of the behaviour.
>
> (Skinner, 1969, pp. 193–4)

Skinner applies the same interpretation to people's self-explanations or reasons for their behaviour. Reasons, like intentions, are descriptions of contingencies or the consequences of behaviour:

> We often speak of the consequences of behaviour as *reasons*. We cite them in explaining our own behaviour: 'the reason I went to the bank was to get some money'. The term seems more suitable than cause, especially if we have not fully understood the process of selection,

because anything which follows behaviour does not seem to be in the
right place to be the cause of it. Nevertheless a reason which lies in the
future is no more effective than any other future event...The
consequences described or implied in advice, instructions, and laws are
reasons why a person takes advice, heeds warnings, follows instructions
and obeys laws.

(Skinner, 1974, p. 142)

Skinner's ideas here account for people's reasons and, in the previous
passage, intentions, in terms of a fully behavioural framework. It is fairly
clear from earlier pages, however, that Skinner has a substantial ancestry.
The developments described in this section have all contributed towards, or
articulated, an attempt to eliminate the teleological realm of Descartes's
dualism. Nonetheless, strong criticisms have been offered of this viewpoint.

Criticisms of causal accounts

Criticisms of the positivist stance focus particularly on two aspects of the
argument. A first issue is the attempt to reduce the two constituents of
Descartes's dualism (extended and unextended substance) into the one
component, extended substance, or matter. This reduction is tied in with the
idea that scientists must use efficient cause (mechanical) explanations, a
physicalist language, and extraspective observations (the observation of
behaviour). Subsequent references to the positivist position connote these
features. The degree of success of the translations and reductions from
dualism to this monistic psychology is one indication of the success of the
positivist account. A second aspect to be considered concerns the degree to
which the positivist thesis has been a methodological and theoretical, rather
than empirical, exercise.

As an example of reductions of intentional phenomena into efficient
causes, Skinner construes intentions as the consequences of behaviour, and
elsewhere as a description of contingencies. Chomsky (1959) and Giddens
(1977) have pointed out that this sort of translation fails to deal with
phenomena like unfulfilled intentions. For example, a person may intend to
do something but not initiate any course of action to carry out that
intention. Conversely, an intended effect may be realized by a course of
events which is independent of the person's behaviour. Thirdly, as Giddens
(1977) notes, a course of action undertaken with certain intentions may
have outcomes quite different from those intended or anticipated by the
person involved. All these events suggest that intentions cannot be equated
with behaviour or its consequences.

The positivist paradigm attempts to achieve a deterministic account by
the argument that consciousness is epiphenomenal, a mere reflection of the
real events that are occurring. A problem with this position is that it fails to

explain the wide range of relationships between consciousness and behaviour that are distinguished by cognitive psychologists. Schneider and Shiffrin (1977) cite a range of evidence indicating that certain behaviours occur with no conscious accompaniment while others are concomitant with an active awareness. Jaynes (1976) raises a similar question: 'If consciousness is the mere impotent shadow of action, why is it more intense when action is most hesitant? And why are we least conscious when doing something most habitual? Certainly this seesawing relationship between consciousness and actions is something that any theory of consciousness must explain' (p. 11). Clearly the idea of consciousness as an epiphenomenon is inadequate for these relationships between consciousness and actions.

A related difficulty concerns a paradox in positivist explanations which suggests the theory is unable to adhere to either its own requirements or its human subject-matter. Positivist accounts stipulate the mechanistic determination of behaviour as a fundamental tenet. In terms of such teleological concepts as intentions and purpose, people have no choice. Yet such a fatalistic conclusion is accompanied by calls for all manner of intervention in human behaviour and society (e.g., Skinner, 1971). The exhortations to adopt the new world view are expressed in terms of persuasion and argument, tactics of the old intentional world view, rather than through reinforcement and punishment. There is a problematic tension here. If behaviour is determined then people are indeed mere spectators. The conclusion that life is absurd, espoused by certain philosophers, is a more logical reaction to the doctrine of determinism, as is the Eastern world's propensity to non-intervention. It is reasonable to conclude that the positivist attempt to translate human behaviour and experience into the terms of determinism, physicalism and extraspection has not been fully successful. The translation fails to account for several classes of phenomena and results in contradictions and new dualisms in the place of old dualisms.

These criticisms relate very much to the practicality of the theory if applied consistently. Other criticisms can be made, however, of positivism's assumptions and metaphysics. Two central stipulations of these theories are that science and psychology must employ extraspection rather than introspection (to achieve objectivity), and that psychology must explain behaviour in terms of efficient (mechanical) causes. In fact, both of those stipulations have an arbitrary or inaccurate basis. No criterion of objectivity has withstood criticism. An early criterion of objectivity was Mach's conception of immediate perceptions or sensations (Boring, 1950). The Vienna Circle realized the subjectivity or 'psychologism' of such a criterion, and substituted operational definitions, wherein the meaning of a term is determined by a corresponding set of operations (Stevens, 1939). This criterion entailed an infinite regress of definitions, and it was quickly realized that Popper's (1959) subsequent criterion of basic or 'protocol' statements was equally unsatisfactory, in that any statement might be questioned by future research. Thus no criterion was established for an unquestionable perception or assertion.

Subsequent writings of Hanson (1958), Kuhn (1970), Polanyi (1964), and Feyerabend (1965) exposed more of the subjectivity of facts. Studies in the history of science, combined with developments in knowledge of perception, suggested that theories are underdetermined by facts and that no atheoretical observations occurred or were even possible. The implication of subjectivity in extraspective observations dissolved the longstanding partnership of extraspection and objectivity. When positivism in science at large has lost the battle for objectivity in extraspective observation, it becomes increasingly unsatisfactory for psychology to retain a pseudo-objectivism by insisting on the extraspective method. It also becomes clear that this insistence is based on a preferred metaphysic, rather than some unquestionable basis or truth.

In similar fashion, it is increasingly clear that the requirement that all explanations must employ (mechanical) efficient causes rather than (purposive) final causes, derives from a metaphysical rather than empirical imperative. The deterministic model of causality is interwoven with theoretical conceptions from a Baconian philosophy and a Newtonian physics. When other paradigms in physics like quantum mechanics (and Heisenberg's indeterminacy principle) do not stipulate such determinism (Heisenberg, 1971), the insistence on its necessity in psychology is seen to be a matter of belief or preference.

These subjective commitments undercut the positivist aspiration to represent a non-metaphysical stance. Yet evidence of other arbitrary choices reveals a metaphysic underlying the supposedly procedural concerns and definitions of positivism. Examples are the Vienna Circle's choice of physicalism as the language of science and verification as the method of science for establishing truth. In some ways, in fact, the positivist account is a highly metaphysical approach; it tends to be prescriptive and programmatic rather than descriptive or empirical. It is true, as positivists claim, that the projection of purpose on to nature in animistic beliefs derived from a particular metaphysic or world view. But it is clear that the prescription of efficient causes, which introjects the presumed mechanics of natural phenomena into humanity, is no less a metaphysical stance.

Similarly, behaviourism's expulsion of consciousness was achieved not by some experiment deciding between paradigms, but by announcement and procedure. As Jaynes (1976) observes of the emergence of behaviourism:

The single inherent reason for its success was not its truth, but its program...Off the printed page, behaviourism was only a refusal to talk about consciousness. Nobody really believed he was not conscious. And there was a very real hypocrisy abroad, as those interested in its problems were forcibly excluded from academic psychology, as text after text tried to smother the unwanted problem from student view. In essence behaviourism was a method, not the theory that it tried to be.

(pp. 15–16)

It was noted earlier that the new allegiance to behaviourism was partially prompted by the fruitlessness of Wundt's introspective method, particularly as a channel for American concerns. But the rejection of the study of consciousness on the basis of a poor methodology in 1913 does not justify its continued rejection many decades later when completely different, and more fruitful, methods are employed. It would be paradoxical if behaviourism cannot learn.

Since Descartes's dualistic demarcation of the issues concerning philosophy and science, most writers have moved in one of two directions in defining explanations of behaviour and an appropriate observational methodology. The positivist account locates the bedrock in efficient causes and extraspective observations. It has been argued that this approach fails to account satisfactorily for a number of phenomena and that it employs arbitrary and at times unjustified metaphysical assumptions. While positivism laid claim to one of Descartes's two worlds, phenomenology inhabited the other.

Phenomenological explanations

Descartes divided human being into two domains. Extended substance, or matter, was propelled by a mechanistic causality, while unextended substance consisted of the mind, soul, intentions and will. Descartes argued that most human action was the product of free choice. In subsequent developments the associationist and materialist schools encroached on this domain. This advance, however, was and is strongly opposed by critics, especially those espousing a phenomenological perspective.

Actions in intentional terms

It was in response to the associationists' assault on the will, and particularly Hume's erasure of the self, that Kant (1720–1804) wrote his defence of human freedom and choice. Kant argued that a noumenal ego transcends phenomenal knowledge and material causation. His argument articulated a belief in human freedom: 'Freedom must be presupposed as a property of the will of all rational beings' (Kant, 1785/1964, p. 99). Subsequently Maine de Biran (1766–1824) expressed Kant's argument in psychological form. He argued:

> I appeal to the inner sense of each man, in the state of wakefulness and consciousness…to determine whether he is or is not aware of his effort, which is the actual cause of a particular movement that he initiates, suspends, arrests or continues as he wishes and because he wishes; and whether he makes a clear distinction between this movement and another which he senses or perceives in certain cases as being affected effortlessly or against his will – for example, the convulsive movements of habit.
>
> (Maine de Biran, 1804, cited in Bréhier, 1968, p. 84)

With this appeal to introspective proof, de Biran upheld voluntary action. Kierkegaard (1813–55) defended a similar position only a little later. As Kant's argument emerged in response to Hume, so Kierkegaard's conception of existentialism was a response to Hegel's transfer of purpose from the individual ego to a universal consciousness which acts out history. Kierkegaard reasserted individual agency, claiming that the most important human faculty is the choice of freedom. He claimed that freedom of choice is the most basic of values, and that this capacity for choice is the characteristic that makes someone a human being or, in existential terms, an existent individual (Solomon, 1972). Kierkegaard's thinking was to be reiterated by existentialists in this century. Heidegger, the central figure in this school, claimed that a person's 'being in the world' (*Dasein*) entails inescapable alternatives and choices.

Clearly a purposive conception of human action has retained its defenders. The development of methods that might be appropriate for an intentional model of action has been the preoccupation of the phenomenological and hermeneutic school. The hermeneutic branch of social theory holds that 'to understand a human act [is] to grasp the meaning with which the actor's intention invested it' (Bauman, 1978). Bauman outlined the requirements for a programme of understanding intentional behaviour. In human affairs, he writes:

> The presence of design and objectives is unquestionable. Men and women do what they do on purpose. Social phenomena, since they are ultimately acts of men and women, demand to be understood in a different way than by mere explaining. Understanding them must contain an element missing from the explaining of natural phenomena: the retrieval of purpose, of intention, of the unique configuration of thoughts and feelings which preceded a social phenomenon and found its only manifestation, imperfect and incomplete, in the observable consequences of action. To understand a human act, therefore, was to grasp the meaning with which the actor's intention invested it.
>
> (p. 12)

On an individual level this programme was undertaken by phenomenology. Husserl replaced both the extraspective method and Wundt's analytic introspection with the phenomenological method. This type of self-reflection is supposed to provide a description of conscious content that is free of any explanatory or philosophical presuppositions. The phenomenological method proved a more productive form of introspection than Wundt's elementistic method, but it has at least one significant limitation. It lacks a basis for explanations shared by social groups and so fails to capture a shared or intersubjective consciousness. To deal with meanings at this level, alternative methods are required. Dilthey (1853–1911) proposed methods that would grasp the meanings of societies other than one's own. He argued that the understanding of human action required a completely different form of explanation from that of the natural sciences. The human sciences should not employ an extraspective method and deterministic explanations (*Erklaren*), but *Verstehen*, the comprehension of actions in terms of their meaning to the actors performing them (Bauman, 1978). This insight was to be achieved through an empathic re-enactment or re-living of the experience of the group or society being studied. Dilthey insisted that this method could be objective, but did not develop a satisfactory argument that could validate this claim. Furthermore the method, while designed for social analysis, was still individualistic in that it provided no medium for intersubjectivity.

The possibility of establishing any such medium did not arise until the recent emergence of hermeneutic phenomenology. This school, whose most prominent advocate is Gadamer (1975), invokes language as the medium of an intersubjective understanding of actions and meanings. Gadamer proposes that people live and interact through language, and that to understand a language is to understand the society which the language articulates. Language, in this analysis, is not specifically a psychological phenomenon but is the public medium of human societies. This account has much in common with the Wittgensteinian school of Anglo-Saxon philosophy. In his *Philosophical investigations* (1968), Wittgenstein proposed that the flow and form of life is expressed in language; the comprehension and explanation of actions is achieved through a knowledge of the rules represented and expressed in language. Gadamer and the Wittgensteinian school proposed that language is more than a system of descriptions, and is the primary medium through which social life is carried on. Both schools believed that 'language is a medium of doing things through communication with others' (Giddens, 1977, p. 139).

Winch's (1958) writing applies these ideas to the human sciences. He proposes that 'language games' express a society's form of life, its interactions and hierarchies. Winch's precepts are developed in Harré's

(1974) proposals for social psychology. Harré and Secord (1972) link their analysis to ideas in hermeneutic phenomenology: 'We shall find the source of our model in contemporary ideas about the nature of a person which are rooted in the way that concept functions in the grammar of our language, and in the forms and systems of our commonest thoughts' (p. 87). They link human language with an anthropomorphic view of humans, and suggest that the human sciences should 'for scientific purposes, treat people as if they were human beings' (p. 84). The uniqueness of the human species is emphasized: 'We believe that a human being is a system of a different order of complexity from any other existing system, natural or artificial' (p. 87).

In this context Harré and Secord outline a paradigm of the causation and explanation of behaviour. It is argued that people generally understand the causes of their own behaviour: 'Agents must know what they are about to do, what they are doing, and what they have done, in the sense of being capable of giving the appropriate commentary' (p. 86). In an overview of their theory, they argue that because people largely understand themselves, their account of their actions is the primary source of an understanding of those actions:

> The account we have developed so far depends a good deal upon a
> person's understanding and analysis of his *own* modes of action. Every
> person knows he is a conscious self-monitoring organism. That is our
> view of ourselves. But will it do as a view of others? Many psychologists
> have supposed that it would not do for that purpose. We believe that
> their doubts about the anthropomorphic model of man really stem from a
> skepticism about the reports that other people give on the genesis and
> meaning of their actions. This skepticism seems to derive from some bad
> philosophical arguments of the past, which have filtered through to the
> practising psychologists ... We propose to redress this state of affairs by a
> short development of the main lines of refutation of this argument to
> reestablish once again the 'open souls' doctrine, and to allow a man
> once more to be taken seriously as a commentator on his actions, and as
> the main contributor to their understanding.
>
> (p. 105)

Harré and his colleagues sometimes make statements which appear to contradict or qualify this strong stance. These variations in the account are seen as 'subtleties' by sympathetic commentators (e.g., Potter and Wetherell, 1987, p. 177), but could be seen as contradictions, or as a lack of parsimony, from a less sympathetic viewpoint. In many respects, Harré and Secord's proposals for social psychology are matched on many points by Rogers' theory of personality. Rogers makes no claim to have resolved Cartesian dualisms, and he maintains some of the tension between the deterministic and the teleological realms. Nevertheless, the emphasis is on an account wherein people choose and determine their own behaviour.

Rogers argues that behaviour, when it is examined scientifically, is indeed best understood as determined by prior causation. But he holds that responsible personal choice is the most essential element in being a person, and precedes any scientific endeavour. He stipulates: 'Man lives essentially in his own personal and subjective world, and even his most objective functioning in science, mathematics and the like, is the result of subjective purpose and subjective choice' (Rogers, 1959, p. 191).

Because actions are the result of a person's purpose and choice, only that person has an adequate knowledge or understanding of those actions: 'Evaluation by others is not a guide for me... only one person can know whether what I am doing is honest, thorough, open and sound, or false and defensive and unsound, and I am that person' (Rogers, 1961, p. 27). Accordingly, Rogers concludes, like Harré and Secord, that 'the best vantage point for understanding behaviour is from the internal frame of reference of the individual himself' (Rogers, 1951, p. 494). As the individual's internal frame of reference is the best vantage-point for understanding behaviour, that behaviour will be best explained by the person's reasons for that behaviour. Harré and Secord, proposing that people be taken seriously as commentators on their actions and as the main contributors to the understanding of such actions, hold that 'In many contexts, a man's action is adequately explained by reference to his reasons for doing it' (Harré and Secord, 1972, p. 40). Gauld and Shotter (1977) proffer a similar argument (see also Shotter, 1984). In both cases, reasons and self-explanations are upheld as sufficient explanations of behaviour.

In sum, phenomenological positions, in defending the validity of an intentional account, argue that actions including language occur because of and in accordance with intentions or intended meanings of the actor. To understand such language and behaviour, it is necessary and sufficient to understand the intended meaning of the language and obtain the actor's reasons for the behaviour.

The fallibility of self-knowledge

Several objections may be made to the phenomenological position. One objection is that reasons may in themselves be inadequate in some respect. A second difficulty is that actor's reasons may be inadequate to explain some aspect of a behaviour or situation. A final problem is that the hermeneutic and phenomenological methods entail unjustified restraints on both theory and explanations.

A first objection, then, is that reasons and intentional statements may in themselves be inadequate. They may be incoherent, incomprehensible, illogical, or irrational. Habermas (1970) offers an extensive critique of hermeneutic phenomenology on these grounds. He points out that in certain individual or social conditions, communication is systematically distorted. An example is communication that includes alterations from any coherent system of linguistic rules. These alterations may be of an ungrammatical nature, as in sentences which cannot be grammatically transformed. A lack of logical connections may also occur at the semantic level. Habermas cites as instances the use of words with opposite meaning or logically incompatible meanings and the condensation of sentences wherein crucial components are omitted or displaced. Habermas suggests that psychotic communication represents an extreme case of distortion. He also points out that such distortions are not restricted to individuals but may characterize a group or society.

A related difficulty concerns the fact that a person may give one reason for his or her action in one situation and a different and conflicting explanation for the same action in a different situation. These occurrences raise problems for an explanation which is compelled to believe the first reason it hears. Fay and Moon (1977) comment on these various distortions and contradictions in actors' communications and reasons: 'by focusing on the concepts available to the actors involved, we could not explain these phenomena adequately...they are events that require explanations going beyond the self-understanding of the actors involved' (p. 224).

So reasons and intended meanings in language may in themselves be unsatisfactory in some way. A second objection concerns the relationship between reasons and behaviour or between reasons and the context in which the explanation is given. Reasons, accounts and self-explanations may fail to explain certain behaviour or aspects of that behaviour. Much behaviour occurs independently of consciousness. Jaynes (1976) points out that 'we are continually reacting to things in ways that have no phenomenal component in consciousness whatever' (p. 22), and lists numerous activities to which consciousness makes little difference. Schneider and Shiffrin (1977) also point out the large range of tasks which are performed without conscious awareness. Similar qualities apply to language, where people demonstrate a knowledge of grammar yet cannot explain the rules they are applying (e.g., Chomsky, 1965). Fay and Moon (1977) note other categories of behaviour, such as those exhibited in some anxiety disorders, for which the actor either cannot give a coherent explanation or cannot give any explanation at all. Fay and Moon point out that hermeneutic and phenomenological methods fail to explain why certain self-explanations occur more frequently in some environmental conditions than others. This 'bounded' quality of consciousness (Giddens, 1977, p. 87) may also be seen in the consequences of behaviour, rather than the behaviour itself. Unintended consequences of behaviour are not captured in an account restricted to the actor's reasons and intentions. There are several ways, then, in which phenomenological accounts may fail to deal with the relationships between self-explanations and behaviour or the conditions in which actions occur.

This point leads to a further objection. Hermeneutic and phenomenological methods place restraints on permissible explanations of a situation. The methods preclude the possibility that certain self-explanations and reasons may be not merely erroneous but may also function to conceal information or some other aspects of a situation. If researchers accept the reasons of a person or a group for their behaviour, they will not see what is concealed; they are prevented from seeing any mechanisms of repression that operate in a social group or individual. Such an analysis not only prevents the scientist from perceiving phenomena such as repression; it also prevents an explanation of such processes. A purely hermeneutic account, Fay and Moon write, deprives the researcher 'of the means necessary to understand the phenomena, namely, a categorized scheme which allows him to speak about the relevant social order in terms... opposed to that of the participants' (Fay and Moon, 1977, p. 226).

In conditions where the participants' self-explanations conceal, distort, or misrepresent aspects of a situation, this constraint can only be seen as unsatisfactory. Billig (1977) similarly protests that phenomenologists have gone from the unseeing scientism and unfeeling detachment of positivism to an equally blind and unthinking sentimentality. He argues that to accept on principle every person's or group's reasons for their behaviour necessitates surrendering one's own values. As he points out, one cannot, and would not want to, explain phenomena such as Nazism by restricting oneself to the explanations given by adherents of such a movement for its actions.

The evaluation earlier of positivist explanations criticized their insistence on deterministic causes and the exclusive use of extraspection, axioms which entailed the a priori exclusion of all intentional and mental phenomena. The central problem with the phenomenological stance lies with the fact that it has replaced one a priori starting-point with another – human consciousness. Ricoeur (1970) suggests that phenomenology disposed of one illusion in philosophy (objectivism) and replaced it with another: the self-reflective revelation of the subject. As Giddens puts it:

> The quest for unassailable foundations of empirical knowledge is one
> which has occupied Western philosophers since Descartes, and has been
> pursued in modern times by empiricists and phenomenologists alike. Both
> come up with answers that presuppose an essentially passive relation
> between subject and object: in the first case, the bedrock is found in
> sense-experience, in the second, it is found in ideations that are regarded
> as distinct from experience and instead inform it.
>
> (1976, p. 134)

In advocating their more humanist approach, Harré and Secord (1972) proposed that psychology should adopt a model which anthropomorphizes humans. But in designing a model which attributes to humans self-understanding and accurate self-revelation, they have not anthro-pomorphized humans, but deified them. Furthermore, restrictive constraints are imposed by employing phenomenology as a necessary and sufficient means of explaining behaviour.

Positivism attempts to make a sufficient explanation of behaviour from one constituent of Cartesian dualism; phenomenology attempts such an explanation from the other. In each case, the paradigm's premises are its conclusions and its conclusions are its premises. Humans become machines or 'Persons'. Both attempts systematically fail to deal with major classes of phenomena. It would seem that a third form of explanation is required. Ricoeur (1970) suggests that the human sciences require a theory that permits explanations in terms complementary to those of subjects, yet which recognizes that intentions may have significant relationships to behaviour; a theory which includes consciousness as significant but which is not forced to treat it as unassailable; a theory which permits and propels a critique of consciousness. The form of explanation which is most in sympathy with these requirements is the form of explanation used by critical theories (Buss, 1979a, b; Habermas, 1971; Ricoeur, 1970; Sampson, 1983).

Critical explanations

It has been suggested that both the positivist and the phenomenological forms of explanations of human behaviour have crucial deficiencies. It might well be asked at this point what other options there are. Mechanical causality and purpose are the only conceived forms of propelling cause, and introspection and extraspection (the observation of behaviour) are the only known avenues through which to acquire data. What options are there if both of these are inadequate? One possibility is that the two forms of propulsion and the corresponding methods of investigation are com-plementary, and that introspection and extraspection report complementary data. It might also be argued that the inadequacies of each method of investigation are also complementary in some way. This idea suggests that the two explanations and avenues of investigation might be combined, although it does not indicate how this might be done.

Deciphering illusions
One attempt at this combination of introspection and extraspection is contained in critical theories. Critical models of cognition assume, in

agreement with phenomenology, that the perceptions of consciousness are significant and affect behaviour, but they also assume, in contrast with phenomenology, that these perceptions can be false and illusory. As Smart (1976) expresses it, the origins of critical theory 'lie in the critique of appearances' (p. 174). Some statements of critical theory could be read to imply that consciousness is generally or always illusory. However, critical theories postulate illusions only in relation to particular conditions, and they specify ways in which these illusions may be reduced and replaced with more accurate perceptions. Nonetheless, emphasis is often placed on the tenacity of illusory perceptions and on the strength of the changes required if illusions are to be removed.

Hegel initiated this form of inquiry. In his *Phenomenology of mind* (1807), Hegel proposed that the human condition is subject to humanly produced constraints. These constraints exercise distorting pressures which shape people in their evolving self-formation (Connerton, 1976). Later, Nietzsche argued that the awareness and self-explanations of individuals regarding the motives of their behaviour actually constitute distortions and mystifications of their real motivations and desires. Marx and Freud, writing in the same period, developed a similar view of mind and behaviour in the context of the human sciences. They accepted the tenet that the constraints of certain conditions had such an effect that people's explanations of their own behaviour were distorted. Ricoeur writes of this common feature in the theories of Nietzsche, Marx and Freud:

> If we go back to the intention they had in common, we find it in the decision to look upon the whole of consciousness primarily as 'false' consciousness. They thereby take up again, each in a different manner, the problem of the Cartesian stronghold. The philosopher trained in the school of Descartes knows that things are doubtful, that they are not such as they appear; but he does not doubt that consciousness is such as it appears to itself; in consciousness, meaning and consciousness of meaning coincide. Since Marx, Nietzsche and Freud, this too has become doubtful. After the doubt about things, we have started to doubt consciousness.
>
> (1970, p. 33)

In this perspective, people's consciousness concerning their actions or conditions is seen as potentially inaccurate, as an awareness which may be illusory. Freud advised that people should adopt a critique of conscious perception analogous to Kant's critique of empiricist accounts of perception: 'Psychoanalysis warns us not to equate perceptions by means of consciousness with the unconscious mental processes which are their object. Like the physical, the psychical is not necessarily in reality what it appears to be' (Freud, 1915/1956, p. 171). Freud argued that unconscious material is often falsified when it reaches consciousness. He claimed that 'Mental processes are in themselves unconscious and only reach the ego and come under its control through incomplete and untrustworthy perceptions' (Freud, 1917/1957, p. 143). Contemporary developments in critical theories may not share many aspects of Marx and Freud's specific theories, but they do share a similar perspective on consciousness, and examine, for example, the common mechanisms underlying social and individual illusions (e.g., Fromm, 1970). Other authors apply a critical analysis to many specific aspects of psychology and related disciplines (e.g., Buss, 1979a, b; Sampson, 1983). Key examples of these analyses are reviewed in the following chapter.

A model that treats illusory perceptions as characteristic of much of the human condition requires a different method from positivist and phenomenological models. When behaviour is seen as determined by material events, the observer seeks relationships between material events and employs behavioural observations (extraspection). When behaviour is seen as intentionally propelled, the scientist obtains reasons from the actor, a form of introspection. What method should be used to explain consciousness and behaviour when both are considered constrained and distorted? The concept of critique is central for this purpose; criticism involves reflection on a set of distorting constraints. The reflective component of criticism focuses on 'objects of experience whose "objectivity" is called into question' (Connerton, 1976, p. 19).

In the initial critique of Hegel, the process of critical reflection was tied to a spiritualized view of the human condition. By contrast, later writers were to take critical reflection and apply it to analysing concrete situations of human experience. This process begins in the deciphering of falsified consciousness. Ricoeur suggests that 'the distinguishing characteristic of Marx, Freud and Nietzsche is the general hypothesis concerning both the process of false consciousness and the method of deciphering. The two go together since the man of suspicion carries out in reverse the work of falsification of the man of guilt' (Ricoeur, 1970, p. 34). This deciphering requires a science which can comprehend meaning yet which is not restricted to meanings expressed in the conscious articulation of the subject. As Ricoeur (1970) observes, critical analyses have developed 'with the means at hand, with and against the prejudices of their times, a mediate science of meaning, irreducible to the immediate *consciousness* of meaning' (p. 34).

Interpretation and explanation
Critical analyses use both interpretation and explanation. Like hermeneutic models, critical accounts see interpretation as necessary to understand the

intentions of the actors they are observing, including the rules and meanings of the actors' social order. Unlike hermeneutic and phenomenological explanations, however, a critical analysis recognizes that many of the actions people perform are caused by conditions that they do not control, and that much of what people do to one another is not the result of conscious knowledge and choice (Fay, 1975). A critical account attempts to explain these causal influences on people. Some critical theorists, such as Freud, have been highly sympathetic to the positivist ethos and have supported a materialistic philosophy and deterministic theories. Yet, unlike the positivists, these writers employed intentional and semantic concepts in addition to causal explanations. Freud initially intended to provide an entirely materialistic and causal account (e.g., Freud, 1895/1953, p. 265). Yet he found this formulation unworkable because it could not tap the interpretative meanings which people place on their circumstances, and which affect their reactions to those circumstances (Rychlak, 1973).

At the social level, a critical analysis focuses on the linguistic representations of a social structure or group. Analysis of these representations, including illusions, is the avenue which leads to understanding the social structure. So the hermeneutic component of this method consists of a critique of ideology; the language and thought which characterizes and justifies a social system. This analysis reveals distortions in the categories used to describe and interpret the world, and contradictions and illogical connections between different statements or arguments. Unlike hermeneutic phenomenology, the analysis goes beyond the semantic analysis, and looks for the causal determinants of the distorted meanings in the person's perceptions. These distortions and contradictions in the language of a society are a guide to the nature of that society. Critical theories attempt to explain how the distortions and illusions came into existence.

The joint use of semantic interpretation and causal explanation also applies at an individual level. Habermas (1971) upholds Freud's analysis as an exemplar of the integration of interpretative and explanatory methods (cf. Giddens, 1976). Symptoms and peculiar actions and statements have to be understood in semantic terms; they can be related to their origins only by grasping their meaning. Freud used interpretation to reconstruct the meaning of events, and likened this task to the translation of ancient scripts with distortions in the text. But explanations of the causes of distortion are also necessary to fully understand the occurrence of these statements and symbols. To understand why statements are distorted or contain major omissions, semantic interpretation is insufficient and causal explanations are necessary. In the clinical context, the therapist must reach beyond the client's descriptions to explain causally why those descriptions are distorted, or why they conceal material that is inaccessible to consciousness. The two forms of explanation supplement each other; one accounts for the expression of a particular condition, such as neurosis, while the other provides the cause of the problem (Wollheim, 1971).

As following chapters will describe, the deciphering of illusions and ideologies is applied in contemporary critical perspectives to many other topics including people's attributions, their perceptions of fairness, and their attitudes to other groups (e.g., Billig, 1977; Buss, 1979b; Sampson, 1983). Critical explanations are free from the important limitations that apply to positivist explanations, which attempt to translate mental content into material terms, and use self-contradictory concepts like 'private stimuli' and 'cognitive behaviours'. On the other hand, a critical model also avoids being restricted to the explanations or reasons offered by actors, in the way that hermeneutic and phenomenological models are.

A template of theories

The paradigms of metatheory reviewed in this chapter form a template of positions which is produced to varying degrees in social cognition and abnormal psychology. But discussions of these theoretical positions in those contexts base their conclusions on experimental evidence, rather than the more conceptual arguments described in this chapter. They shall be discussed accordingly in those terms. The positivist and phenomenological paradigms are well articulated in social cognition and abnormal psychology, but a critical perspective has been applied less in these domains than in other fields, such as perceptions of equity and justice (e.g., Sampson, 1983). Apart from Buss's (e.g., 1979b) work, there has been little development of a critical theory of self-explanations and illusions in social cognition. Partly to rectify this situation, chapter 3 reviews specific critical theories and discusses their applications to specific issues. This review provides a basis for a critical perspective that is applied and evaluated in the discussions of social cognition and abnormal psychology in subsequent chapters.

3 Consciousness and illusions: critical perspectives

The discussion of positivist and phenomenological paradigms in the previous chapter argued that key inadequacies in these approaches are resolved in critical approaches. This chapter reviews critical theories of explanations and perceptions, particularly illusory perceptions. Hegel's ideas form the initial basis for critical accounts, but the first attempts to channel a critical theory into scientific form were proposed by Marx and Freud. Contemporary critical theories reject many of the axioms of these earlier theories, but some of Marx's and Freud's ideas about illusions form a kernel of concepts that influence contemporary research. The chapter begins with a summary of these formative accounts of consciousness and illusions and Fromm's synthesis of these theories. This is followed by a review of the Frankfurt School, focusing on the work of Adorno, Horkheimer, and Marcuse. The discussion then turns to Habermas's current extensions of critical theory, which revolve around his integration of linguistic models into the analysis, and the role of different human interests in human sciences. The following sections review analyses of ideology in psychological theories, and critical perspectives on two issues in social psychology: intergroup relations and the psychology of justice.

Formative concepts

The social origins of illusion

Accounts of the social basis of illusions tend to draw on Marx's categories, even while many authors apply those categories to different targets from Marx. Marx's analysis was formed in the context of expanding European industrialization, which presented horrific conditions for the labouring sector of society. At this time, industrialization was interwoven with a capitalist economy, and Marx identified the poor conditions of workers specifically with capitalism, a linkage that subsequent critical analyses question. Marx emphasized the deceptiveness of people's understanding of their conditions and their actions, often referring to these perceptions as 'illusions'. More recent analyses often use Lukács' term, 'false consciousness'.

25

Marx referred to several social beliefs in these terms. He claimed that religion, rather than offering people real happiness, comprises an illusory happiness, where it encourages people to seek a happy or fair world in a future life, rather than in their present conditions. He argued that the appearance of community in capitalist society is equally illusory, when one group was being exploited by another. Similarly, the belief that certain structures in capitalist society are natural rather than social phenomena is an illusion. In this account, the dominant consciousness of feudal and capitalist societies is a façade for exploitation. Marx claimed that these illusions are, in the first place, produced by the ideologists of society. The function of ideologists, Marx wrote, is to 'develop and perfect illusions' (1845/1961). These illusions serve to conceal important aspects of social conditions and to justify or legitimize those conditions. For example, the perception that particular social conditions and categories are natural and necessary conceals the social origins of those conditions, and at the same time serves to legitimize the social structure. Through ideology, the ideas and perspectives of the most advantaged sector of a society are promulgated through all sectors of that society.

Although ideology functions to conceal social conditions, Marx claimed that it also reflects those conditions. He proposes: 'It is not the consciousness of men that determines their being, but on the contrary it is their social being that determines their consciousness' (1859/1961, p. 67). Marx claimed that illusions in feudal and capitalist societies reflect distortions and contradictions in the economy and social structure. For example, the monetary value placed on goods and labour 'actually conceals, instead of disclosing, the social character of individual labour' (1867/1961, p. 97). Marx argued that relations between the production groups in his society resulted in an increasingly distorted consciousness: 'the more...the conditions of the ruling class come into conflict with the developed productive forces...the less veridical naturally becomes the consciousness which originates from and expresses this form of intercourse' (1845/1961, pp. 95–6). While in one sense illusions conceal aspects of society and entail a 'false' consciousness, yet in another sense they accurately reflect a distorted society.

As a consequence, Marx believed that change in perceptions required changing social structures, and not merely increased awareness, as Hegel had implied. Marx claimed that a particular social order is not undone 'merely by dismissing the idea of it from one's mind, but only by the action of individuals who establish their control over these material powers and abolish the division of labour' (1845/1961, p. 253). He believed that when the economic basis of society changed, the beliefs, laws, and values of society would also be transformed. He claimed that an undistorted consciousness would emerge in a society with no classes or conflicting interests, and where the interests of all sectors coincide. The illusions that characterized his own society would disappear when capitalist society was supplanted by a socialist one, where individual interests would coincide with the general interests of humanity. The economic conditions of this society, because they are not in themselves distorted or constraining, would neither require nor generate a distorted consciousness. Marx did not anticipate that socialist societies might develop their own class structures and inequalities and a false ideology that would justify and legitimize these conditions.

The psychological basis of illusion

Whereas Marx's theory focused on socially shared beliefs and illusions, Freud's theory centred on the individual personality. While Marx's obsession was with capitalism, Freud's psychological economy was coined in neurosis. Freud's account of consciousness related to several aspects of his patients' behaviour. Early in his career, Freud observed that hypnotized patients released information that was previously inaccessible, accompanied by a wave of emotion (catharsis). Focusing on this inaccessible yet existent knowledge, Freud sought to explain how people could be unconscious of knowledge that was laden with emotion and that seemed to be held in some 'internal foreign territory' (Habermas, 1971). Freud noted that patients' statements relating to their condition were often distorted or peculiar, either because they deviated from grammatical or semantic rules, or because they entailed an illogical or peculiar relation to the person's situation. Memories and dreams relating to life incidents were distorted – altered or forgotten in a particular fashion – and were also associated with aroused emotion.

To explain these distorted perceptions and memories, Freud invoked defence mechanisms: 'The defense mechanisms of the ego are condemned to falsify one's internal perceptions and to give one only an imperfect and distorted picture of one's id' (1937/1964, p. 237). When describing these mechanisms, he sometimes used linguistic metaphors which anticipate later linguistic approaches (e.g., Habermas, 1971). Freud described ways that offensive passages in a book are rendered innocuous:

> One way would be for the offending passages to be thickly crossed through so that they were illegible. In that case they could not be transcribed, and the next copyist of the book would produce a text which was unexceptionable but which had gaps in certain passages, and so might be unintelligible to them. Another way, however, if the authorities were not satisfied with this, but wanted also to conceal any indication that the text had been mutilated, would be for them to proceed to distort the text. Such words would be left out or replaced by others, and new sentences interpolated. Best of all, the whole passage would be erased and a new one which said exactly the opposite put in its place...If the

analogy is not pursued too strictly, we may say that repression has the same relationship to the other methods of defense as omission has to distortion of the text.

(1937/1964, pp. 236–7)

The concept of repression explains gaps in people's memories, dreams and descriptions. Other defence mechanisms create distortions in knowledge, such as a partial release of memory intertwined with additional false information, or false connections between two pieces of information. In defence mechanisms such as substitution, isolation and projection, the conscious representation of knowledge is 'falsified', producing distorted perceptions of the person's situation.

Rationalization introduces distortion at a later point. Whereas manipulations such as projection involve the release of information which is in itself distorted, rationalization involves a release of undistorted information accompanied by a false explanation. Freud describes such a case: 'this explanation struck me as unconvincing. Inadequate reasons like this usually conceal unconfessed motives. They remind one of Bernheim's hypnotized patients. When one of these carries out a post-hypnotic suggestion and is asked why he is acting in this way, instead of saying that he has no idea, he feels compelled to invent some obviously unsatisfactory reason' (Freud, 1900/1953, pp. 147–8). Rationalization articulates patients' misunderstanding of the causes of their behaviour. In relation to compulsive actions, for example, Freud claimed: 'The patient's consciousness naturally misunderstands them and puts forward a set of secondary motives to account for them – rationalizes them, in short' (1909/1955, p. 192).

This process of falsification functions to reduce anxiety that would result from a conscious awareness of certain wishes or memories. Freud notes: 'we welcome illusions because they spare us unpleasurable feelings' (1915/1956, p. 285), and claimed: 'The psychical apparatus is intolerant of unpleasure; it has to fend it off at all costs, and if the perception of reality entails unpleasure, that perception – that is, the truth – must be sacrificed' (1937/1964, p. 237). These illusions are not incidental or accidental. Ricoeur (1970) refers to this point in discussing the relationship between illusions and wish-fulfilment:

> The essential character of illusions is not their similarity to error, in the
> epistemological sense of the word, but their relationship with other
> fantasies and their inclusion within the semantics of desire. This properly
> analytic dimension of illusion was very precisely delimited by Freud
> in... *The Future of an Illusion*: 'What is characteristic of illusions is that
> they are derived from human wishes... Thus we call a belief an illusion
> when a wish-fulfilment is a prominent factor in its motivation, and in

doing so we disregard its relation to reality, just as the illusion itself sets
no store by verification.'

(p. 234)

Freud also discussed the removal of illusions and distortions. His therapy
is commonly described as an 'insight' therapy, where insight merely
involves the patient's acquisition of knowledge. Klein (1977) voices this
understanding of Freud: 'As is common knowledge, a chief objective for
Freud as therapist was to help his patient gain insight and this means help
in gaining more revealing self-knowledge' (p. 227). This reading of Freud, or
of common knowledge, interprets the theory in purely educative terms, and
emphasizes concepts such as self-knowledge, information, and insight. This
interpretation draws on statements made by Freud, such as 'The method by
which we strengthen the weakened ego has as a starting point, an
extending of its self-knowledge' (1937/1964, p. 177).

However, Freud's theory of change involved more than this, as its target
was not merely ignorance. Freud's patients disliked having to look into
themselves, and would attempt to manipulate the therapy, trying, as Freud
saw it, to maintain the status quo in their perceptions. Freud called these
continuing defensive efforts resistance. He locates the core of therapy not in
the information given to the patient, but in resistance: 'The crux of the
matter is that the defensive mechanisms directed against former danger
recur in the treatment as resistance against recovery. It follows from this
that the ego treats recovery itself as a new danger' (1937/1964, p. 238).

Resistance includes transference, where patients displace their feelings
toward another person onto the therapist. Here, the patients' actions
involve acting out and working through underlying conflicts. It was
because transference enabled patients to work through relationships, that
Freud saw it as potentially psychoanalysis' 'most powerful ally' (1937/
1964, p. 174). For transference to reach a satisfactory solution, the patient
must see the relationship as being that with the parents. Freud writes: 'It is
the analyst's task constantly to tear the patient out of his menacing illusion
to show him again and again that what he takes to be new real life is a
reflection of the past' (1938/1964, p. 177). The analyst's role is not simply
one of supplying information but of actively encountering the resistance of
the patient. Acting out was also employed in the earlier method of hypnosis,
where patients re-performed scenes from their lives. So providing information is only part of Freud's therapy. A second constituent is
overcoming resistance and transference.

The integration of the psychological and the social
Fromm's (1970) analysis integrates common features in the social and
individual processes underlying illusions. He links ideology at a social level

to defence mechanisms at an individual level, and claims that ideology and rationalization are equivalent. Fromm asserts 'Psychoanalysis can show that man's ideologies are the products of certain wishes, instinctual drives, interests, and needs, which themselves, in large measure, unconsciously find expression as rationalizations, i.e., as ideologies' (p. 172; see also pp. 83, 150).

There are clearly common features in ideology and rationalization, but Fromm's matching is not the only possible parallel. Social ideologies do not simply rationalize social conditions, but make distorted assertions and conceal problematic information. So ideology is analogous to all individual defence mechanisms which distort information. Freud claimed that rationalization can be achieved by other defence mechanisms, such as substitution (e.g., Freud, 1915/1956, p. 182). A common characteristic of the agencies of social ideology (law, religion, literature, illusions, etc.), and the Freudian defensive processes is that they have to do with words and ideas. So both theories propose verbal or cognitive defence mechanisms and ideologies that produce illusions that serve a purpose.

Fromm (1970) suggests a second parallel between the two theories. He matches the 'id' or 'instinctual structure' (p. 151) at the individual level, and the social infrastructure, or economy, at the social level. He suggests that the instinctual structure may be modified by social forces, but remains the centre of the human psyche, which, as a single entity, interacts with society (p. 152). A problem with this synthesis is that it blurs the distinction between the arenas in which the struggles are fought and the various parties involved. In Marxian accounts of exploitative societies, the parties are the different social groups or classes, whereas the arena is the economy, including the relationships between the social groups. Freud's account invokes three parties: the instinctual id, the socializing superego and the arbitrating ego. Conflicts between these three occur in the individual's mind, but this internal arena reflects the relationships in the person's life, such as relationships in the person's family. In both the internal and the external arena, psychopathology reflects problematic relationships between these parties. It is these relationships that the defence mechanisms obscure, just as social ideology obscures the relations between social groups.

Fromm's synthesis of the social and individual domains exchanges the arenas and parties. His account reduces the social and individual spheres to a single sphere where society and the individual are the only parties. Hence society itself cannot be conceived of as an arena in which conflicts occur, and nor can the individual. This synthesis precludes the possibility of parties within either individual or society, and hence the possibility of conflicting parties in either domain which underlie illusions. This account somewhat undercuts the basis for an explanation of illusions. A more consistent synthesis of the formative critical accounts of illusions would construe several parties interacting at the social or individual level.

Fromm did not focus on how illusory perceptions are removed, but there are common features in the early critical theories. Marx argued that the social structure which requires illusions must be replaced by a new one which would neither require nor engender illusions. Such a change, while concomitant with a self-awareness of the situation, derives from action in changing social structures. Freud gives insight an important role, but in therapy the client must also work through crucial relationships and events. Marx's account places less weight on knowledge than Freud's account, but both predict change when relevant knowledge is present.

In sum, several common features may be seen in these formative critical theories of illusions. First, the illusions of interest are not adventitious but are a function of human motivation or interests. At a social level, they prevent people from seeing aspects of their social structure, and legitimize an inequitable society. At the individual level, illusions defend consciousness from knowledge which would produce anxiety. Second, illusions are produced by processes such as defence mechanisms or ideologies, which propagate false or distorted information that conceals and legitimizes a situation. At a social or interpersonal level the cognitive distortions reflect a relationship between parties that usually involves some conflict. For the removal of illusions, information alone is inadequate because the motivation which produced the illusions exercises resistance to its removal. This resistance can be overcome only by combined knowledge and action.

Instrumental reason and sexual politics: the Frankfurt School

The last fifty years have seen numerous proposals for change to both social and personality theories of illusions. It will be seen, in fact, that the two lines of development do not remain distinct. Since Freud formed his account of personality and perceptions, various changes have occurred. Neo-Freudians advocate that defences should be exercised less harshly in the repression of unconscious desires and thoughts; the evaluating superego is viewed accordingly in less sympathetic terms. By itself this tilt in the balance of power between the various parties does not fundamentally alter Freud's framework, as it assumes the same arena and same participating parties. But other modifications to Freud's account are more far-reaching, particularly relating to Freud's synthesis of extraspective and introspective data and explanatory and interpretative concepts. Several authors have rejected this synthesis by moving toward either an extraspective and explanatory account or toward, conversely, an introspective and interpretative model. In other words, they have moved towards the positivist and the phenomenological paradigms.

Paradoxically, both moves were anticipated in one author's theory. Adler (1933/1956) moved toward a model using only efficient causes, by explaining many conditions, such as the inferiority complex, in largely physical terms. His eschewing of mentalistic terminology developed into Sullivan's (1953) interpersonal theory and Dollard and Miller's (1950) translation of psychoanalysis into learning theory. Yet it was Adler also who anticipated shifts to an introspective and intentional model. Adler rejected the view that conscious perceptions are frequently illusory, arguing instead in favour of consciousness' common sense. Adler's placing of faith in conscious self-perceptions was complemented by Jung's (1953) shift from Freud's goal of a deterministic theory to a position giving more emphasis to human choice. This trend arrived at an anti-deterministic zenith in theories espousing phenomenology and existentialism. Maslow (1970) and Rogers (1961) emphasized self-determination and placed a corresponding emphasis on the validity of immediate perceptions of the phenomenological field and consciousness.

From Freud, then, many authors have shifted towards the two polarities discussed in the previous chapter: the positivist with extraspective method and data, and the phenomenological with its introspective, phenomenological method and data. These changes entail that the theories no longer reflect a critical perspective. The validity of these positivist and phenomenological stances was discussed in chapter 2, and further comment on their applications to therapy is made in chapter 7.

Changes have also been made to critical accounts of social phenomena. In some cases the basic structure of Marx's theory is retained and brought to bear on a new milieu (Feuer, 1969). The categories of exploiter and exploited are applied to new sets of groups; most recently to 'first' and 'third' world relations, to racial conflicts and to sexual relationships (e.g., Jaggar, 1983). These developments frequently involve a rejection of Marx's view that the exploitative conditions underlying illusions are intrinsically linked to capitalism. However, they retain a critical interpretation of consciousness and illusion in terms of one party misleading another to serve that party's own interest.

Other changes in critical theories modify this interpretation of illusions. These changes relate to an increased emphasis on the effects of the ideological mechanisms of society. Many authors have rejected Marx's emphasis on the determining influence of the economy. This change emerged in the 1920s when the appropriate economic conditions in Europe did not result in the revolutions and change to socialist economies that Marx predicted. Lukács and Korsch argued that although the social conditions conducive to transformation were present, the social con-sciousness was not yet ripe for change (see Jay, 1973). This idea attributes more influence to consciousness in preventing change than Marx had done. This emphasis was furthered by the Frankfurt School, a group of investigators who worked at the Institute of Social Research at Frankfurt in the 1920s and early 1930s and emigrated to the United States of America on Hitler's rise to power. This school became influential in the 1960s and 1970s when their works first became available in the English language, and when their analysis was thought to capture important aspects of contemporary society (B. Brown, 1973; Jay, 1973).

Two central members of this group, Adorno and Horkheimer (1944/1972), claimed that important aspects of modern societies were not anticipated by Marx's analysis. They argued that Western societies, while remaining capitalistic, were no longer structured primarily in terms of classes and that workers were no longer subject to the poverty and abysmal working conditions of the nineteenth century. They claimed that the new technological media resulted in the economy and ideology being less differentiated. Western societies had shifted from the economic manipulation of labour to the socio-psychological manipulation of consumption through marketing psychology. In fascist societies political propaganda infiltrated the economy and technology upheld the status quo rather than compelling change.

In the context of these views, social analysis shifted from a critique of political economy to a critique of instrumental reason, the mentality preoccupied with technological control and the domination of nature and people. Social systems such as capitalism are re-located as an expression of an instrumental reason which both precedes and will supersede it. Poverty and alienation are no longer defined in economic and material terms but portrayed as cultural or psychological phenomena. Adorno and Horkheimer rejected the views that consciousness reflects the economy and that the removal of illusions results from a combination of change in economic structures and insight. But they provide few alternative ideas as to how illusions are removed, and do not indicate the source of a new consciousness. Adorno and Horkheimer imply the constant presence of illusion, and support this view by pointing out that the illusions associated with instrumental reason apply to diverse societies, including communist ones. This universalistic view, however, does not explain changes in perceptions that do occur; nor does it explain illusions specific to particular social conditions or societies.

It was in an attempt to regain the transformative thrust of critical theories that a third member of the Frankfurt School, Marcuse (1955), developed the fusion of the social and psychological. He pursued Reich's (1934/1972) linkage of political and sexual repression, where Reich tried to explain why European nations in economic crises chose fascism rather than socialism. He identified repression in society with the repression of sexual dynamics proposed by Freud. Between the two, and linking them, stands the authoritarian family that exercises repression on behalf of the state. Reich's political psychosomatics identified the constriction of sexual energy with the fascist personality. The therapy of sexual liberation would clear the way for the dissipation of fascism.

Marcuse (1955) placed this scenario in a socio-historical setting. The sex drive, he wrote, had hitherto been displaced into labour, and necessarily so during the development of civilization and in times of scarcity. In contemporary society such displacement was no longer necessary. Sexual freedom would lead in turn to political freedom and a consciousness that would neither require nor contain illusions. Marcuse's model fuses Freud's emphasis on sexual dynamics with Marx's perceptions of the need for social transformation. A transformation of sexual relationships would produce the transformation of society, including its 'consciousness'.

This theory initially omitted any role for insight or consciousness in the elimination of illusions, but Marcuse (1964) subsequently incorporated the cognitive level. While he reiterated Adorno and Horkheimer's criticism of instrumental reason, he argued that modern culture could retain industrialization and technology yet still be emancipated from an instrumental rationality. Marcuse did not make it clear how two facets of modern culture might be separated. Nonetheless, the two aspects of Marcuse's theory, the emphasis on actions in his earlier theory and the emphasis on the consciousness in the more recent theory, are consistent with earlier critical views of change in perceptions that specify both information and action.

Language, interests and ideology

The turn to language
A recent development in critical theory has been the introduction of linguistic concepts and methods. This move is closely related to the school of hermeneutic phenomenology described in the previous chapter. Habermas (1970), a central figure in this development, proposes that researchers can use analyses of distortions in language to represent social and psychological processes, including perceptions and illusions. In the previous chapter the existence of distortions in language was invoked to challenge the hermeneutic axiom that language is a clear indicator of intentions. Distorted language, however, not only indicates that self-explanations are distorted; it also provides a means of analysing those distortions.

The use of language as an indicator of cognitions was implicit in earlier critical theories, but receives its first explicit focus in Habermas's theory. Habermas's (e.g., 1970) analysis of language modifies the post-Wittgenstein hermeneutics of Gadamer (1975) and Winch (1958). This school employed language to capture and interpret the intended meaning of human statements and activities. As noted earlier, however, interpretation is by itself insufficient to explain distortions in language, the relationship between language and action, or the relationships between language and the environment. Habermas accepts language as the datum expressing intentions and meanings, but he yokes these interpretations with the causal explanations that are necessary to explain the relationships which transgress the self-imposed boundaries of a hermeneutic interpretation.

Habermas applies the linguistic model to individual and social change, which he sees as following from self-reflection. Drawing on hermeneutics and psychoanalytic theory, Habermas argues that as in psychoanalytic therapy self-reflection on the patient's speech leads to change, so also reflection on social forms of pathological speech, assisted by a hermeneutic knowledge of language, will remove pathological conditions. Habermas claims that his model generalizes Freud's technique of creating change. As was noted earlier in the chapter, this reflective view of Freud's method omits a key aspect of Freud's technique, where in both hypnosis and transference the patient re-enacted and worked through events and relationships in his or her life. Habermas's proposals thus leave out a key aspect of Freud's account, and assumes a more educative model of change. Habermas supplies no clear grounds for accepting that change occurs in this way.

Nonetheless, Habermas's proposal that people's language can be treated as the representation of perceptions and illusions provides a valuable development. The linguistic model supplies a tangible criterion of cognitions and illusions (distorted language), and an accessible instrument for analysing the perceptions and illusions as they are expressed in explanations. It thus promises to sharpen a critical analysis, a possibility that is significant for critical theories. Many Freudian and neo-Freudian accounts have described the processes of pathology and change in high abstract terms. Glover's (1955) description of events is an example. He writes:

> If we assume that the anal-sadistic phase has been weathered, the stage of infantile, genital or phallic primacy established, the ego advanced from a mainly narcissistic basis to a more organized relationship with objects, the difficulties likely to be observed are those connected with the positive and negative Oedipus relation and the resolution or abandonment of that situation under the spur of castration-anxiety.
>
> (p. 100)

Such abstractions are not only obscure; they lend ammunition to Popper's criticism that critical theories are unfalsifiable:

It was during the summer of 1919 that I began to feel more and more dissatisfied with these three theories – the Marxist theory of history, psychoanalysis, and individual psychology; and I began to feel dubious about their claims to scientific status...I found that those of my friends who were admirers of Marx, Freud and Adler, were impressed by a number of points common to these theories, and especially to their apparent explanatory power. These theories appeared to be able to explain practically everything that happened within the fields to which they referred. The study of any of them seemed to have the effect of an intellectual conversion or revelation, opening your eyes to a new truth hidden from those not yet initiated. Once your eyes were thus opened you saw confirming instances everywhere: the world was full of verifications of the theory. Whatever happened always confirmed it.

(1972, pp. 34–5)

Popper's criticism was directed at not only the adherents but also the masters. And at times the masters were indeed guilty of his accusation. Freud, for example, asserted that: 'Analysis, in claiming to cure neuroses by ensuring control over instinct, is always right in theory but not always right in practice' (1937/1964, p. 229). Against Popper, it could be argued that Freud is no more guilty of disregarding evidence than Einstein, whose theory Popper (1972) upholds as an exemplar of science, but who claimed that he would believe in his theory even if research didn't support it (e.g., Heisenberg, 1971). Whatever the justice of Popper's selectivity in his criticisms, the linguistic representation of illusions proposed by Habermas makes a critical account potentially more tangible. Models which apply linguistic analyses to social cognition will be reviewed in chapter 6, and linguistic applications to therapy are discussed further in chapter 8.

A second aspect of Habermas's theory concerns the link between changes in cognitions and the underlying interests of the three major paradigms of social science. The following section considers these links in relation to contemporary discussions in social psychology about the enlightenment role of the discipline.

The human interests of science
There is a relation between critical theories' emphasis on illusions and the emancipatory interest of a critical approach to science, which Habermas (e.g., 1971) contrasts with the interests of empiricist and phenomenological approaches. Empiricist human sciences, which are represented most definitively in social psychology by behavioural analyses, have a particular interest in prediction and control (e.g., Skinner, 1971). A fundamental interest of this approach is the control of nature, including human nature. The complete antithesis to this focus is seen in the phenomenological or hermeneutic sciences, represented most clearly in psychology by humanistic

psychology, which orient around an interest in communication and understanding (e.g., Rogers, 1961). The central interest here is in achieving understanding of actions in terms of the agent's self-understanding, which constitutes the ultimate explanation of the agent's action. Habermas claims that critical approaches serve a third interest, a focus on emancipation. Critical theories are concerned with emancipating people from the illusions and ideologies that distort their perception of themselves, and from the particular circumstances that generate and sustain those illusions. Habermas likens the process of emancipation to the process of psychodynamic therapies. These therapies increase people's control over behaviour by revealing previously unknown or unconscious processes that affect a client's behaviour, and thereby undermine the strength of those processes.

Critical theories' emphasis on removing illusions is closely related to the widely used concept of consciousness — raising. As Buss (1979c) notes: 'To the extent that people can be made aware of their own situation within society, then there exists the possibility for implementing social change to better their situation' (p. 84). Consciousness-raising involves transforming the way people perceive themselves, a process that involves not only an educative aspect, but also an overcoming of the psychological and social forces that reinforce the existing consciousness. This concept has been applied by feminist and black groups to counter the consciousness that reinforces and legitimizes sexual and racial discrimination. Jaggar (1983) notes that 'the goal of radical feminist analysis is a "change in consciousness", a change that might be described as a paradigm shift' (p. 268). The same principle applies to racial minorities' re-definition of attitudes to certain races (R. Brown, 1986).

Critical theories' emphasis on emancipation from illusions relates to Gergen's (1973) proposal concerning 'enlightenment effects' in the relation between scientific knowledge and society. Gergen suggested that the dissemination of scientific knowledge from social psychology informs people about processes which affect their behaviour. As people become aware of those processes, they are not affected by them in the same way. So laws of social behaviour can become invalidated as soon as they are publicized. For example, Gergen suggests that when women read the finding that women are more easily persuaded than men, they may react by becoming less easily persuaded, and the initial finding thereby becomes invalidated. This enlightenment effect is like a feedback loop between science and society.

Gergen embeds this idea in a broader argument that social psychology should be considered a form of history rather than science. In addition to his proposition about enlightenment effects, Gergen claims that many social psychological theories are socially or historically relative, quite apart from people's awareness of them, and they consequently cannot specify general laws of behaviour. Gergen concluded from these arguments that social psychology constitutes a socially relative progression of historically bound propositions, rather than a form of universally applicable scientific knowledge. Not surprisingly, given the strong concern that many social psychologists have in establishing the scientific status of their discipline, these conclusions did not pass without comment. Cronbach (1975) agreed with Gergen's claim that there is a science–society feedback loop, but suggested that this principle does not entail that human social processes are unlawful. Cronbach accepted that empiricist writers have tended to make sweeping generalizations that apply across societies and historical epochs, and he conceded that these analyses have assumed that social psychological processes are stable and fixed, which is often not the case. But he points out that feedback processes do not necessarily entail unlawful relationships. He notes that in biology, evolutionary theory has had some success in specifying a model of feedback interaction over time. Gottlieb (1977) offers a similar argument concerning Gergen's claim that social laws are historically bound, and suggests that historical variables should be included in the analysis. In fact, this principle is already being realized in life-span research on development, where the cohort that a person is born into is included as a factor in the analysis, and historical changes in developmental processes are traced systematically (e.g., Nesselroade and Baltes, 1974).

Neither of these counter-arguments refutes Gergen's claim that there is an enlightenment effect in the relation between science and society, where people's learning about the processes affecting them leads them to react differently to those processes, thereby invalidating previously valid predictions. In the context of the empiricist paradigm, this enlightenment effect may be accidental and unintended, and in relation to making generalizations about the way people behave, the effect may be seen as a methodological nuisance. In relation to critical theories, however, enlightenment effects are closely related to a central purpose of critical scientific enterprise, which is to clarify the source of illusions and distortions, so that those illusions can be eliminated.

Ideology in psychological theories
The various interests underlying the major paradigms of inquiry relate closely to the ideological implications of these paradigms. Many ideological aspects of the major approaches in psychology have been pointed out elsewhere (e.g., Billig, 1982; Broughton, 1986; Buss, 1979c; Larsen, 1986b), so they will not be extensively documented here. Nonetheless, they are important for the current discussion, because the analysis of ideological aspects of psychological theory is continuous with the early critical analyses

of ideology. The present discussion focuses on the ideological aspects of positivist and phenomenological approaches.

In (social) psychology the positivist perspective has been represented most explicitly in behavioural and biological perspectives. The behavioural emphasis on prediction and control reflects the interest of technical rationality that underlies positivist science (Habermas, 1971). The behavioural technology reflects an interest in the control of persons rather than an increase in their freedom (Skinner, 1971). At a less explicit level, behavioural technologies accept the status quo in society and concentrate on the manipulation of individuals. Buss (1975) links the flourishing growth of behaviourism in American society to the compatibility between the behavioural emphasis on control and the pragmatism of American society. However, the early roots of behaviourism lie in Europe, particularly in the ideas of Comte, who developed a 'positive' philosophy for maintaining social order as an alternative to the 'negative' philosophies of social transformation that had produced the French Revolution. Comte hoped that positive science would replace religion as a stabilizing force in society.

A second major articulation of the positivist ethos is in theories that emphasize biological determinism, particularly in relation to sex differences and race differences. Evolutionary theory is used to reinforce views that assert inherent differences between males and females, and between different races, particularly blacks and whites in the United States. Biological accounts of sex differences, for example, attribute to men and women instincts that justify their respective traditional places as domestic servant and money-earner (Shields, 1975). These accounts also assert the inherent superiority of men, claiming, for example, that the larger brain size of males implies the intellectual superiority of males. These propositions function ideologically to justify 'traditional' sex roles for men and women, and different treatment of men and women.

Similar implications follow from theories proposing genetic differences between races. Intelligence tests that show differences between blacks and whites are used as justifications for claiming that the differences are genetic and that educational and social changes will make little difference (Jensen, 1969), despite the fact that there is strong evidence to the contrary (e.g., Scarr, 1981). Again, these findings function to justify the advantaged position of a particular group in society, in this case whites. It is significant that the authors who expound these views do not claim that the higher scores of Japanese on intelligence tests by comparison with white Americans or Europeans (e.g., Lynn, 1982) indicate the genetic superiority of Japanese people. The positivist interest in control and domination is channelled in theories that involve that control and domination of particular groups.

As was noted in chapter 2, the antithesis to positivist theories such as behaviourism and biological determinism is seen in humanistic and phenomenological approaches, which emphasize agency and introspection rather than deterministic causes and extraspective observation. Humanists emphasize the sufficiency of actors' accounts of their action (Harré and Secord, 1972), and the humanistic treatment of actors reflects an interest in communication with actors to interpret their actions (Habermas, 1971).

The ideological implications of humanist approaches have been pointed out by several authors (e.g., Broughton, 1986; Buss, 1979a; Larsen, 1986a; Lasch, 1978). These analyses focus on the humanist assumption that people can achieve transformation of themselves and of societies through changing individuals, and through concentrating on self-actualization. The humanist approach implies that people can achieve self-actualization and freedom through an inner psychological state rather than through changes in their outer conditions. This emphasis on the individual has conservative social implications, as it redirects people's attention away from those social conditions that contribute to their discontent. It thus serves the status quo in any society. For members of social groups whose 'actualization' is inhibited by social norms or political legislation, the encouragement to self-actualize is self-defeating. A necessary condition for people to experience numerous choices and freedoms is the existence of social conditions that permit those choices and freedoms. Lasch (1978) claims that the individualistic emphasis in the humanist doctrine of self-actualization has contributed to the development of a 'culture of narcissism', where self-concern and the pursuit of self-fulfilment displace a concern with social change and community. The ideals and hopes placed in humanist analyses can only be realized through an analysis that incorporates change to the social conditions that surround individuals.

Specific applications in social psychology

Specific critical applications in social psychology share many of the features of the critical analysis described in previous sections. Central to these accounts is the analysis of illusory cognitions and ideology that are the focus in general critical theories, both in respect to the illusions of the persons being described and examined by theories, and the ideological implications of the theories themselves. As Gergen and Morawski (1980) observe, critical analyses focus on ways in which social psychological theories and research are shaped by the broader social context. Critical analyses value research that uncovers the more social and historical aspects of cognition and action (e.g., Nesselroade and Baltes, 1974), but they do not share the absolute aversion to experimental findings that characterizes several other schools of inquiry. Rather, different interpretations are often made of certain experiments, and the experimental situation is frequently perceived as a microcosm of larger social relations. The authors included here are not doctrinaire adherents of a critical school, but their work includes theory and research drawing on that perspective.

Intergroup processes

A critical style of analysis is exemplified in Billig's (1976) analysis of intergroup processes, and in particular his interpretation of Sherif's (1966) classic experiments on intergroup conflict. Sherif, using the naturalistic setting of a boys' holiday camp, examined the effect of competitive goals and superordinate goals on two groups' interactions. In conditions with competitive goals, where only one team could win a prize, there was considerable conflict, but in conditions with superordinate goals, where the two groups had to work together to achieve a goal, there was moderate harmony, although a degree of conflict lingered. As Billig (1976) observed, this situation has generally been interpreted as involving two parties, the two groups of boys, and extrapolations are made from these studies to actual conflicts involving two parties, such as conflicts between the United States and the Soviet Union. Billig points out that this interpretation of the Sherif studies omits and obscures the role and actions of a third group in the situation, the experimenters, who were present in the guise of camp authorities. Billig notes that it is necessary to invoke the role of the experimenters to explain several important aspects of the study. It was the camp authorities who determined whether and when the two groups of boys had conflicting or coinciding goals, and whether friends could go together in the same group or be placed in the two opposing groups. So the camp authorities controlled and defined key aspects of the situation in order to produce a particular effect. Billig suggests that rather than exemplifying conflicts involving only two parties, the situation is a case of 'divide and rule', where a ruling group furthers its interest by creating divisions and hostilities between two subordinate groups.

Billig claims that the situation created in the Sherif experiments is an instance of false consciousness, in that the subordinate groups do not see the manipulations of the experimenter group as the cause of their conflicts, and where they consequently attribute all the negative qualities and vices to the other group. Billig notes that it cannot be assumed that the boys would have developed the same ingroup and outgroup perceptions if they had been aware of the experimenters' manipulations of them. For example, in relation to friends who had been deliberately separated and placed in different groups to see if their friendship would survive, and who actually came to blows in the group situation, it cannot be assumed that this same hostility would have occurred if the friends had known that their separation was a deliberate strategy of the experiments. As Billig observes, this question can only be examined experimentally, but it should not be assumed that behaviour produced in a state of false consciousness, where the situation is partly hidden from participants, would be produced in a situation of true consciousness, where the participants know as much about the situations as the experimenters.

Billig suggests that the social identity theory of intergroup relations (e.g., Tajfel, 1978) also omits ideological components in group conflicts. Studies applying the social identity model show that conflicting interests are not necessary for group conflict to occur, and that it is sufficient for groups to be placed in distinct social categories (Tajfel, 1978). Group differentiation occurs as groups form an identity with a social category, and the process of social comparison is applied at a group level. Groups achieve a positive social identity by selecting dimensions on which their own group compares positively with others. Billig claimed that the social identity model, no less than Sherif's model, needs to be integrated with wider aspects of social processes, and with ideological aspects of social identity. Billig argues that a positive group identity incorporates the ideological beliefs that a group produces, in addition to beliefs that group members develop through their individual psychological processes. Billig's argument could be applied to the categories constructed in the social identity experimental situation to suggest that group identity incorporates facets defined by authorities. For example, while Tajfel (1974) claimed that 'social categorization can be understood as the ordering of the social environment in terms of groupings that make sense to the subjects' (p. 9), in several experiments the subjects are placed in groups by the experimenters, and the categories are provided by the experimenters, not the subjects. The groups are not 'categories which make sense to the subjects', but are constructed by the experimenter.

Social identity theory emphasizes that groups may achieve a positive identity irrespective of the objective conditions that exist, and Billig notes that this emphasis can obscure the actual social conditions of a group. A situation of intergroup domination is resolved, not by changing the surface features of a group's identity (e.g. 'Black is beautiful'), but by changing the actual circumstances of domination. Social change may of course follow from a 'raised' consciousness, but the change in consciousness is not itself a complete social change.

Justice and equity

A second key issue in human relationships concerns the allocation of resources in ways that are seen as fair for the parties involved in the relationship. In social psychology, the most influential framework has revolved around various versions of equity theory (Walster, Walster and Berscheid, 1978). Equity theory proposes that people's sense of justice reflects the extent to which the benefits gained from a relationship (frequently referred to as outcomes) are proportional to the contributions made to the relationship (frequently called inputs). According to equity theories, people are most satisfied when the ratio of the outcomes that they and other people receive from a relationship is proportional to the inputs that are made to the relationship. All parties in a relationship are happier if those who contribute more to a task are allocated greater rewards than those who contribute less, and they perceive this situation as just. The theory implies that people accept inequality in society, and believe it fair that rewards are unequally distributed among individuals, because they assume that citizens do not make equal contributions to society. Equity theorists imply that the equity norm is a natural tendency that applies as a general psychological principle in human affairs.

Sampson (1975, 1983) has challenged the suggestion that equity is a universal or necessary psychological principle. He claims that the equity norm is a reflection of a particular society, contemporary American society, which has a capitalist and individualist ethos. Sampson reinforces this claim by drawing on research showing that some groups do not adhere to the equity principle; they believe instead that rewards should be distributed more on the basis of equality. In equality allocations, everyone in a relationship receives the same reward irrespective of the contribution they have made. For example, in the United States studies have found that female participants allocate more equal portions of prizes and rewards to participants in various distributive situations than males (e.g., Kahn *et al.*, 1971). Sampson attributes these sex differences to the different socialization of men and women in the United States, claiming that men have been socialized into economic roles and values more than women.

Other significant deviations from the equity pattern have been found. In both Britain and the United States, where groups that are better off within the current social system believe that the prevailing equity, or distribution of resources, is fair, those who are not so well off believe that an equality-based distribution would be more fair (Robinson and Bell, 1978). Specifically, non-whites, particularly those in the United States, perceive equality as fair, whereas other groups that are getting what they think they deserve from society judge equality as unfair. Sampson applies a similar analysis to the finding that people in the more socialist Western European nations, such as Sweden and Denmark, show a stronger equality orientation to distributing allocations than people in the United States (Block, 1973). These findings suggest that some groups prefer allocations based on equality rather than equity.

Sampson (1975) notes that equity theorists have tended to treat these sorts of finding merely as a deviation from an equity principle, rather than as evidence that people are fundamentally motivated by the principle of equality, or by a tension between equality and equity. Sampson suggests that equity is not so much a basic psychological law about human nature as a psychological outcome of a particular culture's socialization practices. The close fit between the equity principle and the dominant ethos of the culture in which it has flourished has encouraged researchers to perceive equity as a natural state, and to perceive deviations from the equity principle as unnatural or problematic. But Sampson claims that the equity principle comprises a marketplace psychological principle that closely reflects a marketplace economic system. Equity theory construes human relationships in terms of the exchange of goods or commodities. It reduces all human functions and actions to a common currency. The equity equation views people as calculating their own ratios of investments and outcomes and comparing these ratios with the ratios of the people they choose as a comparison group. It portrays the 'economic person' as a fundamental principle of psychological functioning. Sampson counters that the equity principle is socially and historically situated, and that research supports his view. He claims that people in some cases are motivated toward distributions of equality, and that principles of justice vary in different human relationships.

In a more recent discussion of equity, Sampson (1983) argues that the equity studies of justice have inadvertently functioned to legitimize the existing configuration of society, and, by excluding important socioeconomic factors, they have deflected attention from understanding and changing actual conditions of injustice. This is partly a consequence of the subjective emphasis in equity research, where justice is defined predominantly in terms of actors' phenomenology and examined purely from the actor's point of view. In adopting this framework, equity theory fails to investigate whether the actor's framework reflects an ideological stance, or a form of false consciousness. Sampson notes that by not comparing the perceptions of actors with material circumstances, equity theory fails to investigate key issues, such as the ways in which actors' judgements may already reflect a social process. Sampson (1983) argues that 'whether or not this phenomenology reflects justice must be determined more critically by probing beneath and beyond the actor's phenomenology rather than being defined only in its terms' (p. 146).

Sampson notes that the highly subjective approach to justice has led investigators to examine people's judgements about allocations that are predetermined. In this framework, justice is defined after the allocation has occurred, and in cases where allocations may be unfair, after an injustice has been committed. The social mechanisms that make the particular allocations are not examined in equity theories. Sampson suggests that 'insofar as the psychological investigator is content to examine how people make seemingly rational choices in allocating the scarce resources presented to them by an underlying allocation process that is itself unjust, we in psychology will contribute more to mystifying the understanding of justice than helping probe its real operations' (1983, p. 149). An adequate analysis of justice requires the inclusion of processes of distribution, as well as *post hoc* appraisals of that distribution.

A critical perspective

The critical analyses in social psychology show how theories such as equity theory reflect a particular set of values and a particular society. They show how the design of the research on the issues serve to construct the inquiry in ways that reinforce the theory, and how changes in that design can produce findings that test and lend support to alternative theories. Some critical analyses reinterpret experiments in ways that include the subjects' history and immediate context, including the experimenter or the experimental situation, where this is relevant. Chapter 7 applies this sort of perspective to research dealing with cognitive distortions in attributions, locus of control, and helplessness. Before moving to that discussion, we consider models dealing with self-perception and explanations in social cognition and in paradigms that have been posed as alternatives to social cognition in chapters 4, 5 and 6.

4 Self-perception and social cognition

Scepticism as to whether people understand either their cognitive activity or the causes of their behaviour has been articulated afresh by researchers in social psychology in the 1970s and 1980s (e.g., D. J. Bem, 1972; Nisbett and Wilson, 1977; Wilson, 1985; Wilson and Stone, 1985). This new affirmation of the sceptical stance derives its impetus from research and theories in social psychology. A synthesis of these theories was persuasively presented in Nisbett and Wilson's (1977) review of research that examined verbal reports; according to Nisbett and Wilson, this research shows that actors' understanding of their behaviour is no better than that of observers. This conclusion was compelling partly because it reinforced the predictions of D. J. Bem's (1967, 1972) self-perception theory, which proposes that actors' and observers' attributions for actors' behaviour should not significantly differ. This lack of difference was predicted on the assumption that the causes of behaviour are publicly available, in the form of stimuli and cultural norms, rather than being hidden inside the actor's head.

Any research supporting this sort of conclusion carries significance as it bears on the perennial philosophical–psychological issue of the causes and the explanation of behaviour. The major views on this issue were reviewed in chapter 2. The conclusions reached by D. J. Bem and by Nisbett and Wilson support the classical philosophical view, promulgated from Hume to Skinner, that the causes of behaviour are external to the organism and that there is no internal propelling agent or self (Rychlak, 1977). Given this significance, it is not surprising that D. J. Bem's and Nisbett and Wilson's claims have frequently been challenged (e.g., Buss, 1978; de Charms and Shea, 1976; Ericsson and Simon, 1980; Harré, 1981a, b; Shotter, 1984; Smith and Miller, 1978; White, 1980). Some of the arguments of these critics resemble the arguments that Kant and phenomenological theorists presented to the claims of classical positivist writers such as Hume and Skinner (Rychlak, 1968). The developments in social psychology, particularly in attribution theory's analysis of lay epistemology, re-enact the perennial epistemological battles between the empiricist and rationalist paradigms of philosophy and psychology. The significance of the claims

46

made in contemporary social psychology lies less in reiterating classical positions than in claims that psychologists are forced to these positions by experimental demonstration rather than by axiomatic philosophy. Theorists on both sides of the dispute claim that empirical support gives a scientific validity and legitimacy to their position.

In the 1980s several other theories and concepts relating to the self have been developed in the field of social psychology referred to as social cognition. This chapter begins with a discussion of the positivist account of self-perception and self-explanations, and then turns to recent developments in social cognition dealing with perceptions of the self and explanations of actions. These include self-schemata, person memory and the theory of action identification.

The positivist indictment of self-knowledge

D. J. Bem's and Nisbett and Wilson's arguments concerning self-reports are jointly termed the positivist case because, as Bem (1972, p. 4) notes, they affirm classical positivist (or empiricist) axioms. Nisbett and Wilson (1977) contend, in the first of two arguments, that relevant research on attribution, cognitive dissonance, subliminal perception and problem-solving demonstrates that people frequently mistake the causes of their behaviour, and that people's self-explanations derive little or no assistance from introspective access. Experimental subjects are often unaware that a stimulus influenced their response, and are frequently unaware that they have even made a response in certain stimulus conditions.

Nisbett and Wilson's second claim is that actor and observer judgements of the actor's behaviour are equally accurate, and that in situations where observers misattribute the cause of the actor's behaviour, actors make the same errors. Nisbett and Wilson report that observer subjects, who did not participate in experiments but simply read verbal descriptions of them, made predictions about stimuli that were remarkably similar to the reports about the stimuli by subjects who had actually been exposed to them. In experiments by Latané and Darley (1970) and in several of Nisbett and Wilson's own studies, subjects were asked to predict how they or other people would react to stimulus situations that had been presented to other subjects. These 'observer' subjects made predictions that in every case were similar to the erroneous reports given by the actual subjects. Any actor–observer differences that do occur can be explained in terms of exposure to different information or stimuli, such as that resulting from the different positioning of actor and observer. Nisbett and Wilson, like Bem (1972), allow that actors' knowledge of their personal history and their greater access to internal private stimuli can lead to some superiority over observers, but they maintain that these differences are purely quantitative, rather than reflecting a functional or qualitative difference.

Given the premise that people often mistake the causes of their behaviour and that actor and observer attributions do not significantly differ, theorists in a positivist tradition cannot fail to reach the conclusion that displaces intention: actors and observers employ the same mechanisms in their explanations of actors' behaviour. Like Bem, Nisbett and Wilson conclude that 'If the reports of subjects do not differ from the reports of observers, then it is unnecessary to assume that the former are drawing on a "fount of privileged knowledge"' (p. 248). This significant conclusion is accompanied by full-fledged alternative theories which readily accommodate the decisive evidence. Bem proposes that self-explanations derive from people's observations of their behaviour and its surrounding circumstances. An example is the treatment of self-attributed emotions and states. These events are considered to be equivalent to or inferred from such stimuli as heart-rate feedback or trembling hands. A typical experiment illustrating this position is that of Valins and Ray (1967), using people with snake phobias as subjects. The experimenters wired the subjects to false-feedback heart-rate recordings and gave them shocks accompanied by (false) heart-rate increases, followed by slides of snakes which 'elicited' no such increase. The experimenters predicted that subjects would infer from the feedback that they were not so afraid of snakes, and subjects did appear to do this. This type of study is taken to show that people infer their emotions from external stimuli, not introspection. In contrast to Bem, Nisbett and Wilson claim that explanations of self and others express theories of causal relations that are learned within a culture. In the new framework, intentions are redefined as information or content, rather than as a causal process, by Nisbett and Wilson, and as an inference from the stimulus conditions that accompany behaviour by Bem.

In both cases, psychology is being employed here not so much to make new discoveries as to give a new legitimacy to an historic philosophical position. Bem's and Nisbett and Wilson's conclusions affirm Hume's claim that people derive self-knowledge from their perceptions of themselves: 'For my part, when I enter most intimately into what I call myself, I always stumble on to some particular perception or other, of heat or cold, light or shade, love or hatred, pain or pleasure. I can never catch myself at any time without a perception, and can never observe anything but the perception' (Hume, 1739; cited in Copleston, 1958, p. 302). In 1972, Bem reached the same conclusion: 'Self-attributions are made from an individual's observations of his own behaviour and/or the circumstances in which it occurs' (p. 5). Of course, most scholars already know that modern positivism belongs to an ancient tradition. But given the aura of progress that pervades modern science (Skinner, 1971, saw his formulation of positivism as entailing changes on the scale of a Copernican revolution, and Bem's 1972 theory appeared in a series entitled Advances in Experimental Social Psychology), many researchers at the same time fail to realize how similar much of the reasoning and conclusions of contemporary theorists is to that of earlier epochs. But while the conclusion is the same, it is attributed to a different source: experimental evidence. The authors claim that scientific methods justified their claims. The conclusion can nonetheless be disputed on a number of grounds; the following sections of this chapter comprise an evaluation of the positivist argument.

Problems in the positivist account

There are a number of concepts and inferences in the positivist argument that are problematic in some respect. The discussion here will focus first on certain concepts in that argument.

Problematic concepts

Several concepts in the positivist analyses of Bem (1972) and Nisbett and Wilson (1977) are problematic, self-contradictory, or otherwise inadequate. The first of these concepts is the frequently referred to phenomenon of self-attributed emotions and states. These events are said to be inferred from stimuli like heart-rate feedback or trembling hands, as in the experiment with snake phobias by Valins and Ray (1967) described above. While this analysis may parsimoniously explain some events, it cannot deal satisfactorily with sensations outside its focus of convenience. For example, as Malcolm (1964) argues, people do not come to know that they have a headache from taking an aspirin. It is to deal with this sort of difficulty that most positivist accounts commit their own unforgivable sin by invoking 'private stimuli'. Skinner (1953) decreed that of the three classes of events affecting human behaviour (stimulus–organism–response), science must consider only the observable (i.e., extraspectively observable) events: stimuli and responses. And as responses are a function of the organism and the organism a function of the stimuli, science *need* only correlate stimuli and responses. Yet in the same work he finds it necessary to invoke 'private' stimuli to explain certain behaviour (e.g., p. 262). Similarly, in attribution theory, D. J. Bem claims to represent radical behaviourism (1972, p. 55), yet he finds it necessary to invoke private stimuli to explain self-explanations (pp. 3, 4, 55). He argues that 'such concessions to expositional clarity do not, in my view, add anything to the explanatory power of the theory; it remains formally equivalent to its earlier, albeit nearly incomprehensible, incarnation in the more rigid and arid vocabulary of radical behaviourism' (p. 55).

Considering that the term 'private stimuli' covers most of the phenomena being disputed, Bem's disclaimer is most unconvincing, and remains so until behaviourism proffers some operational definition of its 'private' stimuli. The intrinsic contradiction in this terminology is a consequence of the positivist model's inability to provide an adequate explanation of cognition, especially intention. The attempt to translate intention into positivist terms has entailed several other tortuous concepts, one of which is Bem's (1972) definition of intention as the stimuli at hand. As Chomsky (1959) and Giddens (1977) have already pointed out in other contexts, such definitions fail to account in any way for such phenomena as unfulfilled intentions. A person may plan something, but not initiate any course of action to bring it about. Conversely, a plan may be realized by events that are independent of the actor's conduct.

Nisbett and Wilson's (1977) redefinition of intention is equally problematic. They argue that intention, not being a 'process' affecting behaviour, is 'content' or information. Nisbett and Wilson's classification of cognition into process and content, or process and product, has been challenged by a number of authors. Ericsson and Simon (1980), Smith and Miller (1978), and White (1980) have all pointed out that Nisbett and Wilson's decisions as to what counts as process are quite arbitrary, and that the authors did not define the criterion by which their decisions are made. White observes that this omission enables Nisbett and Wilson to construe any kind of evidence to support their position, and to call everything that the subject is conscious of, a product, and everything that doesn't enter consciousness, process. Smith and Miller specifically contest one instance of this in Nisbett and Wilson's claim that the rules that people report using on a task (such as long division) are not the process operating.

There are other difficulties with the process/content dichotomy as it relates specifically to intention, and to Nisbett and Wilson's claim that intention is content rather than process. In their discussion of intentions, Nisbett and Wilson write that 'an individual may know...that he was or was not pursuing a particular intention' (p. 286). The word 'pursue' here is a cue to the non-equivalence of intentions and information. As Nisbett and Wilson imply, one may pursue an intention even if that intention is something that one has at the present time. But if one is pursuing information, then that information is something that one does not have at the present time. The difference derives from the peculiar temporal relationship between intentions and behaviour wherein intentions precede the behaviour that they are expressed in. By contrast, if one is pursuing information, the act of pursuing precedes the ownership of the information. The functional difference between intentions and information in their temporal relationship to behaviour is an important matter that will be returned to below.

There is another relevant difference between information and intention. Intentions comprise people's perceptions of efficacy; rightly or wrongly, people have the impression that they are activating their behaviour, as de Biran (see p. 14) and deCharms both claimed. It follows that if an intention is not the origin of the behaviour, then the self-perceptions of intention are illusory. Nisbett and Wilson come close to recognizing this fact; they claim that people's belief that intentions are the cause of their actions functions 'to sustain the illusion of introspective awareness' (1977, p. 255). If intentions are not causal, then they are illusory, in that they comprise people's impression of causal efficacy. This characteristic of intentions distinguishes them from information or content, as information does not of necessity become illusory when it is categorized as content. The positivist account does not explain either the perception of efficacy that inheres in intentional behaviour or the differences between intentions and content that are pointed out here.

One further unsatisfactory concept in the positivist account is the term 'observer'. In experiments supposedly demonstrating the equivalence of actor and observer explanations (Nisbett and Wilson, 1977, p. 247), 'observers' are people saying how they or other people *would* react in a given situation. These are observers only in a conditional sense of saying how someone would act, rather than being actual observers, who say how someone is acting. Furthermore, in several cases (those saying how *they* would act), they are not conditional observers but conditional actors. People saying how they or others *would* act are not observing but speculating. These procedures differ from an instance of an actor performing a behaviour followed by the actor and an observer proposing a cause for that behaviour.

In its argument about the sources of self-knowledge, the positivist house leans heavily on concepts of sand. In addition, the argument employs several inferences or generalizations that are problematic or unjustified. These inferences are linked to a looseness in terminology which charac-terizes discussions of explanations of actions, and attributions in particular. Discussions of access to causes of actors' behaviour include cognitions as diverse as states, attitudes, problem-solving and attributions of the causes of behaviour. These various cognitions are different, and represent responses to different questions or situations. Furthermore, the indiscriminate labelling of all references to causes of behaviour as attributions fails to differentiate intentions, or plans for behaviour, from reasons for or rationalizations of that behaviour. These various cognitions will be defined for the purposes of the following discussion. Four definitions are proposed:

1.   *Intentions.* Intentions inhere in a plan of action, and can be operationally defined as the (class of) response, if one is given, to such questions as: 'What are (or were, will) you (or they) planning to do?' in reference to a particular action.

2.   *Reasons.* Reasons express a motive or rationale for an action, and can be defined as the (type of) response, if given, to such questions as 'Why are (or were, will) you (or they) perform, performing this action?'

3.   *States, attitudes, emotions, traits, and sensations.* These phenomena, which as a group shall be called states, are indicated in replies to such questions as 'What do (or did, will) you (or they) think, feel, or like?' with regard to some object, issue, or event.

4.   *Problem-solving.* This category includes the (kind of) response, if one is given, to such questions as 'How do (or did, will) you (or they) do this?'

These four definitions do not restrict the concepts defined to either past, present or future, and they do not imply or entail the prerogative of actor or observer. The definitions thus have more in common with those of Boden (1973) and Antaki and Fielding (1981), who define the constituents of explanations in term of their function, than with those authors such as deCharms (1976), who define the concepts in terms of the person giving the explanation, and give an a priori advantage to the actor with regard to intentions and reasons. These categories also differ from the classification of Buss (1978), who proposes that actors give only reasons for their behaviour, whereas observers give both reasons and causes. Even when actors explain their behaviour in causal terms, he suggest, they really mean a reason-type explanation. The rationale for using definitions that do not themselves entail the prerogative of either actor or observer is to prevent those tautologous situations where psychologists set out to demonstrate an advantage for actor or observer which has already been assumed in the definitions they embrace.

Of the four categories above, the first two, intentions and reasons, together comprise an explanation of an anticipated or actual action. An intention describes the action, while a reason comprises a motive explaining why the act is being carried out. Thus an intention and reason together explain an action, although, as Boden (1973) has pointed out, any single intention may be conceived for a number of different reasons, or to serve one or more of a number of motives. Although intentions and reasons may be treated as distinct levels of explanation (cf. Heider, 1958; Schank and

Abelson, 1977), it is difficult to draw an absolute or clear-cut distinction between them. Intentions correspond to what Vallacher and Wegner (1985) refer to as lower-level identifications of actions, whereas reasons and motives involve higher-level identifications. The third category of cognition, states, differs from both intentions and reasons in that whereas intentions and reasons are directly related to actions, states may have no relationship to actions. These distinctions are overlooked in several inferences or generalizations in the positivist argument.

The inference across cognitive classes

Although the four categories of cognition listed above refer to different kinds of cognitive content or operation which correspond to different questions or situations, the positivist account lumps the categories together, treating them as interchangeable and functionally equivalent. For example, Nisbett and Wilson (1977) group together questions corresponding to states, problem-solving, and reasons: 'Why did you like him? How did you solve this problem? Why did you take that job?' (p. 231). They similarly group together 'choices, evaluations, judgements, and behaviour' (p. 231), and 'causes of attitudinal, emotional, and behavioural responses' (p. 233). This lumping together of several cognitive categories allows advocates of a positivist account to make inferences across those categories. Writers generalize from experiments providing evidence about people's states to conclusions including intentions, reasons, and causes. Nisbett and Wilson (1977), for example, claim to be analysing people's 'reports about the causes of their behaviour' (p. 234), or their 'reasons for [their] behaviour' (p. 232). Similarly Bem (1972) claims to have re-explained intentions in his behavioural analysis. He stipulates that 'the intent or meaning is inferred from the stimulus conditions that appear to be controlling the observed behaviour' (p. 6).

While these conclusions refer to intentions and reasons or causes, the experiments from which the conclusions are inferred mostly manipulate states, not explanations of behaviour. Typical is the Valins and Ray (1967) experiment outlined earlier which analysed subjects' accounts of their emotions. The experiment employs the Schachter and Singer (1962) paradigm, which is not concerned with people's intentions or reasons for actions undertaken. Subjects in these experiments are asked how frightened they are, not what they plan to do or why. This observation applies equally to the many other experiments with the same basic design (see Kleinke, 1978, for numerous examples). Yet it is primarily on the basis of this form of experiment that the positivist analyses reach conclusions about all cognitions, including intentions, reasons and causes. Nisbett and Wilson thus generalize too broadly in concluding their review of research: 'The evidence indicates it may be quite misleading for social scientists to ask their subjects about the influences on their evaluations, choice or behavior. The relevant research indicates that such reports, as well as predictions, may have little value except for whatever utility they may have in the study of verbal explanations per se' (Nisbett and Wilson, 1977, p. 247). This generalization from research with states and emotions to conclusions about choices and explanations of behaviour probably suggests that positivist models are more successful in explaining states and emotions than they are in explaining intentions and reasons (Morris, 1981).

More recently, authors have challenged positivist accounts even as they apply to states and non-intentional cognitions. Sears (1986) suggests that the low level of self-knowledge demonstrated in research with college subjects, who are at a stage when the self-concept is in flux, would not be replicated in research with adults whose self-concept and attitudes have crystallized. This interesting speculation has not been examined in research, but recent research on people's detection of stimulus information of their judgements suggests that actors are superior to observers in detecting influences on their behaviour, even in cases that do not involve intentional behaviour (Gavanski and Hoffman, 1987). But the central argument here is that research comparing actors and observers has not examined intentional action, and has generalized about intention from studies examining other classes of cognition.

Nisbett and Wilson's failure to distinguish between different classes of cognition relates to their not distinguishing between automatic and controlled cognitive processing (Morris, 1981; Schneider and Shiffrin, 1977). Automatic processing involves the effortless processing of information that requires little attention or consciousness, and applies particularly to well-rehearsed tasks. Automatic processing is triggered by environmental stimuli, without necessitating conscious attention or control. By contrast controlled processing, which applies particularly to new tasks or to processing novel stimuli, involves the conscious attention of the person. Bargh (1984) has discussed the relevance of this distinction for social cognition. Bargh focuses particularly on attitudes and scripts, and does not examine the relevance of the automatic/controlled distinction for the difference between actors' knowledge of their own cognitions and the causes of their actions by comparison with observers. This particular connection is made by Morris (1981) and Scott (1989), who point out that Nisbett and Wilson's claim that people have no access to cognitive processes and the causes of their actions is based largely on phenomena involving automatic processing, and pays little attention to phenomena involving controlled processing. Nisbett and Wilson have tended to generalize about all cognitive processes on the basis of tasks involving automatic processing. A comprehensive strategy for examining actors' and observers' knowledge of actors' cognitions and actions would include the study of intentions and controlled processing.

The inference across independent and dependent variables

A second inference underlying the positivist argument is the extrapolation from experiments in which cognitions are the dependent variable to conclusions that would be valid only if cognitions had been the independent variable. This inference relates to Bem's (1972) discussion of dependent and independent variables in attribution research. Bem distinguished three response classes: behavioural, physiological and cognitive (p. 46), and points out that in all the research carried out on self-perceptions:

> Cognitions or self-attributions are the dependent variables. Instrumental behaviours, consummatory responses and physiological responses (real or falsified) are among the variables which can serve as antecedent or independent variables, the stimuli from which self-attributions of beliefs, attitudes, or internal states can be partially inferred by the individual. Attribution models are thus very explicit about the direction of the causal arrow, and they remain mute about any phenomenon in which the noncognitive response classes play the dependent variable.
>
> (p. 47)

Bem recognizes that there is a bias or asymmetry built into the positivist designs, in that they do not treat cognitions, overt behaviours, and physiological responses as functionally equivalent response classes. The asymmetry reflects a limitation in the self-perception model of which Bem is fully aware: 'How do attribution models account for noncognitive response classes? They don't. Self perception theory can get us from the stimulus manipulation to the attribution. It cannot get us from the attribution to anything beyond that' (p. 47).

Bem allows that because of these limitations, 'additional machinery must be added if attribution models are to deal with behavioural or physiological responses as dependent variables' (p. 60). As he observes, the results obtained are an artifact of an experimental design in which the experimenters' asymmetrical treatment of different 'response' classes has always categorized attributions as the dependent variable. But what he doesn't point out is that the conclusions that are inferred from the research would only be justified if attributions had been treated as independent variables. An example is Nisbett and Wilson's (1977) suggestion, cited above, that they had explained people's choices and explanations for their actions. But neither actions in the absence of changes in observable stimuli, nor self-attributions of intentions or reasons have been investigated in attribution research as independent variables. More recent articulations of the same paradigm persist in focusing on the effects of stimuli on cognitions such as liking and states, rather than examining cognitions as determinants of actions (Wilson, 1985). This bias in the positivist designs becomes clearer when we consider a third inference in the positivist argument concerning the temporal relationship between cognitions and behaviour.

The inference across temporal relationships

The temporal relationship between cognitions and behaviour is related to the causal relationships considered in the previous section. In bringing attention to constraints on temporal relationships, S. E. Taylor (1976) points out that there is a temporal restrictiveness in contemporary research in cognitive social psychology. She notes that in nearly all of this research, subjects are asked to state their reactions to the manipulations at the close of the experiment. Experimenters ask subjects what they conclude, rather than asking them how they are putting information together when they are doing so.

S. E. Taylor suggests that social psychologists, even when studying cognitive processes, have acted like behaviourists in adopting an S–R approach which obtains retrospective and outcome reports, instead of an S–O–R approach which analyses ongoing processes. She suggests that cognitive processes would be better understood by studying process over time, and by obtaining concurrent reports from subjects. Ericsson and Simon (1980) and White (1980) also focus on this temporal parameter and point out that a far wider range of accurate reports can be obtained from subjects if researchers use concurrent, rather than retrospective, reports.

The important point here for the current argument is that the research from which the positivist theorists infer their conclusions about intentions and self-perception contains an asymmetrical temporal relationship between cognitions and actions, with the cognition always subsequent to the action. Yet inferences are made which would be legitimate only if researchers had used concurrent reports. It is the use of asymmetrical temporal relationships, coupled with designs that limit cognitions to dependent variables and that make inferences across different cognitions, that underlies the claims made by advocates of the positivist stance. It has been wrongly inferred that this research has accounted for intentions, reasons, and perceived causes, and found no significant differences between actors and observers. But this conclusion would be justified only if research obtained no significant differences in actors and observers when actually testing intentions, reasons and causes, and when testing all causal and time relationships between attributions and behaviour.

The effect of removing asymmetries

In fact, the science of psychology as conceived in social psychology has not yet done away with intention. The concept has hardly been put to a genuine test. But the very attempts to dispense with intention, including the biases in the selection of parameters to achieve this purpose, assist in pointing to how investigation might get closer to the concept. This was partially realized by S. E. Taylor (1976), Ericsson and Simon (1980), and White (1980), who proposed that research should supplement recall experiments, where self-reports follow behaviour, with concurrent reports, where people answered questions like 'What are you doing?' and 'Why are you doing this?' This change produces different results, but the design retains an unnecessary restriction on temporal relations between behaviour and cognition, a restriction probably resulting from the influence of information-processing conceptions. A full range of temporal relations would include reports *preceding* behaviour, in addition to reports following and concurrent with behaviour.

The effect that this manipulation of the time parameter could have on differences between actors and observers can be illustrated in a thought experiment which employs the cognitive class of intentions and a temporal relationship where the report precedes behaviour. We instruct an actor to formulate an intention to be carried out at a subsequent time. We also instruct an observer to formulate what he thinks the actor will do at that subsequent time. Both parties write down their prediction, and at the appropriate time the actor performs an action. We then evaluate actor–observer differences in accuracy of prediction.

Most people's experience of functionally equivalent situations requires no further test to know that such a situation would challenge the positivist claim that there are no significant differences in actors' and observers' explanations and that they have displaced the concept of intention. Is it not likely that there would be a significant actor–observer difference in predictions and that the difference would be one of accuracy, and thus superiority? The imagined situation may seem absurdly simple, but it represents a reversal of the asymmetries and inferences which dominate current research. Instead of inferring across cognitive classes from states to intentions, it examines intentions. Instead of the unilateral causal relationship wherein cognitions are always the dependent variable, it examines cognitions as the independent variable. Instead of the unilateral time relationship wherein reports are always subsequent to behaviour, it places the behaviour after the report. These reversals would demonstrate significant actor–observer differences in accuracy of prediction. Intention is the fount of knowledge which qualitatively distinguishes actor and observer.

Boundaries to the actors' privilege

What holds for intentions, however, does not necessarily hold for reasons and motives, the second category of explanations. Actors' privilege with regard to their intentions does not automatically extend to their reasons, their perceptions of the motive for their behaviour. This is apparent if we extend the thought experiment outlined above a stage further. After actor and observer have made their predictions, the actor performs the intended action and tears up a photograph, as an arbitrary example. Actor and observer are then asked to provide a reason or motive for the action. They give different explanations: 'Because I wanted the paper to write on'; 'Because the photo reminded him of his brother.' When comparing actor and observer on predictions of actions from intentions, comparisons in accuracy of prediction could be made. But this is not so simple to achieve with reasons and motives. There are no grounds like 'greater accuracy' on which one can establish actor superiority in reason explanations. Did the actor tear up the photo because he wanted the paper to write on or because it reminded him of his brother? The phenomenological school wants to take the actor at his word in such situations. But as critical theorists (e.g., Habermas, 1971) have emphasized, there are a number of ways in which the actor's self-explanations or reasons may be unsatisfactory. People sometimes simply cannot explain their behaviour; they do not know why they do certain things. In other circumstances people do explain their behaviour but their explanations include recurring distortions and self-contradictions (Habermas, 1971; Ricoeur, 1974). People also give conflicting explanations across settings, as where people give one explanation for their behaviour in one setting and a different explanation, conflicting with the first, in another setting. People's explanations of their actions may additionally include falsity or deception, and can function to conceal one or more motives for the action undertaken. These characteristics are evident in social groups as well as in single actors.

In fact it is possible that an observer may proffer a better explanation (reason or motive) of the actor's behaviour than the actor. It is because people sometimes cannot understand why they do what they do (as well as for other reasons), that they consult clinical psychologists, psychiatrists, and other specialists. An observer's explanation of a person's behaviour may be more convincing to that person than their own explanation. So while it can be demonstrated that actors are privileged with regard to their intentions, the same decisive superiority does not extend to their reasons or their explication of their motives.

The suggested distinction between intentions and reasons may contribute to a resolution of the long-standing conflict between phenomenological writers who insist that people have the experience of generating their own behaviour and researchers of a more positivist bent who point to the evidence that people make numerous errors with regard to their behaviour (e.g., Nisbett and Ross, 1980). The distinction between intentions and reasons, along with the imaginary and actual situations described above, supports the notion that people at least partially generate their behaviour voluntarily, but it is also in harmony with the vast array of research indicating that people often misattribute the causes of their behaviour.

This analysis also suggests that authors who argue that there are intrinsic differences between actor and observer explanations are mistaken to try to locate the actor's advantage in the reasons given for the behaviour (e.g., Buss, 1978; Shotter, 1981a). Actors are indeed privileged with regard to their intentions, but observers may be as good or better at discerning or proposing the reasons or motives for the actors' behaviour. Perhaps it is because people are aware of a reason for an action when they are forming an intention that they think that they have privileged access to their reasons and motives. But although people may have a very clear reason in mind when they conceive or carry out some action, that reason may not reflect any or all the motives underlying the behaviour.

The procedure which has been suggested here to compare actors and observers requires an actor to generate an intention and then predict his or her action, and compares that prediction with an observer's prediction. The principle behind this procedure relates to Popper's (e.g., 1959) theory as to the feature that distinguishes superior scientific theories. Good scientific theories make falsifiable predictions, such that they can be rejected when their predictions are falsified. 'Pseudoscientific' theories are less susceptible to falsification and are based more on *post hoc* explanations of events, readily assimilating unanticipated outcomes as supportive. The procedure typically used in social psychology experiments that demonstrates equivalence between actors and observers asks *post hoc* an action why the actor did it. The complementary procedure proposed here, of asking actors and observers to make predictions of the actor's actions, applies a more falsificationist criterion to the study of the explanations of actors and observers. Rorty (1970) has made similar claims about mental states: 'Statements about beliefs, desires, emotions, and intentions are implicit predictions of future behavior, predictions that may be falsified' (p. 420).

The idea that predictive power and falsifiability are distinguishing features of successful scientific theories has itself been challenged and falsified (e.g., Kuhn, 1970; Lakatos and Musgrave, 1970). Even 'good' scientists do not readily accept falsifications of their predictions and hypotheses. Fischhoff (1980) has demonstrated that lay people also do not change their beliefs when their predictions are falsified, and that they assimilate non-predicted outcomes into their existing understanding of events. What starts as surprise is soon assimilated as 'just as I thought'. After elections, neither individuals nor newspaper editors lack explanations for outcomes they did not predict. The *post hoc* explanation is a leveller of theories as it is of actor and observer differences. It is in predicting the subsequent actions that the actor is distinguished from the observer. When it comes to articulating reasons and motives, which is the point at which many theorists have located the actor's superiority, this demonstrable advantage disappears. People often do not and sometimes cannot report their reasons and motives accurately.

It could be argued that the actors' superiority in predicting their actions is due to some process like a self-fulfilling prophecy, where actors' performance of the action they predict is due to a desire to prove their prediction correct (cf. Sherman, 1980). This process could explain the actors' motive in performing the predicted action, but it does not explain the actors' antecedent advantage in knowing what their intention is in the first place. This source of information needs to be explained, as well as the action that follows a self-prediction.

Are empirical demonstrations relevant?

Earlier in this chapter it was noted that the issues being disputed here address questions that have been disputed for centuries by writers addressing philosophical–psychological questions. It can reasonably be asked whether such issues can ever be adequately approached by psychology conceived as a science. Is the question more appropriately dealt with by the philosophy of mind or the philosophy of action? Or isn't the question of whether human behaviour is intentional simply an assumption that a viewpoint either espouses or rejects while investigating more specific propositions?

These are questions to which any reply is itself a matter of opinion, subject to territorial imperatives as well as epistemological constraints. It is important to note that in reaching or rationalizing this opinion, the definitions given to both methods and subject-matter play an influential role. People can define scientific method itself in such a way that science a priori cannot examine mental events or processes, as in a strict methodological behaviourism. In such cases one cannot study intention scientifically because of one's chosen definition of science. Alternatively one can define intention as an expression of free will that cannot yet or cannot ever be explained by science (Shotter, 1980). Such formulations have similar logical implications to the 'God of the gaps' position which locates God's presence and efficacy in those mysteries which elude science's grasp (Coulson, 1955;

Flew, 1955), and commit intention to a shrinking domain if the human sciences increase their capacity to explain human thought and action.

If these sorts of preconditions are not stipulated, there is no reason in principle why concepts such as intention cannot be defined and examined in empirical terms. The task may be difficult or impossible in practice, and those who do wish to put such concepts into testable form should heed Rychlak's (1968) observation that when mentalistic concepts are put into testable terms, the form into which the concept is channelled frequently fails to capture the essence of the original concept. Despite these hazards, it seems reasonable to accept that if theoretical models, supported by research, can parsimoniously explain people's actions and their awareness of efficacy without reference to intention or some equivalent concept, then they can reasonably claim to have established the dispensability of the concept of intention as an explanation. This is precisely what D. J. Bem and Nisbett and Wilson have attempted to do. What is argued here and in evaluations by others is not that Nisbett and Wilson and Bem are mistaken in principle for attempting to do so, but that in practice they have failed, and thus the evidence not only fails to justify many of their conclusions, but it militates against them.

New self concepts in social cognition

In recent years perceptions and explanations of self and other have been widely conceptualized in terms of processes of social cognition. The cognitions accompanying and underlying social interaction have been construed in terms of models of the general processes of memory and cognition. Within the domain of social cognition, several major topics of interest are relevant to the perception of self and of others, particularly self-schemata and person memory. Research in these areas relies heavily on the information-processing metaphor. A further development, the theory of action identification, represents a substantial shift from this metaphor to a more action-oriented model.

Self-schemata
The concept of self-schemata is one of several concepts in contemporary social cognition that concern the perception of self and of others. Self-schemata are defined as cognitive structures relating to the self that contain information about a person's traits and appearance (Markus, 1977). The full range of a person's self-schemata comprise that person's self-concept. Research examining self-schemata has concentrated on the issue whether people are schematic (have a schema) or aschematic (have no schema) in relation to various traits and attributes. For people who are schematic for a

trait such as independence, independence is an important aspect of their self-concept; their independence is important to them and they see themselves as extreme or prominent on that trait. To people who are aschematic on a trait, the trait is not salient and not central to their self-concept. Research examining this distinction uses reaction time judgements as a measure of judgements; people who are schematic in relation to the trait 'sporting' process information relating to sport more rapidly than people who are not schematic on that trait. In essence, this framework examines people's judgements and inferences about information describing themselves.

The study of self-schemata places self-knowledge in the context of an information-processing model of cognition. It provides one tangible channel into people's perception of themselves as personalities, and into their processing of information relating to their self-concepts. Greenwald and Pratkanis (1984) suggest that 'the conception of the self as a system of schemata provides a welcome means of accommodating the self as knower alongside the self as object of knowledge' (p. 147). What the study of self-schemata appears to leave out is the intentional aspect of the self as agent; it includes the cognitive but omits the conative. Although it does examine people's predictions of their own behaviour, these predictions are based on schema, rather than on people's intentions. Research on self-schemata pays little attention to people's perceptions of their own intentions, despite the fact that research on person schemata (schemata of other people) examines people's perceptions of other people's goals and intentions, in addition to inferences about traits (e.g., Taylor and Crocker, 1981). Research that examined goals and intentions in relation to self-schemata would capture more of the intentional aspects of cognition and would provide a more dynamic treatment of self-perceptions. People's self-concept is likely to be coloured by their intentions and wishes, their desires and plans, and not merely by their traits (cf. Schank and Abelson, 1977; Vallacher and Wegner, 1987).

Person memory
The research on self-schemata is closely related to the concept of person memory, which is memory of the appearance, behaviour, and traits of other persons (Hastie and Kumar, 1979). The accuracy of memory of other persons is an important issue in relation to issues such as eye-witness identification in the legal context. Person memory is considered to operate largely on the principles that apply to memory in general, particularly the operation of memory networks. This feature extends to explanations of an observer's understanding of an actor's behaviour. For example, the understanding of another person's actions in empathy is explained in terms

of the operation of the memory networks that underlie person memory. While it is recognized that empathy with another person involves 'more psychological engagement' and 'deeper processing' than forming personal impressions (Fiske and Taylor, 1984, p. 228), the phenomenon is nonetheless explained primarily in terms of its effect in improving memory. This view of empathy at the same time acknowledges and yet skirts around the intentional or action-based nature of the phenomenon. It is acknowledged that research shows that people who are told to empathize with a person make many more attributions about the person, explaining why the person is doing certain things, than detached observers (Harvey, Yarkin, Lightner and Town, 1980). This focus on causes for actions suggests that the actor's perspective which is appropriated in empathy involves a sense of carrying out reasoned actions, rather than simply a sense of static attributes such as traits or schemata. However, authors dealing with person memory do not consider this implication of the finding, and restrict their account to the operation of memory. For example Fiske and Taylor (1984) suggest that 'the additional work that goes into constructing explanations' improves memory, and provides additional memory retrieval routes. The implication of this interpretation is that understanding people's actions in empathy revolves around an enhancement of the memory process, rather than an understanding of the intentions of the actor.

This purely memory-based interpretation is maintained despite the fact that research indicates that empathy is assisted by knowing actors' intentions or goals. Fiske and Taylor (p. 228) recognize that when reading stories, 'understanding someone's goals enables readers to build links among the person's various actions', and that if 'you are told' what someone's goal is, a series of disconnected actions 'take on new meaning'. Fiske and Taylor infer from these findings that 'empathy promotes a focus on the other person's goals, and as we have already noted, goals provide a strong memory aid' (p. 228). But the findings in the empathy research involve features in addition to memory. As Fiske and Taylor recognize, the literature indicates that actions are better understood if people understand the intentions that generate and coordinate the actions. The literature also suggests implicitly that actors have special access to their intentions, and that knowing those intentions derives in Fiske and Taylor's terms from 'being told', presumably by the actor or by someone who is privy to the actor's intentions. These findings suggest that intentional actions are an important component of people's actions, and that knowing those intentions enhances both apprehension and memory. The explanation of empathy purely in terms of memory appears to invert the memory and understanding processes, implying that the key process involved in empathy is a memory process. By contrast, several aspects of the research on empathy suggest that a key facilitative component of empathy involves 'understanding' the intentions in the action, and the improvement in memory follows as a consequence of this effect. In one sense, actors' knowledge of their own intentions can be seen as a form of private expertise that operates in the same facilitative way as expertise in the normal sense.

The analysis here supports the view expressed by Ostrom (1984) that the role of action in cognitive processing 'has been neglected by social cognition researchers' (p. 27). Ostrom notes that 'most analyses of cognitive processes have dealt exclusively with the issues of representing and processing passively received information about other persons... They have ignored the companion obligation to work toward an understanding of how action goals are formulated, behavioural plans are structured, and muscle movement instructions are initiated' (p. 26). In relation to conceptions of the self, Ostrom asserts that 'self-knowledge is not a trait label plus its schematic implications. Instead, self-knowledge that is drawn upon in the midst of social interactions derives from the store of actions previously engaged in' (p. 27). We might add the actions being currently engaged in and about to be engaged in. The analysis here supports Ostrom's assessment that social cognition should incorporate the action-related dimensions of cognition, but critical perspectives also propose that people's self-knowledge and their understanding of their own action may involve errors, omissions and distortions that serve some functional purpose.

The theory of action identification

Vallacher and Wegner have recently developed a theory of action identification, where they attempt to reconcile the seeming conflict between intentional or 'unbounded' consciousness on one hand and bounded lawful behaviour on the other (Vallacher and Wegner, 1985, 1987; Wegner and Vallacher, 1986). They note that theories in social psychology have examined retrospective reflections on actions, but have failed to directly examine the intentional prospective link between cognition and action. They note that a direct analysis of how people think about their more significant actions, and how those thoughts affect the nature of those actions is largely missing from contemporary psychology. Their theory of action identification attempts to address this problem, and integrates retrospective and prospective conceptions of action. The conception of an action, of what a person is doing, is referred to as an action identity. For example, a single action may be identified as 'dialling the phone' or 'making a complaint'. Actions may have many identities, and these are arranged hierarchically, extending from lower level identities, which describe the more behavioural details of an action, to higher level identities, which convey a more general understanding of the goal of an action. For example, in relation to a telephone call, 'turning the dial' is a lower level identification, whereas 'flattering the boss' is a possible higher level identification for the same action. This hierarchy corresponds in broad terms to the distinction between 'what' and 'why' explanations introduced above. Lower level identifications correspond to what is being done, or the intention of an action, whereas higher level identifications indicate the reason why the person is carrying out the action, or the motive for the action.

Vallacher and Wegner propose that actions are guided by their identities in the actor's mind: by the actor's cognitive representation of an action. Consequently, although this corollary is not stated explicitly, their position implies that actors' understanding of the causes of their action is superior to observers'. In relation to differences in actors' and observers' attributions to personal and situational factors, they claim 'without knowledge of a person's phenomenal organization of action, it is difficult for an observer (lay or professional) to determine whether the person's behavior reflects personal considerations...or responsiveness to contextual cues that provide meaning for an action undertaken at a relatively low level' (Vallacher and Wegner, 1987, p. 11). The theory implies that observers who are not 'privy to' the identification that the actor holds in any situation may not correctly identify the person's intentions or motives. In contrast with Nisbett and Wilson's claim that people's accounts of their own action involves telling more than they can know, Vallacher and Wegner emphasize that people know what they are doing. They assert that the theory 'can be portrayed as one of those theories that says people know what they are doing' (Wegner and Vallacher, 1986, p. 557). They suggest that this knowledge is particularly evident in relation to higher level identifications for actions. A person who has higher level identifications for an action is more resistant to alternative conceptions of the action because 'a person with a relatively high level understanding already knows what he or she is doing' (Vallacher and Wegner, 1987, p. 8).

Action identification theory provides a substantial advance over the more positivist accounts of self-perception, as it incorporates intentions and cognitions that precede actions in addition to explanations that follow actions. The theory may be questioned for assuming too much in relation to actors' knowledge of what they are doing, and actors' advantage over observers. Vallacher and Wegner emphasize that in their higher level identifications of their actions, actors know what they are doing, and their understanding of their action derives from their cognition accompanying their action. However, it is not clear that this 'knowledge' is always present. Actors and observers are more likely to agree on low level identifications, such as whether the actor is turning a door-knob, than on higher level identifications, such as whether the actor is flattering the boss. But it is disputable whether one can assume that actors' higher level identifications necessarily constitute knowledge of the reason or motive for an action. It is possible that observers' higher level identification might be more plausible than an actor's. If a policeman finds a person inside a locked bank at night, and the person claims to be looking for a friend while the policeman believes he or she is robbing the bank, the policeman's identification may be more plausible. To some extent, even higher level identifications can be tested by predictions. For example, actor and observer may agree on a lower level identification of a person's action in a public situation, such as giving to charity. But they may have different higher level identifications 'because I care about the refugees', 'because he wishes to impress his girlfriend'. Predictions of behaviour in other (e.g., private) situations would not necessarily support the actor's identification for the action.

In short, whereas action identification theory implies that people 'know what they are doing' at higher level identifications, it can be suggested that people sometimes may not know what they are doing, or they might not report certain higher level identifications that they are conscious of.

What do we know?

Positivist analyses in social psychology (e.g., D. J. Bem, 1972; Nisbett and Wilson, 1977) claim that research validates the view, long held by positivist philosophy, that behaviour is environmentally determined rather than intentional, and that verbal reports do not assist an understanding of cognition or behaviour. It is argued here that Bem and Nisbett and Wilson fail to demonstrate that actors are not advantaged over observers by their knowledge of their own intentions. This theoretical framework can be inverted to demonstrate that actor reports on certain tasks are superior to observer reports, and thereby illuminate the efficacy of the ever-exorcised fount of intention. But actors' distinct privilege in knowing their intentions does not extend to a necessary advantage in comprehending the reasons or motives for their behaviour. In fact an observer may offer a more satisfactory rationale for a person's behaviour.

Theory and research on self-schemata and person memory capture certain cognitive and perceptual aspects of self-perception, but they lack an account of the more conative or action-related aspects of cognition. This aspect is however examined in action identification theory, which explores aspects of people's identifications of their actions. but which places too much confidence in people's knowledge of what they are doing, at least in higher level identifications. If this aspect of the theory is modified, however, the paradigm provides the potential for valuable inquiry into actors' and observers' explanations of actions.

5 New accounts: ethogenics and hermeneutics

Several authors have recently challenged the adequacy of social cognition and attribution theory for the analysis of explanations. Critics propose the modification or the entire replacement of the attribution-oriented approach in social cognition. A central issue in these evaluations is the conceptual distinction between reasons and causes; authors have queried how, or indeed whether, attribution theories and related models can deal with both of these types of explanation (Buss, 1978; Locke and Pennington, 1982; Shotter, 1981a, 1984). A second issue is the question of whether the analytic mode of reasoning described by several attribution theories captures the imputations and rationalizations characterizing explanations in everyday life. Critics concerned with this issue argue for a more functional model that emphasizes self-presentation and related functions of explanations and discourse in general (Harré, 1981a, b; Michael, 1989; Neisser, 1980; Potter and Wetherell, 1987).

Frequently these issues are not discussed in isolation, but are linked to proposals for replacing the attribution approach with an ethogenic, hermeneutic or discourse analysis framework (Gergen, 1980, 1982; Harré, 1981a, b; Michael, 1989; Shotter, 1981a, b; 1984). Critics also suggest that conventional approaches to explanations have been selected and retained more as a consequence of ethnocentric and ideological influences than scientific or theoretical merit. These challenges have stimulated some sharp exchanges between those who would retain and possibly modify an attribution approach and those who would altogether reject that approach (Harré, 1981a; Harris and Harvey, 1981; Harvey, 1981; Kruglanski, 1979).

This chapter and the following one focus on these criticisms and proposals. The reason–cause dispute is discussed in this chapter, and the criticisms are considered in terms of a set of definitions and parameters which allow the concepts and arguments to be clearly defined and evaluated. The discussion examines the reason–cause distinction in relation to actor and observer differences and the temporal relationship between explanations and actions. The following chapter discusses the idea that research should adopt a self-presentational analogy as its primary metaphor, and examines the related developments in discourse analysis.

A number of papers have attempted to establish the way in which the distinction between reasons and causes should relate to attribution theory and social cognition. Locke and Pennington (1982) attempt to integrate that distinction in attribution theory by a combination of empirical research and conceptual or necessary truths. Shotter (1981a) defines actor and observer differences in relation to the distinction between reasons and causes by claiming that the distinctive features of each type of explanation is indicated in its unique temporal relationship (i.e. retrospective or prospective) to behaviour. Both Gergen (1980, 1982) and Shotter (1981a) have discussed the issue of how ambiguity in explanations may or may not be resolved in relation to differences between actors and observers. This section discusses each of these aspects of the reason–cause distinction, employing definitions that serve to illustrate and test the various claims made, and relating the various arguments to three parameters: the class of explanation, the person giving the explanation and the temporal relation between an action and an explanation.

Arguments of necessity

Buss (1978) and Locke and Pennington (1982) focused on differences between reasons and causes in relation to the different perspectives of actors and observers. Both papers deal with the relationships between reasons, causes, actors and observers by introducing conceptual or necessary truths, whereby the authors stipulate a necessary or a priori relationship between the class of explanation and the person giving the explanation.

Conceptual distinctions

Buss's (1978) paper has received considerable discussion elsewhere (Buss 1979b, c; Harvey and Tucker, 1979; Kruglanski, 1979), but the course and outcome of that debate is illustrative for the current discussion. Buss proposed that whereas observers may explain an actor's behaviour in terms of either reasons or causes, actors only use reason explanations. He thus proposed an a priori or necessary relationship between the class of explanation and the person giving the explanation. Buss (1979c) later relinquished this pairing, which was central to his thesis, in response to Kruglanski's (1979) observation that actors sometimes do give causal explanations for their behaviour. The supposedly necessary relationship was thus challenged and rejected on empirical grounds. Buss (1979c) nevertheless retained the view that the distinction between reasons and causes is necessarily conceptual and that this characteristic entailed that those concepts could not be defined in empirical terms. He queried: 'How could one operationally define a reason or a cause, an action or an occurrence? I cannot think of any simple way' (p. 1458).

Locke and Pennington (1982) take up this issue, and set out to clarify the relationship of reasons and causes to the different perspectives and advantages of actor and observer. Whereas Buss (1978) postulated a single necessary relationship between the class of explanation and the person giving the explanation, Locke and Pennington introduce three distinctions that are immune to empirical impression on the ground that they are conceptual distinctions or conceptual and necessary truths. The conceptual distinction they make, which they suggest is not subject to empirical test, arises in their description of distinctions between reasons and causes. They propose that: 'If there is any difference between reason and cause, it is the difference between the *content of* some belief, which provides the agent's reason, and the *existence* of a belief with that content, which provides the cause' (p. 214). Locke and Pennington claim that 'this distinction between reasons and (other) causes is a conceptual distinction. Like the distinction between husbands and bachelors, it neither requires empirical confirmation nor permits empirical refutation' (p. 214).

Despite their claim of empirical immunity, Locke and Pennington's distinction makes two assumptions that are subject to empirical refutation. In the first place their definitions propose that the existence of beliefs with reason-type content causes behaviour, whereas the reason itself does not provide the cause. If we found a case where a reason provides the cause, then this distinction is called into question, as would the husband–bachelor distinction come into question if we found husbands who were also bachelors. Yet Locke and Pennington themselves in the course of their exposition describe cases where reasons do indeed provide the cause; they claim that 'insofar as behaviour can be explained by reference to the agent's reasons, agents will have privileged introspective access to the cognitive causes of their conduct' (p. 221). Other passages make the same observation (e.g., p. 217). In suggesting cases where reasons themselves provide the cause of behaviour, Locke and Pennington are acknowledging empirical situations that conflict with the proposition that underlies their own distinction between reasons and causes.

Considerably more difficulty arises in relation to a second assumption in their definitions, the assumption that the mere 'existence of a belief with reason-type content...provides the cause' of the behaviour being explained. The assumption that the mere existence of a reason-type belief provides the cause of an action is challenged by the many instances where a person's belief about why he or she performs an action occurs or exists after the action occurs. Explanations commonly follow behaviour, sometimes emerging or altering after many years, as in people's reflections on their youthful actions. In these cases the mere existence of the explanatory belief can hardly have caused the behaviour that it follows. Unlike the husband–bachelor distinction, Locke and Pennington's distinction, that neither requires empirical confirmation nor permits empirical refutation, makes empirically unsound assumptions. This is not to imply that authors should not make distinctions between reasons and causes, or any other conceptual distinctions, but rather to suggest that we should not bolster our preferred distinctions by invoking philosophical necessity, a strategy that protects our concepts from both analytic evaluation and empirical test. A set of distinctions or assumptions do not become immune from empirical confirmation or refutation simply as a consequence of someone declaring them to be so. Such a status has to be established, rather than asserted without any further justification. Locke and Pennington write as if they assume that simply because they call their distinction a conceptual distinction it consequently becomes a watertight distinction equivalent to the distinction between husbands and bachelors.

Necessary truths

The comments made about Locke and Pennington's conceptual distinctions also apply to the necessary or conceptual truths put forward in the same argument. They claim that 'it is a conceptual truth – guaranteed by the philosophical notion of a reason for action – that there are reasons for behavior only to the extent that it is intentional' (p. 217). Locke and Pennington do not explain the implication in their assertion that there is a single philosophical notion about reasons for actions. There are many such notions, some of which demonstrate considerable insight, but none of which guarantees the conceptual truth which Locke and Pennington propose. Indeed, the claimed conceptual truth can be challenged. The question of whether people ever proffer reasons for unintentional behaviour can be posed empirically. Whatever some philosophical relationship between teleological concepts may imply, there is no conceptual truth that precludes the possibility that people may offer reasons to explain their behaviour even when their behaviour is not intentional. If David pushes Mary, and Mary consequently bumps Astrid, and Astrid asks Mary why she bumped her, it is possible that Mary may offer a reason explanation, even though her bumping Astrid was unintentional. Claims to authorship of accidental or unintended but commendable outcomes are common in everyday life. The projection of purpose into causal events is not merely a possibility, but is a characteristic feature of animistic beliefs. Similar projections can be experimentally induced by simple temporal contiguities (Michotte, 1963). It is not only the case that people offer reason explanations for unintended events; it is also possible that people may present causal explanations for intentional events. Moscovici (1981) has pointed out an example of this in the Nazi ideological strategy of publicizing causal accounts of disastrous or harmful events that were deliberately or unintentionally brought about. Both of these cases (reason explanations for caused events and causal explanations for intended events) negate the apparently commonsense proposal, which Locke and Pennington present as a guaranteed conceptual truth, that there are reasons for behaviour only to the extent that it is intentional.

A final appeal to necessity occurs in Locke and Pennington's claim that 'Agents are necessarily in a better position than observers to know their reasons, precisely because they are their reasons (i.e. beliefs)' (p. 217). This is peculiar logic. If we were to suggest that observers are in a better position than actors to know their (the observers') reasons or explanations for the actors' behaviour simply because those reasons are their reasons, our suggestion would be seen as somewhat circular and non-significant. Yet such a suggestion has the same logical structure as Locke and Pennington's original circular claim. For their claim to have any significance, there has to be an unstated premise that allows the conclusion to assert more than can be derived from the stated premises. Their claim only has significance if we make the assumption, unstated in the claim itself, that the agent's reason is the correct or superior explanation of the agent's behaviour. And indeed this is Locke and Pennington's position; they claim that 'insofar as behaviour can be explained by reference to the agent's reasons, agents will have privileged introspective access to the cognitive causes of their conduct' (p. 221). So the significance of their claim that actors are advantaged over observers rests on an empirical condition, rather than a conceptual necessity. Once again, the invoking of necessity is unsatisfactory. All three instances of necessity or conceptual truth that Locke and Pennington propose make problematic assumptions and/or conflict with empirical conditions. This confusion about conceptual distinctions and necessary truths, and about the relationship of those supposed givens to empirical findings, is reflected in the contradictions and about-faces in Locke and Pennington's claim:

> It is our reasons for acting, and not the other causes of our behaviour, to which we appear to have privileged, introspective access; and if an agent necessarily knows what his reasons are...there is a sense in which he cannot be mistaken or ignorant about them – though this philosophical claim may already be challenged by the findings of psychopathology, as well as those of Nisbett and Wilson.
>
> (p. 220)

Given these difficulties, it seems that Locke and Pennington have not completely succeeded in their stated intention of eliminating confusion in the area by their integration of philosophical and empirical resources. This is not to devalue all attempts to integrate philosophical or analytic approaches in the study of explanations. It is rather to point out the difficulties in Locke and Pennington's attempt to achieve this integration by resorting to claims of conceptual truths and philosophical necessity. It should be noted that the practice of invoking necessary and conceptual truths is not in itself an analytic strategy, but more the opposite, in that it proposes concepts or axioms which may not be subjected to further analysis. Such strategies are rarely employed by authors dealing with similar issues in the philosophical sphere (e.g., Davidson, 1963; C. Taylor, 1964) and in social theory and social philosophy (e.g., Giddens, 1976; Habermas, 1971; Ricoeur, 1974), or by authors who have considered the same issues in relation to psychology specifically (e.g., Rychlak, 1968, 1977; Smith, 1974). Perhaps most significantly, they have not been employed by authors who have successfully developed models of lay epistemology incorporating intentional categories such as goals and plans (Heider, 1958; Schank and Abelson, 1977). This should encourage us to believe there may be alternatives to the sorts of definitions and stipulations introduced by Locke and Pennington. We may recall Buss's (1979c) sceptical query mentioned earlier, as to how one could possibly construct an operational definition of reasons and causes, which he saw as being the empirical alternative to conceptual and necessary truths. But it is not necessary to agree with the negative implication in Buss's question, or with his juxtaposition of the conceptual and the empirical dimension. In the first case it is possible to define reasons and causes in operational forms. This can be illustrated with operational definitions of intentions and reasons that have been introduced in the previous chapter (McClure, 1983), and which represent a conceptualization similar to that of Heider (1958; see especially Heider's distinction between intentions and reasons e.g., p. 110), and Schank and Abelson (1977; see especially the discussion of plans and goals in chapters 4 and 5). They are as follows:

Intentions
Intentions inhere in a plan of action, and can be operationally conceived as the (class of) response, if one is given, to such questions as 'What are you (or they) planning to do?' in reference to a particular action.

Reasons
Reasons articulate a motive or rationale for an action, and can be operationally defined as the (type of) response, if given, to such questions as 'Why are you (or they) performing this action?'

States

States represent an affective or dispositional condition on some dimension (e.g., hunger, arousal), and are indicated in replies to questions like 'Are you (or they) hungry, thirsty, angry?' etc.

If we extend this series of definitions to include causes, we can define causes in the following manner:

Causes

Causes comprise a mechanical explanation of a behaviour, and can be defined as the (type of) response, if given, to such questions as 'What is making you (or them) do this?' in reference to an action.

Whereas intentions and reasons explain an outcome in terms of teleological (final cause) concepts (aim, purpose, intention, reason, goal), causes explain an outcome in terms of mechanical (efficient cause) concepts. (This is defining the concept of cause in what Kruglanski (1979) calls the exclusive sense, which excludes teleological explanations, rather than the inclusive sense of denoting any explanation including the teleological. As Kruglanski observes, the exclusive use is usually adopted or assumed in discussions of attributions.) States differ from intentions, reasons and causes in that they may have no relationship to actions or behaviour. A person may be hungry, angry or content without taking any action and without wanting to. But states can instigate actions, as when a person is thirsty and takes some action to change that state (Schank and Abelson, 1977). When used thus as an explanation, states express an explanatory hinterland between intentions and causes. They may entail a goal-directed action, as in the statement 'I/he was hungry so decided to buy some food and cook a meal', or they may explain an action without reference to or implication of intentions or goals: 'He was so angry (uncontrollably angry) that he hit her.'

These are operational definitions of intentions, reasons, states and causes. But while they were introduced in the context of disagreeing with Buss's (1979c) implication that such concepts cannot be operationally defined, it is not necessary to agree with Buss's and Locke and Pennington's tendency to consider conceptual distinctions and operational or empirical definitions as mutually exclusive or inherently opposed to the ways of conceiving terms. The definitions presented here, while operational, make conceptual distinctions. An operational definition is simply a particular type of definition; it *assumes* conceptual distinctions between the concept it is defining and other concepts. The particular significance of the definitions given here, in relation to Buss's and Locke and Pennington's positions, is that they do not a priori link or confound the class of explanation (reason, intention, cause, etc.) being examined with the perspective of the person (actor or observer) who is giving the explanation. This enables us to treat the type of explanation and the person giving the explanation as distinct dimensions. We can then establish empirically whether and when actors and observers actually do give different kinds of explanation. For example, we can design situations where different kinds of behaviour occur and can ask the actor and an observer for their explanations of that behaviour. However, when we construct situations to illustrate this point, a further dimension, the temporal relationship between the explanation and the behaviour, is always implicated. Examples will be discussed in relation to that dimension in the following sections.

Temporal relations between behaviour and explanation

Shotter (1981a, 1984) explains actor and observer differences with regard to different classes of explanation (telling and reporting) in terms of the temporal relationship between the explanation and the behaviour; that is, whether the explanations are retrospective, concurrent, or prospective. While Shotter uses a different terminology for classes of explanation to that employed by Locke and Pennington, the issues that arise are the same; Shotter's 'tellings' correspond to reasons and intentions while his 'reportings' correspond to states and causes. Shotter suggests that reports comprise people observing and reporting on themselves: 'In formulating ... a report upon the events leading up to and constituting one's current state, one's self is split: an aspect reports while an aspect is reported on' (p. 160). Shotter proposes that reports correspond to the processes postulated in D. J. Bem's (1972) self-perception theory, which claims that people's perceptions of themselves are based on their observations of their own behaviour, emotional states and environmental conditions. Shotter also proposes that reports are always retrospective, and follow behaviour. By contrast, tellings have prospective implications. Tellings do not derive from self-observation, but involve status-assertions. The pronouncement 'I love you' is offered as a status-assertion; by this Shotter means that the pronouncement functions as a declaration intended to change the status or nature of the relationship. Shotter writes of tellings:

> The fact is that here my declaration is not a reporting but a telling; it is a moral statement which once uttered (whatever its causes) commits me to going on in the future with the woman to whom it is uttered in a way different from my relationship to her in the past. Now, my status in relation to her is changed; that was my reason for my utterance.
>
> (1981a, pp. 159–60)

So tellings have a prospective, rather than a retrospective, use. They are attempts to project oneself in a particular way towards the future (p. 160). Shotter claims that tellings are not based on data, and thus cannot be checked out with data. They can be checked for their sincerity only by observing the subsequent actions of the person doing the telling.

Shotter's account introduces a promising direction in channelling the general axioms of ethogeny into specific claims relating to the class of explanation and the temporal relationship between explanation and behaviour. Yet the attempt still leads to difficulties; Shotter's distinction between telling and reporting is not clear, and the proposed relationship of that distinction to the temporal parameter is unsatisfactory. In distinguishing tellings and reportings, Shotter writes:

> It is in their 'logical grammars' (Ryle, 1949) that telling and reporting may be distinguished...that is, it is in what they imply for one's future action, being in receipt of one or the other of them, that is important. While statements or actions used as reports or appraisals may be checked out for their truth or falsity by reference to observational data, to establish whether the state of affairs depicted in the statement exists in reality, tellings or avowals are treated in quite another way. For someone to demand that I make available to them the particular observational data upon which I based my avowal 'I want coffee' would be distinctly odd, for in fact, as I mentioned before, there are none.
>
> (pp. 170–1)

If there is any intrinsic difference between reports and tellings, it cannot be that which Shotter proposes, as reports cannot always be checked by reference to observational data in the way that Shotter suggests. If a person reports that they see red or that they feel hungry, their report cannot be checked out by observational data. Their report's validity is contingent on the person's sincerity, which Shotter treats as the distinguishing feature of avowals or tellings, and not reports. So reports and tellings cannot be distinguished purely by whether they can be checked through observational data.

There are also difficulties in Shotter's claim that reports and tellings have an intrinsically different temporal relationship to behaviour. On this matter, Shotter writes that:

> Avowals do not have to be warranted like reports, by reference to facts, to any antecedently or currently existing states of mind, body, or anything else, as they simply are not used like reports. They are used by people to reveal to others what they currently have in mind – what their needs, interests and desires are, etc. – in an attempt to order future action: executed now, they function to change the shared social reality within which the next action must occur.
>
> (p. 171)

Shotter's description suggests that people's tellings or avowals can be distinguished by the way in which they are used to order future action or events. But this feature does not define or distinguish tellings and avowals, as people often reveal their 'needs, interests and desires' to others without attempting to order future events. At the same time people sometimes do use reports, which Shotter identifies with antecedent or concurrent events, in attempts to order future action. A baby's crying, or a child's irritated, 'I'm hungry', or an adult's, 'I'm tired tonight', are reports all functioning to influence future events.

Shotter's linkage between the type of explanation and the temporal placing of the explanation thus entails several difficulties. Shotter is correct in claiming that attribution research has focused primarily on retrospective accounts and on reports, which are only one class of explanations. This provides good grounds for his suggestion, also made by Taylor and Fiske (1981) in a somewhat different framework, that research should focus on prospective or forward-looking statements and cognition. But Shotter, like Locke and Pennington (1982), makes unsupportable claims in suggesting that reports necessarily have concurrent and retrospective implications and that tellings or avowals have prospective implications. Instead of confounding the two variables (the class of explanation and temporal relations) in the very way we define those parameters and the concepts, which produce the problems discussed above, we can initially treat each dimension as independent, and then examine the ways they do and do not relate to each other. This can be done by using an extension of the taxonomy outlined earlier; extending that taxonomy to include the temporal dimension we have:

Intentions
Intentions articulate a plan of action, and can be operationally conceived as the (class of) response, if one is given, to such questions as 'What are (or were, will) you (or they) planning to do?' in reference to a particular action.

Reasons
Reasons express a motive or rationale for an action, and can be operationally defined as the (type of) response, if one is given, to such questions as 'Why are (or were, will) you (or they) performing this action?'

Causes
Causes comprise a mechanical explanation of a behaviour, and can be operationally conceived as the (type of) response, if one is given, to such questions as 'What is (or was/will) making you (or they) do this?' in reference to an act or behaviour.

If we define the terms and concepts in this manner, the definitions of the concepts do not *presuppose* that there are differences between actors and observers, or that there is an a priori or necessary temporal relationship between classes of explanations and behaviour. Research may establish a relationship between the class of explanation (e.g., tellings or reports, intentions or reasons) and the behaviour, but an adequate empirical demonstration of this relationship is only possible if the concepts are defined in such a way that the relationship is not assumed by the definitions themselves. In fact the definitions and parameters proposed here do enable us to establish certain differences between actors and observers, particularly if we use a time relationship where the attribution precedes behaviour. An example discussed in the previous chapter is a situation where we ask a person to formulate an intention to be carried out at a subsequent time, and ask an observer to formulate what he thinks the actor will do at the subsequent time. If both parties then write down their predictions (i.e. prospective reports) and the actor then performs an action, we see the actor's superiority in prediction, an advantage which derives from the actor's ability to generate intentions which he or she is aware of and may then carry out. The procedure thus demonstrates empirically an advantage in the actor that concurs with many of the ethogenic and hermeneutic axioms about human agency.

However, as has been noted in chapter 4, actors' clear advantage with regard to intentions does not extend to their explication of their reasons or motives – their explanation of why they did (or are doing) some act (McClure, 1983). Actors' rendering of their reasons and motives can even be less plausible than that of observers, particularly when they can offer no explanation for their actions, as sometimes happens, or when they offer an explanation that contradicts itself. So in disagreement with ethogenic and hermeneutic models which hold that actors will reveal their reasons and motives, it is suggested that we may not necessarily establish people's reasons and motives simply by asking them.

To recapitulate: it is suggested that Shotter, like Locke and Pennington, is pursuing a valuable direction in extending the scope of models of lay explanation to include intentional explanations and in focusing on the temporal relationship between explanations and actions. But his account in several places deals with these dimensions by stipulating necessary relationships that lack an adequate conceptual basis and that conflict with empirical situations. Yet several of the points which Shotter attempts to demonstrate in relation to the time parameter can be established, using the framework of definitions and parameters presented here. In the following section on ambiguity in actions, this point can be elaborated and illustrated in relation to examples which Shotter himself employs.

Ambiguous actions

The discussion so far has examined actor and observer differences in relation to a single intention or cause. Shotter (1981a) and Gergen (1977, 1980, 1982) have also discussed these differences in relation to actions that are ambiguous and have an indefinite number of motives. Shotter and Gergen both propose that the meaning(s) of any given action is not self-evident, but is ambiguous, and that the clarification of meaning requires a form of interpretation. They suggest that a suitable framework for such interpretation is provided in a hermeneutic approach, and that a more empiricist approach, as exemplified in most theories in social cognition, fails to capture this dimension of the explanation of actions. Both of these discussions, and Shotter's paper in particular, address these issues in terms of relationships between the three parameters discussed in previous sections: the class of explanation, the person giving the explanation, and the temporal relationship between the explanation and the action. Shotter's position on the ambiguity of actions will be considered first.

Making intentions clear

Shotter (1981a) focuses on the ambiguity of actions and the ways whereby ambiguity is reduced by the actor's explanation of those actions. He writes: 'The aspect of "ordinary explanations" which interests me is how, when the indications in people's actions are insufficiently clear as to the uses they intend them to serve, these indications are "explained" or made clear' (p. 165). He illustrates this question in relation to the following episode: 'They were walking very close now. Her hand brushed more than accidentally it seemed against his. He grasped it. She turned towards him, startled, eyebrows raised, a questioning look. He smiled and squeezed her hand more tightly in his. She turned away, head slightly bowed. He loosened his grip and silently her hand slipped away', (p. 165).

Shotter points out that in this episode the man's intentions in taking the woman's hand are ambiguous until he makes them clear in subsequent actions. The woman also makes her intentions clear in her subsequent actions. Thus the precise meaning of an action is established by soliciting the actor, through speech or gesture. Shotter suggests that these events bear little correspondence to the inferential processing of information described by attribution theories, which he claims deal only with antecedents of behaviour (p. 166). Shotter proposes that such events require a hermeneutic theory whereby one establishes the intention or meaning of an action by soliciting the author of the action. Shotter also claims that the difference between attribution theory and hermeneutic or interpretative theories is analogous to the respective perspectives of third persons (observers) and first persons (actors) or second persons (the addressee, or person acted upon). He proposes that whereas first and second persons, as illustrated by the couple in his illustration, can intervene in an action, third persons may only infer about behaviour. He also suggests that third persons may note unintended behaviour, while second persons 'do not have that right' (p. 168).

Once again we can query Shotter's distinctions between the possibilities and 'rights' of first, second and third persons. With regard to Shotter's claim that first and second persons can intervene in episodes while third persons cannot, one can make the rejoinder that observers, bystander apathy aside, sometimes do intervene or join in transactions, and that this is precisely what third-person observers do in typical experiments. Third persons can and do ask actors what they are doing and why, just as second persons can. And against Shotter's claim that second persons 'do not have that right, unless we are physicians or ophthalmologists, etc. to step out of our "personal involvement" with people, and attend to aspects of their behaviour to which they do not intend us to attend' (p. 168), one could point out that second persons, like third persons, do this much of the time. Furthermore, those who are incapable of doing so may have more difficulties with social interaction than those who can, because they fail to pick up many of the messages that are not intentionally transmitted but which communicate people's wishes, for example, to terminate a conversation.

Yet there is a difference between the parties in the situation Shotter describes which he is driving towards but which he mislocates in his distinction between the 'rights' of second and third persons. The important distinction is between the first person (the actor) and the second and third persons (the addressee and observer). In Shotter's example both actors make their intentions clear by their subsequent actions; they could have achieved this equally well through words. The qualitative difference in the transaction is not so much between the person being addressed and the observer as between the actor and two others; the actor knows his intentions before he acts and communicates them, whereas the other two do not. This conclusion corresponds to the points made earlier about actors' advantage with regard to their intentions. The same qualifications also apply. While the man in Shotter's illustration may know that he wants to alter the relationship before he makes that intention known, his companion and the observer may have a more plausible view of his motives (or reasons) than the one he himself offers or believes.

So there are certain misconnections in Shotter's tying together of the class of explanation parameter and the person parameter. There are different problems in his treatment of the time parameter. Shotter claims that on the one hand the attributional approach focuses entirely on antecedents of behaviour, whereas the hermeneutic approach focuses on the consequences of behaviour, or the uses to which behaviour is put (e.g., p. 164). It is difficult to see how Shotter obtains these temporal differences. Attributional models, such as Kelley's (1972a), do emphasize inference as a means of establishing a cause of an action, but these inferences are subsequent to behaviour, attempting to ascertain the cause of an action or event that has already occurred. In this respect, inferences are no different to the hermeneutic querying and interpretation that follows an action. Both follow behaviour. A more significant difference is that whereas attribution theory has commonly focused on the question of whether the propulsion or locus of causality of behaviour is internal or external, a hermeneutic model assumes that an action had an intention (an internal source), and attempts to find out what the intention is, from a myriad of possibilities.

Thus Shotter deals with the issue of ambiguity in actions by stipulating inherent differences between the perspectives and privileges of first, second and third persons; he relates these differences to the differences between attribution and hermeneutic theories. Most of these stipulations can be questioned, but Shotter's examples can be reinterpreted in a way that does clarify differences between actors and two classes of observer, although they do not establish all of the differences that Shotter stipulates.

Mixing hermeneutics and empiricism

A somewhat different mode of argument is employed by Gergen (1977, 1980, 1982) in dealing with similar issues in relation to a hermeneutic perspective. Gergen does not invoke philosophical necessity or the 'rights' of different persons, but argues on the basis of empirical evidence and theoretical elegance. Gergen's treatment of ambiguous actions differs from Shotter's in a second respect. Whereas Shotter deals with the question of how a motive may be established in terms of actors' advantage over observers, Gergen argues that an 'actual' motive cannot ever be definitely established. Gergen builds his analysis around the following type of example. We see our friends Ross and Laura at a social gathering, and notice that Ross touches Laura's hair. Gergen asks how we identify the action, and how we determine what the action suggests about Ross and Laura's relationship and the manner in which we should regard it if we wish to retain their friendship. As Gergen argues, the action in itself tells us little, in terms of its interpersonal significance. It could mean that Ross is in love with Laura, or that Ross wants Laura to think he is an affectionate person, or perhaps that Ross knows Laura dislikes being touched and touches her to deliberately irritate her. Gergen proposes that all actions can similarly be interpreted in a number of ways, and that people draw on contextual information, such as what they heard about Ross the day before or after the incident, to reach an interpretation. Using this example and others, Gergen argues compellingly that all interpretations are subject to infinite revision in the light of additional information.

In his 1980 paper Gergen does qualify the degree of revision possible in interpretation by allowing that some interpretations are less valid than others; he suggests that one would not interpret Ross's actions in the illustration above as jumping in the lake, for example. He thus implies an approximation or hierarchy of accuracy in interpretations, which qualifies the general postulate that interpretations are subject to infinite revision. But Gergen subsequently (1982) withdraws this qualification by proposing that an interpretation of Ross's action in the illustration as 'jumping in the lake' is not less valid, but simply less plausible, and that implausibility does not equate empirical inaccuracy. It is simply an implausible interpretation because it does not conform to normal social usage. The phrase 'jumping in the lake' may simply be a rhetorical way of suggesting that Laura is likely to react angrily. Thus Gergen retains the position that all interpretations of actions are subject to revision.

Gergen also rejects the possibility that the meaning of the actor's action can be obtained by asking the actor. He differs from Shotter (1981a) in suggesting that 'it would not appear that the actor is necessarily privileged by virtue of his or her private access to internal experiences' (1980, p. 244). In arguing for this position, an extension of the argument dealing with self-knowledge in his (1977) paper, Gergen draws on a wide range of research demonstrating that internal identification of emotions and mental processes are subject to error and bias. He proposes that internal identifications are in a continuous state of reconstruction. Gergen (1982) later reinforces this empirically based argument with the further claim that the idea of people being aware of their own cognitions or intentions forces theoretical speculation to the borders of incredulity. It requires a mental process in which one level of process acts as a sensing and recording device and a second process furnishes the material to be sensed and recorded. Gergen suggests that this way of conceptualizing self-perception involves an imitation of models of external perception, and implies an awkward subject–object dualism in internal perception. Gergen juxtaposes dualistic self-reports with a stream of consciousness, which he sees as a legitimate epistemological resource.

Gergen argues his case very effectively, and in place of the questionable stipulations of necessity used in the arguments discussed earlier, he bases his argument on empirical evidence and principles of theoretical elegance or parsimony. But we can still query whether that argument justifies the conclusions Gergen reaches. With regard to actors' access and the dualism of internal perception, Gergen is correct in suggesting that such models can take on a dichotomous connotation, as in Shotter's (1981a) suggestion that 'In formulating ... a report upon the events leading up to and constituting one's current state, one's self is split: an aspect reports while an aspect is reported on' (p. 160). But the fact that a model of introspection is analogous to or derived from a model of extraspection is not in itself a weakness. It isn't self-evident that a dualistic model of introspection should be a priori more unsatisfactory than the dualism in extraspection that scholars have attempted to transcend for decades. It is also not necessary that self-reports would force theoretical speculation to the border of incredulity (although that in itself would not necessarily be a weakness). Several influential theories in psychology have adopted such a perspective (e.g., Harré and Secord, 1972; Rogers, 1961). Gergen contrasts dualistic self-reports with a stream of consciousness, which he sees as a satisfactory epistemological resource. But verbal reports can themselves be seen as articulating a stream of consciousness (Ericsson and Simon, 1980). Gergen does not make clear his criterion for his distinction between a stream of consciousness, which he sees as acceptable, and the perception of self that he argues is theoretically unsatisfactory.

A second argument that arises in Gergen's (1977, 1980, 1982) discussions of this issue is his contention that evidence has demonstrated that people do not have access to their internal processes. In the two earlier papers (1977, 1980), Gergen refers more particularly to Nisbett and Wilson's (1977) argument that people do not have access to their behavioural causes or mental processes and actually articulate socially derived scripts. He also refers to the research demonstrating that people's identification of the emotional states is subject to their context (e.g., Schachter and Singer, 1962). Gergen (1982) later adds Freud's observations that defensive processes distort and conceal people's desires and motives.

While all of these lines of evidence are significant and compelling, they do not justify all the conclusions that Gergen draws from them. Freud indeed considered that conscious levels of awareness were subject to distortion and bias. But just as the words bias, distortion and illusion assume a potential state of non-bias, or an undistorted account, so Freud (1915/1956) aimed to establish the reality behind the ego's defensive fabrications, and his therapy included this goal. Nisbett and Wilson's (1977) paper, and other similar papers, again provide strong evidence implying the limitations of introspective access. But Nisbett and Wilson's conclusions and generalizations have been challenged by Ericsson and Simon (1980), White (1980) and others, and can no longer be cited as unequivocal evidence for general claims about verbal reports and introspective access. An additional point pertinent to Gergen's position is that Nisbett and Wilson's criterion for the subjects' error is the subjects' failure to report the actual cause of (their) behaviour, a presumption of actual causes that is incommensurable with Gergen's view of the infinite revision of possible meanings of the behaviour.

No objections could be raised here to Gergen's third premise, that people's perception of their emotional states is highly capricious and subject to its social context. But the arguments in chapter 4 apply equally here; emotions and states are only one cognitive class, and we may not legitimately generalize from research on states to conclusions about, for example, intentions (McClure, 1983, 1984; Wilson, Hull and Johnson, 1981). We also should not generalize about human capability from research using retrospective reports, unless we obtain similar results using concurrent and prospective reports (McClure, 1983, 1984; Taylor and Fiske, 1981). To return to the point made earlier, if research focuses on plans or intentions (rather than states or emotions), and if the temporal relationship is inverted so that the reports obtained are concurrent or prospective rather than retrospective, we can establish certain differences between actors and observers. Gergen's example with the Ross and Laura incident can be adapted to illustrate this point. Instead of retrospectively wondering what Ross's motives were after the event, we ask Ross on arriving at the party what he is going to do, and ask an observer what he (Ross) is going to do, and Ross says he is going to touch Laura's hair while the observer says Ross will go and get a drink. If Ross subsequently touches Laura's hair we might reasonably conclude that Ross has a form of access that the observer doesn't have, and consequently reject Gergen's claim of their equivalence. But this access to intentions is only one part of the explanatory picture, as was noted earlier. If we attempt to ascertain Ross's reasons or motives for his action, and ask Ross and the observer why Ross touched or is touching Laura's hair, we may find the observer's explanation more plausible. On this point we might agree with Gergen and his claim that explanations of the motive for the action are susceptible to infinite revision.

What implications does this conclusion have for the hermeneutic axiom that actions have intentions or meanings and that the task of understanding these actions requires an understanding or interpretation of those meanings? It is argued here that some actions are intentional and that this quality advantages the actor over the observer in certain respects. But the fact that people may either not fully understand themselves or may conceal their motives for their actions requires a more sceptical hermeneutic or interpretation, or what Ricoeur (1974) and others have described as a critical hermeneutic (Giddens, 1976; Habermas, 1971; Thompson, 1981). This requirement is already being realized in part in the linguistic sphere by empirical analyses concerned with deciphering linguistic explanations (e.g., Clippinger, 1977; Labov and Fanshel, 1977; Rommetveit, 1974). Research of this nature in the sphere of attributional explanations has been less evident, yet it is a desirable extension of research into attributions and misattributions, with the important difference that it would not be limited to internal–external polarities but would include a full gamut of explanations. Examples of work moving in this direction are Fletcher's (1983) examination of people's explanations of marital breakdowns and Gowler and Legge's (1981) analysis of explanations in relation to conflicts in organizational settings.

Reasons and causes: conclusions

This chapter has focused on a key issue in explanations of actions: the relationship of intentional or goal-directed behaviour to models that emphasize causal explanations, such as attribution theories. The arguments that are considered move beyond the general axiom that behaviour is goal-directed, and attempt to define what difference this quality makes in relation to differences between actors and observers and to temporal relationships between explanations and actions. The types of argument employed and the substantive claims made have both been considered.

In treating reasons and causes, several authors make a number of stipulations in the form of necessary or conceptual truths, or the 'rights' of different persons, that are unsupportable or unsatisfactory, and confound different parameters relating to explanations. Authors go beyond the claim that actions and explanations include an intentional dimension to make the claim that people understand their own motives and reasons. This claim cannot be justified, and has led to a tendency to treat explanations in an unquestioning and naive manner.

Several of the authors' proposals on intentions, reasons, and causes, however, can be reframed in a manner that is free from a priori stipulations and does not confound the type of report, the person giving the report and the time relation between the report and the action. In this framework it is possible to demonstrate the efficacy of intention and to show corresponding differences between actors and observers, but at the same time to clarify and establish limits to actors' self-knowledge and to their advantages over observers. So the flaws in the arguments reviewed here do not nullify the goal of constructing models that incorporate intentional factors.

A second issue focused on by critics of attribution theory and social cognition concerns the analogy between the lay thinker and the professional scientist. It is suggested that this sort of analogy should be replaced by models that capture more functional aspects of explanations and discourse. This issue forms the central focus of chapter 6.

6 Self-presentation and discourse analysis

This chapter continues the previous chapter's examination of alternatives to attribution theory and other orthodox approaches to social cognition. A central issue here is the question of whether explanations are predominantly inferential and logical, as many theories of social cognition suggest, or more functional, in the sense of serving to present an image of self to particular audiences. The chapter begins with arguments for the self-presentational analogy, considers disputes about the ideological variables affecting models, and proceeds to discourse analysis, which examines the discursive quality of people's communications in naturalistic contexts.

Which analogy: scientist or actor?

The critique of inferential models

Harré (1981a) claims that attribution theories and related models suppose that lay explanations are inferential or propositional, a supposition that results in a 'rhetoric of scientism'. This rhetoric is most definitively expressed in Kelley's (1972a) covariation model, which proposes that lay attributors establish the causes of behaviour by employing strategies analogous to statistical procedures used by scientists. Harré claims that in the 'real' world, explanations are functional in a self-presentational sense. They function as a ritual display, as rhetoric, as show; they are designed to impress, and affect others' impressions. Harré proposes that a dramaturgical analogy is more appropriate than an analogy with the scientist or than assumptions that people normally explain actions on a propositional–inferential basis. He suggests that if researchers examined accounts in actual situations (such as gossip), rather than obtaining people's responses to written descriptions of situations, they would find that people operated in a rhetorical impression-manipulating manner. The use of documentary–laboratory methods prevents researchers from capturing the rhetorical self-presentational nature of everyday explanations; methodology has thus constrained the model that is employed. Harré attributes this tendency to the ethnocentricity of American researchers and to an absence of reflexivity, in that exponents of attribution theory fail to apply knowledge about themselves to their subjects, and vice versa. Thus Harré claims that:

> Kelley knows that *he* is not attributing processes, properties, moral qualities, etc. to a target person on the basis of situational determinants. He knows he is a rational being with his own collectively sanctioned personal projects in the light of which he says things about others, e.g. his subjects. Our problem, as reformers, is to persuade Kelley that the people he has studied are rather like himself.
>
> (1981a, p. 141)

Harré's comments raise a number of questions and implications. By suggesting that Kelley's model of the way scientists think does not apply to lay explanations, Harré is implying that scientists at least *do* think in that purely logical inferential manner. Yet this assumption has now been refuted on a wide scale (e.g., Feyerabend, 1975; Kuhn, 1970). Harré is also hereby treating science as separate from the rest of Western culture, yet science is a social institution that is deeply embedded in Western culture, and its modes and theories permeate and in turn reflect that culture (Feyerabend, 1975; Moscovici, 1976). In conceiving of attributions as rational analytic processes, attribution theorists are being reflexive, not because they are themselves purely rational and inferential, but because they genuinely see themselves in terms of a rationalistic ideology or ideal. Kelley's (1972a) 'analysis of variance' analogy is meant to be a projection of what scientists actually do on to the lay person, but it is reflexive projection of the empiricist notion of what scientists do. Thus we might contest Harré's claim that 'Kelley knows that *he* is not attributing processes, properties, moral qualities, etc. to a target person' in the way that his (Kelley's) theory proposes, not simply because we haven't all had the opportunity to read Kelley's mind, but because Kelley's covariation model reflects the empiricist world view dominant in Western culture.

As the previous point implies, we might also question Harré's identification of a mechanistic rationalistic ideal with American ethnocentricity. Kelley's covariation model of lay inference is itself based on a British philosopher's (J. S. Mill) framework. Harré's (1981b) illusion of scientistic rhetoric in social psychology, 'a typically North American idea' (p. 219), is a quotation from a British social psychologist (p. 220), while the example given of a person who transcends these boundaries, Garfinkel, is a North American (Harré, 1981a, p. 142). But irrespective of the specific examples, it is historically untenable to identify an empiricist or rationalistic ideology uniquely with American culture when that ideology has permeated Western intellectual culture at least since the Enlightenment (Adorno and Horkheimer, 1944/1972; Habermas, 1971), if not earlier. Ironically, Harré (1981a) himself, while chastising Kelley's scientism, argues that the ethogenic 'doctrine' is commensurable with structural models in the natural sciences (e.g., p. 156).

What implications do these comments have with regard to the issues of reflexivity and the analogy with scientists? On the question of reflexivity, it would be silly to deny that astute self-observation is a useful resource in our inquiry. But, despite what Harré implies, reflexivity cannot be relied on to support any particular model. Different researchers prefer different models (e.g., Freudian, humanistic or behaviouristic), and interpret themselves and the world around them in terms of those models (Berger and Luckmann, 1966; Bohm, 1973). The models themselves have to be justified and evaluated on other grounds.

As for the analogy with scientists, the recent realization that scientists themselves do not fit the 'purely rational and statistical' prototype suggests that we may not be justified in discarding the analogy with scientists simply because other people do not fit that prototype. A more reasonable response would be to study the actual strategies used by the newly demythologized scientist in his or her explanations and compare these strategies with those of other people. Such work is being undertaken in empirical studies on the behaviour and interactions of scientists (e.g., Mittroff, 1974). Kruglanski and his colleagues are taking a similar approach in relation to social cognition, examining the conditions under which biases and errors like perseveration occur within science and everyday thought (e.g., Kruglanski and Ajzen, 1983; Kruglanski, Baldwin and Towson, 1983). Such comparisons do not require the stronger assumption that there are no differences between scientific and non-scientific inference (Moscovici, 1982). But the realization that scientists are affected by many of the constraints on the lay person does suggest that social psychologists could treat the 'ordinary' person in a less condescending and moralizing manner (cf. Kruglanski, Baldwin and Towson, 1983; Moscovici, 1982).

Reservations can also be expressed about Harré's claim that attribution theories, and Kelley's theories in particular, assume that attributions are made on the basis of propositional or inferential processes. In the first case, there is some ambiguity in Harré's description of Kelley's model. While Harré (1981a) in most part correctly describes Kelley's (1967) covariation model as 'applying logical rules of causal inference to identified causal candidates' or 'a matter of logical information processing' (p. 140), he also refers to it as a stimulus-response model: 'According to this underlying theory Kelley can, for example, talk of the determinants of attribution as "situation and target person"' (p. 140). This sort of talk 'merely asks us to see the attribution as a Humean concomitance between an external treatment and an external response to that treatment' (p. 140). Harré suggests that the question of the reflexivity of attributions 'can be formulated only when the Humean metaphysics of causality has been cleared away' (p. 141). But in Kelley's covariation model the situation and target person are not the determinants of the attribution but the candidates about which attributions are made. Kelley's model does not involve the stimulus-response causality of a 'Humean metaphysics', but an extension of the inferential model put forward by Mill. Nevertheless, Kelley clearly does treat certain processes underlying attributions as inferential, as Harré suggests. But it is less obvious what proportion of attributions Kelley believes to be accounted for by those models. Kelley (1972a) did propose that the covariation model was applicable only to 'ideal' situations, and he described a number of biases deriving from functional or motivational factors which operate in other situations. Subsequent papers (e.g., Kelley, 1973) have continued to acknowledge these influences on attributions; and Kelley's (1980) model of strategies used by magicians to mislead audiences, a model which he suggests could apply also to commercial and political propaganda, describes manipulations that are certainly not inferential or propositional in the sense used by Harré. Kelley's earlier models certainly emphasized inferential factors, but they did not overlook other factors to the extent that Harré suggests.

Similar comments can be made about Harré's charge that conventional (American) research on explanations has adopted a purely inferential–propositional model and ignored self-presentational factors. Reeves, Richardson and Hendrick's (1979) bibliography of papers in social and personality psychology includes a category of papers on self-presentation – mostly articles in American journals. This itself is not evidence that the self-presentational dimension has been integrated into work on attributions and explanations, but Kelley and Michela's (1980) review of attribution research includes a category on self-presentational factors, and Baumeister's (1982) review indicates that an interest in such factors is increasing. From these sources it would seem that work on self-presentational factors is being undertaken in mainstream research in social cognition. This seems to challenge the claim that most (American) research ignores self-presentational factors and presumes that only inferential processes are at work. In fact there may be fewer differences between Harré's (1981a) position and the mainstream paradigms than Harré implies, particularly if one accepts his contention in another paper that 'the most powerful analytical model combines an overall dramaturgical approach to social reality with a problem-solving analysis of the performances staged by ordinary folk playing themselves' (1981b, p. 214).

Several of the major criticisms made by Harré, then, may be challenged. Yet while it can be suggested that Harré has failed to capture the letter of attribution theory on many points, we might be unwise to conclude that he has therefore wholly failed to capture the spirit of the enterprise. Certainly there is much research on self-presentational factors in relation to attributions, contrary to what Harré's evaluation implies. Yet at the same time there are large areas of inquiry in which such factors are likely to be significant but where they have been completely overlooked or ignored. Neisser (1980) has pointed out conspicuous examples of this. It does seem that many social psychologists in the 1970s were sufficiently mesmerized by the information-processing paradigm to have emphasized inferential processes at the expense of more functional and manipulative ones. And while method has not determined theory as much as Harré suggests, in that the predominant use of the experiment has not prevented authors from considering self-presentational factors, it is probable that methodological zealotry has led to a considerable under-appreciation of the importance of those factors. As Taylor and Fiske (1981) suggest, 'The notion that we must become even more rigorous in our methods (a goal inspired by our association with cognitive psychology) has led to premature rigor...social cognition needs a little less rigor mortis' (p. 508). The clear implication is that a methodological pluralism would encourage a stronger emphasis on self-presentation factors. This raises the question of how much emphasis should be placed on such factors, a question that is now considered in relation to Harré's proposals for an alternative approach to explanations.

Is the dramaturgical analogy sufficient?

Any discussion of Harré's criticisms of existing research in social cognition still leaves us without an evaluation of the primary proposal implicit in Harré's analysis, the proposition that self-presentational factors are the primary motive in explanations and that theory on explanations should accordingly adopt the dramaturgical analogy instead of the analogy with scientists. Certain doubts must be expressed about this proposed analogic hegemony, the principal difficulty being that many explanations and attributions do not seem to be undertaken solely or primarily for the purpose of self-presentation or display. A mundane instance is the not-uncommon situation where a person, or group of people, wonders why a particular incident occurred. For example, when a woman is sitting wondering why the man next to her spoke to her in a particularly blunt way, the woman doesn't necessarily exercise a flight of rhetoric. She may wonder if it was something she said that provoked the bluntness, or whether the man was characteristically blunt, or whether other people also saw the comment as blunt. This sort of lay analysis may entirely lack the display dimension.

On a somewhat different level, the paradoxical perceptions of depressed people which many researchers have considered (e.g., Abramson and Sackeim, 1977) are not likely to be driven by self-presentational motives.

Occasions where people or groups attribute their success on tasks to luck and others' success to skill could in some cases function as a display of humility, but when they reflect a negative self-evaluation such attributions are more a case of self-misrepresentation than self-presentation. Equally important is the armoury of attributions and rationalizations articulated in prejudice, bigotry, racism and sexism (Pettigrew, 1979). Such attributions serve certain interests, to retain a term used by Kelley (1972a, e.g., p. 18), and therein highly functional, but they do not serve the function of display so much as those of discrimination, exploitation and hostility. The same point applies to explanations of social conditions such as poverty and unemployment (Furnham, 1982). Attributions intrinsic to belief systems, wherein people attribute positive and/or negative events to God, gods, demons or witches, articulate beliefs which are not adhered to purely for display, but for which some people live and die. Harré (1981a, p. 169) himself includes several of these instances and others in a valuable list of possible topics for investigation, but in few of these instances is it evident that self-presentation is the primary motive. To Harré's claim that 'we should be asking whether there is anything but self-presentational factors at work', it can be suggested that there is quite a lot else. In fact, Harré weakens his case for a self-presentational model when he attempts to subsume all human affairs into that motive, as when he writes:

> What sort of statements are being made in concrete social activities, such as strikes, riots, parties, working breakfasts, overtakings in the inner lane and so on? Starting with these as rough guides: modern strikes can hardly be seriously taken to be economically motivated. They are best understood as claims to recognition and dignity, as displays of worth; riots too may be something like that: look at me, and take me seriously.
>
> (1981b, p. 213)

Quite apart from its reductionism and conservative ideological implications, this tendency to see a wide range of human affairs including strikes and riots as display, that is, in terms of Harré's own model, would seem to be a case of Harré reflexively seeing the world in terms of his preferred framework, much as he suggested that Kelley did. This leads to a downplaying or overlooking of other functions or motives.

It is suggested, then, that the self-presentational motive is not sufficient as an account of several aspects of lay explanations. But to argue that it is not sufficient is not to argue that it is unimportant or that it is currently being taken adequately into account. As was suggested earlier, such factors have been overlooked in many circumstances where they are likely to be significant. Yet it would seem most worthwhile to examine explanations in relation to the several primary functions or interests they serve, and not merely that of display. This broader view of the functions served by explanations has been explored in recent work on discourse analysis. Before turning to discourse analysis, it is appropriate to comment on certain underlying aspects of the disputes discussed up to this point.

Ethnocentricity, ideology and discrimination

The specificity of ethnocentricity

The discussion of the issues up to this point has focused on specific arguments and substantive claims made in relation to those issues. This is not the only level at which arguments are posed. Questions of ethnocentric or ideological influences on the disputed theories have been raised by critics of attribution theories and social cognition. Harré's suggestion that attribution theories are ethnocentric reflections of American culture has already been mentioned. Other authors (Billig, 1982; Buss, 1979b; Furby, 1979; Semin, 1980) have pointed out and discussed the ideological implications in current attribution theories. Harré implies that these aspects of attribution theories are further grounds for rejecting them in favour of an ethogenic or hermeneutic approach. But it would be a mistake to assume that only attribution theory has ideological implications or that America is the only place where scientists are influenced by their culture. Harvey (1981) is entitled to respond to Semin's (1980) discussion of ideological dimensions of attribution theories: 'Practically all scientists and theorists exhibit degrees of ethnocentricity and ideology in their research and writings. It would be impossible to find any theoretical position that is pure and contains no implied prescriptive stances. Attributional analyses are no exception, and I think that we should welcome clear searching assessment of the ideological features of the *various* approaches' (Harvey, 1981, p. 303).

And certainly there are ideological dimensions to ethogenic and hermeneutic approaches to lay explanations, some of which have been pointed out by Buss (1979a, ch. 14). The central emphasis in those theories is on the sufficiency and validity of the accounts given by individuals and groups for their actions. There is the general implication or explicit injunction that researchers should give considerable credence to these accounts; they should empathize and interpret, instead of observing, explaining and theorizing about their subjects (e.g., Harré, 1974; Shotter, 1981a).

Such an emphasis is not totally lacking in ideological implications. Buss (1979b) has observed that an empathic understanding of people's self-accounts precludes the possibility that the relevant actions may derive from unconscious motives, motives that may be omitted or distorted in the person's account. Habermas (1971) and Ricoeur (1974) have similarly observed that people's accounts of themselves may articulate a 'false consciousness', or distortions and misattributions as to what they are doing or why they are doing it. People's accounts may conceal their thoughts or motives more than revealing them. Billig (1977) has pointed out the difficulties this problem produces for the application of an hermeneutic–ethogenic analysis to social movements like fascism. The same difficulties arise in studying explanations and attributions if we give credence to explanations that include misattributions and rationalizations. If we treat people's perceptions of justice in an inequitable society as self-sufficient or self-explanatory, for example, then we are prevented from seeing how those perceptions function to maintain and justify an equitable access to resources (Hewstone, Jaspars and Lalljee, 1982). Critical theorists (e.g. Habermas, 1971) point out that commonsense understandings are often employed by people to sustain a social order in which they possess power or control.

So there are clear ideological implications of standing in an uncritical or unevaluative relationship to individual self-understandings or to the social understandings enshrined in common sense. Critics of attribution theory, then, should not consider it such a moral victory to have exposed ideological underpinnings to attribution theories when there are also ideological dimensions to the positions they proffer as alternatives. The ideological implications in hermeneutic approaches nonetheless can be combated if authors employ a critical hermeneutic which is not bound to take explanations at face value, and which attempts to decipher the meaning, cause and function of distortions and misattributions (Billig, 1977; Habermas, 1971; Ricoeur, 1974).

Inter-paradigm differentiation

There is a related issue that has been mentioned several times but not discussed directly, and that is the exaggerations of the differences between theories. It was suggested that the differences between the attribution and the hermeneutic–ethogenic approaches to explanation (differences which are described succinctly in Antaki and Fielding, 1981; see also Moscovici, 1981) are somewhat exaggerated in Harré's differentiation of ethogenic and attribution models of explanations. Harré accentuates the difference between ethogenic and attribution models and minimizes the differences (as expressed by different adherents) within those models (cf. Totman, 1980). It appears that authors like Harvey, writing in defence of orthodox attribution theories, have sometimes demonstrated the same tendency. For example Harvey (e.g., 1981) implies that all critics of the attribution approach are of a philosophical (i.e. non-empirical) bent. While such a description is a reasonable assessment of Shotter's (1981b) comments, it is not true of many of the critics of attribution theories, who not only carry out research themselves, but whose criticisms are little different to those made by recognized authors writing within an orthodox attribution (or cognitive psychology) perspective (e.g., Taylor and Fiske, 1981; Neisser, 1980). Heider (1958) is not lambasted for his extensive theorizing. This maximizing of differences between theories and the minimizing of differences within positions, or polarization, as Antaki (1981) describes it, exemplifies intergroup discrimination as characterized by Tajfel (1978), mapped onto intercontinental (Europe/America), national (British/American) or paradigm-based (attribution/ethogenic) categories. This is not to deny the differences between the various perspectives, but to suggest that certain semi-fictitious stereotypes are projected onto those more real differences. This recent emanation of discrimination resembles the intercontinental discrimination that appeared early in social psychology's 'crisis', when again, an established paradigm was being challenged (McClure, 1978). These exaggerations lessen the force of valid criticisms, and reduce the possibility of rational discussion.

Discourse analysis: do words speak louder than actions?

The most recent development in new approaches to social psychology and explanation revolves around discourse analysis. This approach has been advocated for social psychology in general by Potter and Wetherell (1987), and for explanations in particular by Michael (1989). These two lines of analysis will be considered in turn.

Discourse and social psychology

Central to Potter and Wetherell's (1987) exposition of discourse analysis is the idea that people's statements should be seen as functional actions rather than as descriptions of some inner state. This idea extends Austin's (1962) distinction between performative statements which use language as an action, such as a judge saying 'I sentence you to six years in prison', and descriptive or constative statements where the language describes an internal state or attitude, such as someone saying, 'I don't agree with the use of nuclear energy.' Whereas many social psychologists agree that *some* statements and attributions serve a functional purpose, such as self-presentation, rather than describing a cognitive state, Potter and Wetherell argue that *all* statements and discourse should be treated in this way, and that social psychologists should dispense with inner states, attitudes, and other cognitions.

Potter and Wetherell justify their position partly in terms of the variability in people's accounts. For example, they report that their own research on New Zealanders' discourse about Maoris contained numerous contradictions, rather than a clear and consistent prototype or stereotype. People may refer to Maoris as 'lazy' and 'such hardworking people' almost in the same breath (p. 124). As Potter and Wetherell observe, their argument parallels Mischel's (1968) critique of trait theory, which drew on the variability of behaviour across situations to challenge the idea that people have traits which guide their behaviour. Mischel proposed that behaviour reflects the situations in which it occurs, and Potter and Wetherell claim that discourse reflects a particular situation or function, rather than internal attitudes. Potter and Wetherell allow that their position amounts to a non-cognitive social psychology, and claim that the issue of whether self-reports are accurate descriptors of mental states is a non-issue.

In an important respect, discourse analysis improves on the ethogenic perspective. The discourse approach recognizes that people's explanations may not directly reflect their attitudes or intentions, and may actually serve to conceal these cognitions. As was argued earlier in this chapter and in chapter 5, ethogenics tended to take people's explanations at face value to a much greater extent, when there is no adequate basis for doing so, and good reasons not to. However, Potter and Wetherell's argument entails difficulties, including their treatment of verbal reports and people's explanations of their own actions. Rather than explicitly taking a position on the issue of whether and when people's verbal reports are accurate indicators of their mental states, they suggest that the researcher should bracket off this issue, and treat descriptors of mental states as discursive social practices.

What isn't made clear in this argument is how researchers (and lawyers) can reconstruct the distinction between intentional and unintentional actions. Legal distinctions between murder and manslaughter hinge on whether a homicide was driven by intention (Hart and Honoré, 1985). Similarly, aggression is distinguished from accidents causing injury by the presence of intention (Baron, 1977). A key aspect of children's moral development lies in their distinguishing actions that are intentional from those that are unintended, rather than judging an action by its consequences (Piaget, 1965). No less with adults, if a person carries out an action that is insulting to a particular ethnic group in the presence of a member of that group, the reaction of that member is affected by whether they see the action as intended to insult. The issue of intentionality in action is central to social behaviour, and is not simply a conceptual luxury to be indulged in by researchers of a particular theoretical persuasion. A theory that wishes to bracket out mental states must provide some alternative account of these intentional phenomena, as did Skinner, who in identical terms to Potter and Wetherell (e.g., p. 179), claimed that explanations should not move 'under the skull' (e.g., Skinner, 1974).

A second difficulty in Potter and Wetherell's argument concerns their use of the variability of accounts. The variability that Potter and Wetherell found in their open-ended interviews may partly reflect the methods they were using (cf. Bowers, 1988), and is likely to be less evident at the level of behavioural intentions, where attitudes are relatively reliable predictors of behaviour (e.g., Ajzen, 1985). Political parties and commercial enterprises spend much money obtaining people's attitudes and behavioural intentions. This practice would not be worth while or useful if people's attitudes were generally as contradictory and incoherent as Potter and Wetherell suggest.

Even where there is variability, it is not self-evident that the existence of variability in people's discourse is sufficient reason for claiming that we should do away with cognitive constructs or processes. Although Potter and Wetherell argue convincingly that people's discourse shows a variability that would not be expected if people have clear or consistent stereotypes and prototypes, it does not follow that references to dispositional properties are inappropriate. The city where I currently live, Wellington, is known as a windy city. On some days it is extremely windy, yet on other days the weather is totally calm. Does this variability mean that it is a mistake to refer to the city as windy? It doesn't, because Wellington is windy more frequently than other cities, and the wind reaches a stronger intensity than in most other cities. A statement about the dispositional properties of a city or a person does not entail consistency, but implies a distinctive proportion of the property in question, a comparison in which the object has more of that property than other objects. The fact that a person may offer variable or inconsistent statements about a social group does not entail that the person does not have an underlying disposition or attitude, in the sense of an attribute that is present in them more or less than it is in other people.

On the other hand, the variability in people's discourse may reflect contradictions in their attitudes, and these contradictions themselves may be important, either because they reflect contradictions in people's circumstances (Bowers, 1988), or because they may underlie people's actions (Billig, 1982). The discourse approach provides few theoretical links between discourse and behaviour. It is difficult to examine the relation of people's discourse to their actions if there is no theoretical connection between discourse and behaviour or between discourse and cognitions.

This issue has implications for the relevance of discourse analysis to applied issues, such as the role of cognitions in personal problems like emotional disorders and depression. Certain cognitions contribute to depression, evidently because the person believes them (e.g., Abramson, Seligman and Teasdale, 1978). The aim of cognitive therapies is to induce different cognitions and attributions, to get the person to see things differently so that they will feel things differently. If we don't treat people's verbal reports as in some way being reflections of their actual perceptions, then we have no grounds for working with the cognitive component of people's problems. No clear alternative is offered by the discourse analysis paradigm. The sample implications apply at a social level. If we don't treat social groups' self-deprecating attributions and statements as reflections of their cognitions or circumstances, then we lack clear grounds for changing those cognitions, or for 'consciousness-raising'. In this respect the discourse approach, despite its pretension to be 'radical', has certain nihilistic implications in its current form. Parker (1989) comments on this issue: 'If every statement about the nature of social-psychological method or theory can be glossed as rhetorical device, and if truth claims are just sophistic tricks, then how can the analysis of discourse be put to progressive use?' (p. 150). If a model is to have effective applications to the way people think and act, it is necessary to retain the analysis of cognition that was previously banished from psychology by behaviourism, and is rather cheerfully dismissed from social psychology by discourse analysts.

A similar argument applies to the analysis of science in the form of discourse among scientists, a topic much focused on by discourse analysts (e.g., Potter and Mulkay, 1982). It is useful to know that science is a human endeavour, and is subject to social and psychological analysis. But the demonstration that the scientific emperor has no clothes does not come to grips with the power of science in modern society, any more than journalism which exposes or analyses a princess's love letters explains or challenges the wealth or prestige of royalty. An analysis of the discourse of scientists needs to be placed in the context of an analysis of the values and applications of science, and the relation of science to society.

In short, discourse analysis offers an advance on ethogenic approaches which treat actors' accounts as generally valid or accurate. Its cutting-edge is blunted, however, by the way it dismisses the issue of self-reports and cognitions, while presenting no alternative account of the difference that cognitions and intentions make in social behaviour. The exclusion of cognition from discourse analysis also undermines the grounds for changing people's cognitions about themselves and their conditions.

Discourse and explanations
Whereas Potter and Wetherell's analysis applies to discourse in general, Michael (1989) has applied discourse analysis specifically to explanations and attributions. His critique revolves around two issues: the analogy with scientists and the social context of attributions (McClure, 1989b).

Classic attribution theories draw analogies between the ordinary person's attributions for behaviour and scientific inferences about behaviour. This analogy has been questioned before, and critics have suggested that attributions would be better modelled by analogies with lawyers and historians, because people's attributions correspond more to the element of advocacy in legal argument than to the supposed detachment of scientists. Discourse analysts, such as Michael, claim that we should use analogies with the skilled manual or unskilled professions, such as the plumber or housewife. (Michael seems to imply that housewives are unskilled.) Michael claims that the selection of scientists for comparison has occurred because attribution theory did not ground cognition in historically concrete behaviour, and because the theory reflects the division in society between manual and mental labour.

A problem with this claim about attribution theories is that Heider (1958) did in fact draw a parallel between outcomes on a manual task (such as rowing a boat across a lake), and outcomes on a 'mental' task (such as sitting an exam). As Heider noted, outcomes on both sorts of tasks are affected by ability, effort, the difficulty of the task, and luck, however that is defined. Research on explanations of success and failure on mental and physical tasks has shown that there are strong similarities in explanations of the two tasks (McClure, Jaspars and Lalljee, 1989). The key point here is that the attribution paradigm applies to both mental and manual tasks, and is not restricted to the mental or cognitive domain in the way that Michael suggests.

Even if attribution analogies were restricted to psychologists' activity, that activity is not purely cognitive, contrary to what Michael suggests. Psychologists carry out experiments, which are behavioural events, not purely mental events. And the ways in which attributions are affected in these experiments serve as a model for attributions outside the laboratory. For example, the induction of helplessness in learned helplessness experiments, where people exposed to uncontrollable stimulus conditions become helpless, simulates helplessness in natural settings, where people experience circumstances where they do not control their own contingencies (McClure, 1985). Similarly, experiments that induce misattributions in subjects by false information serve as a model for conditions in social life, where people are fed false information concerning the causes of their cognitions of behaviour. Scientists do not simply sit in armchairs; there is a practical aspect to their activity. Michael's proposal to reject parallels with scientists because they deal with cognitions would reinforce any division between manual and mental activity, rather than eliminate it.

A second problem with Michael's claim about the appropriate analogy for explanations is that Michael does not show how the work of manual workers such as the plumber is as useful an analogy as the analogies with scientific and legal inference. The professional task of the psychologist is to provide explanations of behaviour, which is what people do when they make attributions. By contrast, the professional task of the plumber is to deal with plumbing, which does require explanations, but they are explanations of events such as why no hot water is coming out of the tap. The parallel analogy to the scientist and the lay person giving explanations of behaviour is between the plumber and the lay person doing the plumbing. The reason why the plumber was not chosen as an analogy for attributions is probably because the plumber's professional task is not explaining behaviour, just as the middle-class doctor, accountant, and banker, who are equally ignored by attribution theory, are not concerned primarily with explaining behaviour. The selection of analogies for attribution theories is based at least partly on the relevance of the analogy rather than an inherent bias toward analogies with mental or middle-class occupations.

Michael notes that a policeman's explanation of a criminal action such as rape may appear unreasonable in scientific terms, but this does not mean he is a bad scientist, and it may even suggest that he is a good policeman. But few attribution researchers deny that many attributions serve different functions from scientific inquiry. And police officers' explanations serve similar functions to a prosecution lawyer's explanations, and are closer to analogies with lawyers suggested by attribution theorists than to models of manual workers that Michael is calling for in the name of discourse analysis. In short, there are several difficulties in the claim that analogies with scientific and legal inference should be replaced by analogies with manual workers for the purpose of modelling attributions.

The second issue raised by Michael concerns the social origins of explanations. According to the discourse approach, explanations are not the product of individual inferences, but reflect the discourse of a social culture. Michael claims that the discourse approach deals with social functions of explanations. He also claims that these social functions of explanations are invisible to the explainer in a way that individual functions (e.g., self-presentation) are not, although he gives no justification for the view that individual functions are transparent to the explainer. Michael claims that previous extensions of attribution theory in a social direction fail to capture the social dimensions of explanations. For example, Michael claims that social attribution theories, which link attributions to group membership (Hewstone and Jaspars, 1984), 'corrupt' the social, in that they fail to capture the complex totality that explanations reflect; he also claims they retain an individualistic motivational kernel that animates the group member independently of the social milieu.

Michael does not spell out these claims, and in their present form they are not convincingly argued. Research on social attribution does examine the conflicting explanations of different groups for their outcomes, and shows the relation of these explanations to people's circumstances. For example,

Hewstone, Jaspars and Lalljee (1982) showed that boys at private schools attributed their own success to ability and attributed the success of state schoolboys to effort, while state schoolboys attributed the private school-boys' success to their luck in being able to go to better schools. The private schoolboys' explanations reflect and reinforce a genetic viewpoint, and the state schoolboys' explanations contradict this view. These explanations relate directly to the boys' circumstances, and serve in the case of the private schoolboys to justify their advantages.

The same point applies to attributions for the success and failure of men and women, like the widely replicated pattern where men's success on a task is attributed to ability and women's success on the same task to effort or luck. These explanations similarly function to underpin social inequalities (Deaux, 1976). Michael does not show what key aspects of explanations these studies leave out, although from other expositions of discourse analysis one might conclude that studies on social attribution fail to capture the contradictions within a group's arguments (Potter and Wetherell, 1987). This point applies to other features that Michael associates uniquely with the discourse approach, including the way stereotypes shape the self-perception of the stereotyped person, and the way behaviour and explanations work back on people to consolidate their identity and social position. These aspects of explanations are also examined by theories of social attribution and social identity.

The same point applies to Michael's claim that the goal of giving people insight into their conditions is unique to the discourse approach, as this end can result from other approaches. For example, research in the social attribution paradigm has shown that subordinate groups may express the same view of themselves as the dominant group, and make ingroup-deprecating rather than ingroup-supporting attributions (Hewstone and Jaspars, 1984). These attributions reinforce people's subordinate circumstances, but when research findings are publicized, subordinate groups may recognize the cognitive patterns that reinforce their disadvantage, and may change their perceptions and explanations accordingly (and their circumstances). As Gergen (1973) noted, there is feedback between psychology and society whereby findings are disseminated, and people become aware of how they are manipulated and then counter this manipulation, thereby invalidating the processes that previously affected them. So the dissemination of knowledge leads not only to the maintenance of society, but also to its transformation, and this pattern is not restricted to research obtained by discourse analysis. The function of giving people insight into themselves and their world that Michael claims is unique to the discourse/praxis framework, can result from other approaches.

Michael makes useful criticisms of the theory of social representations

(Moscovici, 1984). He challenges the theory's emphasis on making unfamiliar representations familiar, claiming that this process reflects an individualist motivation. Certainly, the theory's emphasis on familiarization implies that people's acquisition of new representations involves cognitive assimilation, rather than accommodation or transformation. By contrast, much research in this paradigm has examined transformations in social representations, such as the way representations of psychoanalysis transformed popular thinking, and Moscovici (e.g., 1984) refers to these changes as revolutions in common sense akin to scientific revolutions. This research is at odds with the dominant emphasis on familiarization in the theory, which should be changed to account for major changes in world view where the unfamiliar conquers the familiar.

Michael also claims that Moscovici's theory neglects the role of power in social representations. In fact, the theory does invoke the power of popularizers who transmit scientific ideas to common sense (Moscovici, 1984). Yet not all representations derive from science. Common opinion is shaped by influential economic theories, for which the powers of advocacy include economists and politicians; there are also, for example, feminist belief systems, with advocates who include writers and academics. As Michael implies, a theory of social representations should describe these other avenues of ideas and power.

Despite these useful comments about the theory of social representations, Michael fails to make a clear case for the distinct value of a discourse approach to the study of explanations. Several of the features that he claims are unique to the discourse approach apply equally to other approaches.

Conclusion

There have been a range of criticisms and attempts to rectify attribution theories' failure to adequate justice to either the intentional (goal-based) dimension of actions and explanations or to the functional nature of explanations. In one sense this trend can only be welcomed, given that much attribution theory and research has diminished, rather than expanded, the conceptual inheritance it received from Heider (1958). But the alternative viewpoints and proposals have not all escaped the 'fuzziness' in theoretical thinking that has characterized attribution approaches (Taylor and Fiske, 1981, p. 515).

But these flaws do not invalidate the attempt to broaden or transcend attribution theory or to give due weight to intentional and functional factors (cf. Ginsburg, 1979). With regard to self-presentational factors in explanations, while it is suggested that those factors do not have the all-embracing importance that ethogenicists suggest, it is agreed that they have been insufficiently acknowledged and examined. And on the matter of ethnocentricity and ideology, while it is pointed out that ethogenic and hermeneutic theories are not free of the ideological dimensions that their exponents have discerned in attribution theories, it is suggested that the negative consequences of these alternative ideological tendencies can be counteracted. In relation to the examination of naturally occurring discourse, it is suggested that this method is useful for exposing the contradictions in people's talk, but that this stance does not justify the exclusion of cognitive processes. The weaknesses in these arguments do not nullify the value of models that do justice to intentional and functional factors, and they provide no excuse for retreating into the 'obsession with methodological exactitude and the craving for scientific status' (Billig, 1977, p. 393) which has often inhibited social psychology.

7 Illusions, control, and helplessness

The discussion up to this point has focused on research in social cognition. In this chapter and the following one, the discussion broadens to aspects of social cognition in personality and abnormal psychology, areas which show important practical implications of the various issues. Critical analyses hold that self-perceptions and cognitions are often illusory, a view shared by discourse analysts and positivist (or behavioural) psychologists. In explaining these illusions, however, critical analyses attribute illusions to motivational factors, rather than the adventitious stimuli or information-processing errors emphasized in other accounts. The critical models also link illusions to relations between two parties, rather than the effect of merely one cognitive agency.

This chapter examines cognitive distortions and illusions produced in research on attribution, locus of control, and learned helplessness. The discussion first considers the information-processing versus motivation dispute, then offers a critical interpretation of illusions produced in studies dealing with attribution, locus of control, misattribution therapy, and learned helplessness. A brief final section examines attempts to demonstrate intentional action by inducing an internal locus control.

The information-processing versus motivation dispute

Several authors advance the idea that illusions are a function of motivation, in the form of people's attempts to raise their own self-esteem. There is a large literature concerned with the contest between these 'motivational' explanations of illusions and 'information-processing' explanations that attribute distortions to the person's normal processing of information, or errors in that processing (e.g., Bradley, 1978; D. T. Miller, 1976; Monson and Snyder, 1977; Nisbett and Ross, 1980; Ross, 1977; Stevens and Jones, 1976). For the purposes of the argument here it is necessary only to summarize the relative success of the two approaches. Some perceptual errors do seem to be best explained in terms of information-processing or similar variables, but with other illusions explanations invoking motivation seem more convincing. For example, researchers have found that people's explanations for their outcomes on various tasks show an asymmetry between success and failure (e.g., Federoff and Harvey, 1976). Subjects attribute success to self and failure to luck and external factors, particularly when they have a choice in selecting the task they perform. Bradley (1978), arguing for the motivational account, claims that such a result derives from the subjects' motivation to protect their self-esteem. This explanation appears at least as plausible as Ross's (1977) alternative and somewhat tautologous argument that such biases must derive from the past experience of actors and observers.

Numerous other biases and illusions have been examined, for each of which some psychologists have proposed an explanation which emphasizes information, whereas others emphasize motivation. Each explanation has its focus of convenience. Certainly for some illusions, a strong case has been made that motivation is the dominant factor (Bradley, 1978; Federoff and Harvey, 1976; Harvey, Harris and Barnes, 1975; Stevens and Jones, 1976). Yet, while researchers have successfully explained a number of illusions in terms of the motivation factor, this element is frequently disregarded or avoided in models of social cognition. Several psychologists imply that information-processing variables will explain most illusions, and that motivation will no longer be required as an explanation (Ross, 1977; Taylor and Fiske, 1978).

Several factors may account for this view. One issue is that assumptions are made which are not questioned even by advocates of motivational explanations. In much of the literature one finds the assumption that the application of an information-processing account necessarily precludes motivation. It is assumed that 'motivation' and 'information-processing' are alternative and mutually exclusive explanations. Miller and Ross (1975), for example, set out 'to compare the explanatory power of the self-serving attributional analysis with that of a non-motivational information-processing analysis' (p. 213). Researchers have inferred that as information and motivation are largely complementary, so information-processing and motivational explanations are complementary. It follows that invoking an information-processing explanation excludes motivation.

This assumption is questionable, as there is more to information-processing than information. Even information-processing machines made by humans are designed to achieve some purpose in their processing: to achieve some end. Simon (1976) noted that concepts such as 'motive' and 'plan' are peculiar to the processes that go on in decision-making systems, and that 'There is no reason, of course, why the decision maker has to be human. There are many cases today...where the decision maker is a computer. The computer has motives (to achieve an optimal balance between the costs of stockouts and of excess inventories and plans)' (p. 257). An information-processing account does not automatically preclude motives. The assumption that it does do this lends unjustified support to the information-processing model of cognition.

A second assumption that reduces the impact of motivational explanations is the assumption that human thinking can be mapped successfully by highly logical inferential models. An example is the analogy between lay attributors and scientists. Reference has already been made to Kelley's (1972a) proposal, similar to many others in the field, that the lay attributor 'generally acts like a good scientist, examining the covariance between a given effect and various possible causes' (p. 2). One could ask whether people also think like bad scientists; but to challenge this analogy, the quibble isn't necessary. Consider some major figures in physics, a highly respected science. Newton's spectrum of seven colours derives from his belief that his God organized the universe according to the number seven (Feyerabend, 1965). This logic is not an analysis of variance. Einstein's refusal to accept the uncertainty principle of quantum mechanics was not because of an analysis of variance but at least in part because 'the Lord God does not throw dice' (Heisenberg, 1971). And was the troublesome principle itself introduced because of an analysis of variance? No; it was introduced so quantum mechanics could escape the falsification occurring in cloud chamber experiments (Heisenberg, 1971). Even if lay persons do think anything like 'good' professional scientists, they are not completely constrained by supposedly rational rules like analyses of variance. This sort of assumption in the literature is based on a legendary view of scientists. In being accepted by many contestants in the field of social cognition, it prevents researchers from examining the influence of motivational factors.

These assumptions can be linked to a type of paradigm shift (Kuhn, 1970) that took place in social psychology in the 1970s. D. J. Bem (1972) observed: 'There is, in short, a shift of paradigm taking place within social psychology, a shift from motivational/drive models of cognitions, behaviours and internal states to information-processing/attribution models of such phenomena' (p. 43). The influence of the information-processing paradigm has encouraged authors to accept questionable assumptions favouring that paradigm. The dominance of the information-processing approach has also affected people's reactions to evidence. It was suggested earlier that research supports the view that motivational factors are a significant variable in certain illusions. This reading of the literature is shared by Ross (1977), even though his argument favours non-motivational explanations. Ross writes (note the implication of the word 'unfortunately'): 'unfortunately the existing attribution literature provides relatively little conceptual analysis of evidence pertaining to non-motivational biases' (p. 183). Whatever the evidence indicates, however, it is motivation that goes by the board. Ross proposes in the same article that a 'fruitful strategy...may be to temporarily abandon motivational constructs and to concentrate upon those informational, perceptual and cognitive factors that mediate and potentially distort attribution judgments "in general"' (p. 183). So, while it was acknowledged that the evidence points to the role of motivation, this evidence is waived in deference to the preferred paradigm.

The 1980s have seen a weakening of this trend away from motivational explanations, and a partial shift back towards models that incorporate aspects of 'hot' cognition, such as emotion and motivation. Nevertheless, the influence of information-processing accounts is still strong, and many authors retain a preference for explaining cognitions and illusions in terms of non-motivational factors (e.g., Fiske and Taylor, 1984). Even where motivation is invoked, however, it is often restricted to explanations of illusions in terms of the person's effort to maintain self-esteem. The following sections of this chapter consider motivational factors in a broader sense, and emphasize the role of a person's context in the formation of cognitive distortions and illusions.

Illusory attributions and locus of control

The pro-motivation theorists' argument about self-esteem is circumscribed in its suppositions; it seeks to demonstrate the effect on illusions of the motivation of one party: the person who holds the illusions. The critical perspective shares the view that many cognitive distortions reflect motivation, but it usually locates the origin of illusions in relationships between two or more parties (see chapter 3). The critical framework can be applied to research dealing with attributions, locus of control, attribution therapies and learned helplessness. The discussion begins with research that manipulates people's perceptions by presenting certain information, usually false, about aspects of their situation. This research comprises experiments designed within the focus of convenience of the behavioural (or positivist) account of perceptions and illusions, which explains the cognitions in terms of the mechanical effects of stimuli, reinforcement, and similar concepts. Although the events in the experiments have been previously interpreted to support this account, it is suggested here that they correspond more closely to a critical analysis.

Deception and control

Phares' (1957) experiment set the pattern for the induction of misattributions in accordance with the behavioural model. Phares manipulated perceived locus of control by falsely informing participants that a task that they were to complete involved chance, where an external locus was intended, or skill, where an internal locus was intended. Subjects then performed tasks, and were given feedback (also false) about their success or failure. Phares predicted that the participants' perception produced by the locus of control manipulation would determine their interpretation of the feedback about whether they succeeded or failed on the task. Phares subsequently measured their expectancy of future success and failure. People who received skill instructions and success feedback were expected to show an increased expectancy for future success, on the grounds that the skill instructions should produce an (illusory) internal locus of control.

Since the Phares (1957) experiment there have been numerous experiments in the areas of learning theory, locus of control and attribution which manipulate false instructions and false feedback in a similar fashion (reviewed in, for example, Kleinke, 1978; Nisbett and Ross, 1980; Nisbett and Wilson, 1977). The outcomes of these experiments are interpreted to support the behavioural account of perceptions and illusions. Phares, for example, claims that his results, as outlined above, support a mechanical model of perceived control. He claims that the illusory expectancies produced in the experiment are a consequence of 'situational variables' and of reinforcement in skill or chance situations (Phares, 1957, p. 341). A similar example in the domain of learning theory is the experiment of Kaufman, Baron and Kopp (1966), where subjects were given false information concerning contingencies. Kaufman *et al.* report that instruction-produced behaviour 'was relatively insensitive to the influence of actually programmed reinforcement' (p. 249), and explain this effect: 'This outcome is consistent with the contention that instructions represent an important source of stimulus control for the operant behaviour of humans' (p. 246). In the attribution arena, many psychologists use similar techniques and employ similar explanations (e.g., Ross, Lepper and Hubbard, 1975). All these accounts interpret their production of illusions with false information to support the behavioural paradigm which interprets cognitions in terms of the concepts of stimuli, reinforcement, and a purely mechanistic causal process.

The behavioural interpretation of these studies, however, entails problems and contradictions, particularly in relation to the number of parties involved and the type of causes present. A first discrepancy concerns the issue of whether an account of the processes in these studies should involve merely one person, the experimental subject, or a second person, the experimenter. It has been recognized by, for example, Nisbett and Wilson (1977), that there are two parties involved in this type of experiment, and that the experimenter's behaviour is a critical factor producing the illusions. Nisbett and Wilson recognized that the results in experiments of this type:

> could never be obtained if subjects were aware of the critical role played
> by the social pressure from the experimenter. If subjects realized that
> their behavior was produced by this social pressure, they would not

change their attitudes so as to move them into line with their behavior, because they would realize that their behavior was governed by the social pressure and not by their attitudes. We concur with Kelley's view that this fundamental unawareness of the critical role of the experimenter's behavior is essential to the erroneous attitude inference obtained in these experiments.

(p. 239)

These statements recognize the role of the experimenter in producing the illusions, yet in theoretical accounts of this research, the experimenter is not included, and the experiments are interpreted in terms of factors affecting the subject, such as stimulus control and subjects' errors in processing information. There is a contradiction between the recognition of the essential role of the experimenter's involvement in discussions of the experiment and the formal interpretation of the experiment in terms of a theoretical model which excludes the experimenter.

The mechanistic account is problematic not only concerning the number of parties involved in producing the illusions, but also the type of cause involved. It is acknowledged that illusions derive from false information. The word false, as in false information, false instructions, and false feedback, permeates the literature (e.g., Kleinke, 1978). Yet what kind of a 'stimulus' is false information? It is information that is not true, and is given knowing that it is not true. It is not an error, accident, or epiphenomenon. The deliberate imparting of false information is usually called deception, and indeed deception is recognized as a common phenomenon in the literature. No writer on the topic denies that deception occurs in these studies. Yet deception is clearly a motivational and intentional concept. The causal processes in these experimental situations are at least partly intentional. The purposive element is compounded when we ask: do not experiments have a design? Indeed they are not only designed to achieve something, which is an intentional situation, but designed to deceive. Only an existentialist should be comfortable with the intentionality saturating these manipulations and such comments as that of Ross, Lepper and Hubbard (1975): 'Every subject was explicitly asked to acknowledge her understanding of the nature and purpose of the deception before the experimenter proceeded to the next phase of the study' (p. 883). Yet in spite of such statements that acknowledge the role of deception, it is claimed that these experiments merely demonstrate the operation of efficient causes, that they show simply the operation of 'stimuli' and 'reinforcement'.

It could be argued that this account excludes earlier steps in the causal sequence, such as the experimenter and the deception, and that the choice of what factors to include is a matter of the particular model being employed. While there is some legitimacy to this argument as a general principle, the purely mechanistic model leads to problematic implications when it is applied to the allocation of responsibility in human affairs. To blame stimuli for the illusions produced intentionally by deception is equivalent to someone blaming the pen for the words they write. When a court imposes a fine for deceptive advertising, it doesn't fine the billboard that carries the advertisement. To take another comparison, to attribute the effect in a deception experiment to the stimulus employed is equivalent to blaming a gun for a murder that is committed. The behavioural interpretation of the processes in these studies is highly problematic when applied to human actions in everyday life. It can be suggested that the experiments that induce illusions by false information include elements that do not fit the behavioural model, but that do fit a critical perspective. This approach incorporates two parties, and recognizes that many illusions result from the motivated propagation of false or distorted information by one of those parties.

The emphasis on the role of experimenter in this analysis is rather different from that focused on in relation to experimenter effects. Several psychologists have demonstrated the influence of the experimenter in research with human subjects, and the strong effects of variables such as the expectancies of subject and experimenter (e.g., R. Rosenthal, 1966; Wuebben, 1975). These artifacts are often seen as lessening or nullifying the validity of the experiments. The argument here, however, is not that the role of the experimenter nullifies the validity of the experiment, but that it supports a different interpretation of the effects being produced in the experiment.

It might be thought that this argument applies only to experiments employing verbal deception, and does not generalize to experiments on attribution and locus of control that induce illusions without employing false information. But this is not the case. In many studies that induce illusions without the use of false information, the events are no less compatible with a critical analysis. An example is the study by Rotter, Liverant and Crowne (1961), where the main difference from the deception studies is in the manipulation affecting the participant's perceptions: this was changed from the instructions in the Phares (1957) study to particular tasks. Rotter *et al.* (1961) examined the effect of tasks that would be regarded as skill or chance tasks on the basis of the previous cultural experience of the subjects. The skill task, which was used to produce an internal locus of control, involved a motor-skill apparatus, while the chance task, used to produce an external locus of control, was a card-guessing procedure. After performing the task, subjects were given success and failure (false) feedback and their expectancies then measured.

The experiment confirmed the prediction that greater shifts in expectancies would follow feedback in skill conditions. Rotter *et al.* interpret the result to support a behavioural account. Referring to perceived locus of control in terms of expectancies, they claim that their study shows that 'under skill conditions positive and negative reinforcement leads to greater increments and decrements in verbalized expectancies' and that 'the extinction of expectancies under continuous negative reinforcement will reverse under chance and skill conditions so that 50 per cent is more resistant to extinction than 100 per cent reinforcement under chance conditions, and 100 per cent reinforcement is more resistant to extinction than 50 per cent reinforcement under skill conditions' (pp. 176–7).

The illusions are thus attributed to skill and chance conditions and to differing reinforcement manipulations, an entirely deterministic account. This interpretation of the situation, however, omits important features of the procedure. In this experiment the situation is intended and constructed by the experimenters to engender a particular effect on perceived locus of control. Rotter *et al.* took some care to select tasks that would achieve this effect. They write of the tasks they were looking for: 'Both tasks must be controlled by E, but in one case S should believe that performance is a matter of his own skill and the other that it is a matter of luck' (p. 163). They report: 'A number of tasks were tried out in an attempt to meet these conditions and finally tasks were found for female Ss which appeared to work with a minimum of suspicion of experimenter control' (p. 163). In this experiment, then, the events are not adventitious but designed to have a certain effect. And why female subjects? 'In pretesting the skill tasks a number of the men expressed some suspiciousness…Consequently, it was decided to run this experiment entirely with female Ss. The men who did express suspiciousness did not know what was happening but felt that in some way the experimenter was controlling the outcome' (pp. 164–5).

So only subjects who believed the experimenters' misleading structuring of events and feedback were employed. In this manipulation, then, only tasks that would succeed in deceiving subjects, and only subjects who were successfully deceived, were employed. Yet the behavioural account attributes the illusions to stimulus conditions and reinforcement. There is a tension between an intelligible account of the events in the experiment and the formal behavioural description. Again, however, the situations produced in this paradigm fit the critical perspective. The situation here was neither adventitious nor determined but was clearly intended, designed and altered to achieve those illusions. The same observations apply to other experiments with similar designs (Lefcourt, 1976; Phares, 1976). While the experiments described here were designed and interpreted to support the behavioural paradigm of illusions, key aspects of the studies do not fit this model and are compatible with a critical analysis.

The psychopathology of everyday illusions

Nisbett and Wilson's (1977) related account of perceptions and illusions in everyday life entails similar tensions. Nisbett and Wilson argue that when people make an attribution, they do so not by consulting introspective knowledge but by applying causal theories. Concerning the origins of these theories, they write: 'Causal theories may have any of several origins. The culture or a subculture may have explicit rules stating the relationships between a particular stimulus and a particular response. ("I came to a stop because the light started to change.")...The culture or a subculture may supply implicit theories about causal relationships' (p. 248).

This account invokes two parties: the attributor and the culture (or subculture). From the proposition that attributions derive from the culture, it follows that misattributions and illusions would derive from the culture's supplying false causal theories. Nisbett and Wilson fail, however, to arrive at this logical consequence; instead they build an unexplained asymmetry into their theory. They are quite clear that correct attributions derive from the culture:

> In general, we may say that people will be accurate in reports about the causes of their behavior and evaluations whenever the culture, or a subculture, specifies clearly what stimulus should produce which responses, and especially where there is continuing feedback from the culture concerning the extent to which the individual is following the prescribed rules for input and output.
>
> (p. 254)

With this conception of accuracy, it is fairly clear where errors are going to come from. Nisbett and Wilson state: 'Verbal reports relying on such theories will typically be wrong not because the theories are in error in every case but merely because they are incorrectly applied in the particular instance' (p. 248). Errors are not blamed on the culture but on the individual or on a particular breakdown in theory. Nisbett and Wilson list a number of factors in individual judgements which lead to errors in attributions. Although cultures are assumed to produce the correct attributions, it is not suggested that cultures also may produce false attributions.

This asymmetry is striking when one recalls the ways in which illusions are induced in many experiments on attributions and perceptions. In these experiments, illusions derive not from subjects' faulty judgement, but from the acts of a second party disguising the experimental situation. In Nisbett and Wilson's (1977) own terms, and against their own theory, the evidence they reviewed demonstrates 'that when even relatively minor steps are taken to disguise the connection between stimulus and response, subjects will fail to report such a connection' (pp. 253–4). This suggests that the 'errors' result from deliberate concealments by the experimenter. The role of the experimenter in producing the illusion is acknowledged; we recall Nisbett and Wilson's acceptance that the several results they cite: 'could never be obtained if subjects were aware of the critical role played by the social pressures from the experimenter. If subjects realised that their behaviour was produced by this social pressure, they would not change their attitudes' (p. 239).

This acknowledgement that the experimenter contributes to producing the illusions in the experiments conflicts with Nisbett and Wilson's own theory that illusions in daily life result from the subject's judgements while correct perceptions derive from an external agent, such as the culture. Nisbett and Wilson go on to suggest that the illusion-producing deceptions in the experiments from which they generalize to daily life do not occur in that same daily life: 'Deceptive practices are often employed in structuring the stimulus situations in such [dissonance and attribution] experiments, and these practices may result in people being misled in ways that do not normally occur in daily life' (p. 242). After conceding that illusions result from deceptions in the experiments, Nisbett and Wilson argue that such deceptions do not occur in daily life. Yet they claim that their experiments apply to and explain illusions in everyday life.

It can be seen that this account contains asymmetries and illogical inferences. The argument concedes that in the experiments illusions result from the actions of two parties, yet claims that in everyday life illusions result from errors within one party. The argument claims to derive its theory of illusions in daily life from the experiments, and admits that the experiments contain deceptions, yet asserts that deceptions do not occur in daily life. Nisbett and Wilson's account actually obscures important aspects of the experiments, while claiming to derive its account of everyday life from them. But while Nisbett and Wilson's account fails to reflect the experiments, there is no reason to believe that what *is* happening in the experiments does not apply to everyday life.

It is suggested here that the critical perspective accounts for the illusions of subjects in these experiments more satisfactorily than behavioural accounts, and that behavioural accounts can only explain the phenomena by incorporating concepts that do not fit their theory. The following sections apply these principles to abnormal conditions, in the first case to misattribution therapy, and then, more extensively, to learned helplessness. Both models draw on the behavioural tradition which explains processes affecting illusions largely in terms of efficient (mechanical) causes. The analysis developed here will suggest that learned helplessness is not only learned: it is also taught.

Misattribution therapy

Misattribution therapy was originally developed by Ross, Rodin and Zimbardo (1969). The procedure typically has two conditions. In the first condition, subjects are classically conditioned to exhibit fear symptoms to a stimulus that is scheduled with an electric shock. The experimenters then deceptively juxtapose stimuli to make the subjects attribute their aversive arousal symptoms to a 'placebo' source, such as noise. The rationale is that if subjects can be induced to misattribute fear to something other than the actual cause of that fear and which is not in itself considered harmful, then that fear will lessen. The technique has been further developed by a number of therapists and researchers (e.g., Holroyd, 1978; Singerman, Borkovec and Baron, 1976; Valins and Nisbett, 1971; Wein, Nelson and Odom, 1975).

The procedures employed in misattribution therapy are similar to those in experiments referred to in the previous section, where cognitions were manipulated in non-clinical situations. There are, however, differences in the procedures and in the descriptions of those procedures, which are significant in relation to explanations of the studies. A first relevant difference from the attribution and locus of control experiments is that the illusions produced are actually called illusions or misattributions. They are no longer described as 'expectancy changes' (Phares, 1957), 'behaviour insensitive to the influence of actual reinforcement' (Kaufman, Baron and Kopp, 1966), or internal or external locus of control. The stated aim of the therapy is to produce misattributions or illusions. The description of the procedure as one that aims at misperception, illusion, or misattribution sheds the rather mystifying jargon of the laboratory-based accounts where terms like 'changing of expectancies' were employed. Valins and Nisbett (1971) include a section justifying the use of the deception which is more conspicuous in this context. They write: 'While we have used deception in our therapy-relevant research, we have done so not because we believe that deception is usually necessary or desirable but because deception techniques are economical ways of asking research questions' (p. 148). In fact, there is no more deception employed in misattribution therapy than there is in the experiments where effects of deception were given different names like 'expectancies', or 'external locus of control', and the deception was less obvious. The description of the induction of illusions as a process of deception, however, does not fit the mechanistic pretensions of the behavioural position.

Misattribution therapy differs in a second way from the laboratory experiments discussed earlier. In the laboratory context, it is easier for the experimenters to maintain that there was only one party involved in the changes occurring, because the role of the experimenter is not usually included in the explanation of experimental outcomes. But in the therapeutic situation, where the experimenter is replaced by the therapist, it is more difficult to exclude him or her from the account. The role of the second party is more conspicuous.

The situation supports the critical interpretation of illusions in terms of the deliberate action of one party manipulating information that is perceived by another. The close match of misattribution therapy to the critical account of illusions is apparent when we recall the role of ideology in critical social theory and the defence mechanisms in critical accounts of individual cognition. Both produce a false consciousness to achieve some purpose – to conceal the nature of society or to conceal the nature of unconscious knowledge or emotion. In like fashion, misattribution therapy is designed to conceal from subjects the nature of their fear symptoms by inducing them to misattribute symptoms to other stimuli. While it may seem obvious that there are both motivation and two parties involved here, both of those factors were more concealed in the equivalent attribution and locus of control research. The following section shows how a similar argument applied to learned helplessness leads to therapeutic applications that extend beyond the solutions that follow from the conventional explanation of helplessness.

Helplessness: taught and sometimes learned

The learned helplessness model applies the behavioural analysis to an explanation of depression (e.g., Seligman, 1975; Abramson, Seligman and Teasdale, 1978). The model relates closely to the research on locus of control discussed in previous sections (Lefcourt, 1976; Hiroto, 1974). The learned helplessness model has undergone much theoretical development, but it has retained several assumptions about responding, reinforcement and contingency that gravitate around the view that helplessness reflects uncontrollable or inescapable conditions. As a consequence of this view, the therapy proposed for helplessness places little emphasis on giving people increased control over the contingencies affecting them. The analysis here questions the 'uncontrollable conditions' assumption of the learned helplessness model and the associated therapy. This analysis suggests an alternative interpretation of the experiments used to induce helplessness, and shows the implications of this analysis for therapies and theories concerning perceptions related to helplessness.

The experimental induction of helplessness

The procedure used to induce learned helplessness was originally administered to dogs (Mowrer, 1948; Seligman and Maier, 1967), and subsequently applied to humans (Hiroto and Seligman, 1975; Roth and Kubal, 1975). In the first stage of the procedure, experimental subjects receive a powerful electric shock that they cannot escape. In the second stage, the same subjects and a control group that has not received the shock treatment are placed in an avoidance apparatus. Shock can be avoided in this stage if subjects run to an adjacent compartment when a warning stimulus is presented. Subjects in the control group learn to run in response to the conditioned stimulus and thus avoid shock, but subjects that have received inescapable shock initially run about in the avoidance apparatus, and then receive the shock without moving. They become 'helpless'. These subjects exhibit many symptoms characteristic of depression: passivity, anorexia, and lower norepinephrine levels. Seligman (1975) has also postulated a cognitive deficit in human subjects, the illusory belief that there is no escape in the second stage.

The helplessness induction procedure has not always produced helplessness in human subjects (Blaney, 1977; Rizley, 1978), and Abramson, Seligman and Teasdale (1978) proposed that the occurrence of helplessness in humans is contingent on the attributions that people make. Helplessness is contingent on stable, global, and internal attributions for negative events. There is much debate on the relation of these cognitions to helplessness, with some researchers claiming that the effect of non-contingency is not mediated by cognitions (e.g., Oakes and Curtis, 1982; Tennen, Gillen and Drum, 1982; Tennen, Drum, Gillen and Stanton, 1982), and two recent reviews concluding that there is little evidence that cognitive factors play a causal role in the onset of depression (Brewin, 1985; Coyne and Gotlib, 1983), although others disagree with this conclusion (Peterson and Seligman, 1984; Sweeney, Anderson and Bailey, 1986). It has been suggested that the cognitions in question may be an effect of helplessness or depression, rather than its cause (cf. Brewin, 1985). Studies on this issue using longitudinal designs (designs that examine attributions antecedent to the measurement of depression) do not provide a clear-cut answer. Whereas some longitudinal studies suggest that a negative attribution set does precede depression (e.g., Golin, Sweeney and Shaeffer, 1981), others find that negative attributions do not predict depression (e.g., Hammen, Adrian and Hiroto, 1988). However, there is strong evidence that the onset of depression does follow negative life events (e.g., Brown and Harris, 1978; Hammen, Adrian and Hiroto, 1988; Parry and Brewin, 1988), so the proposed link between helplessness and loss of control is still central, even if it is uncertain whether this relation is mediated by particular expectations or attributions.

The learned helplessness model interprets the classic experiments inducing helplessness in terms of a learning process that involves a single person. According to this model, 'learning that reinforcement and responding are independent is central to the symptoms and etiology of both learned helplessness and depression' (Miller and Seligman, 1976, p. 7). Helplessness is said to involve one person learning from an immutable situation that responding and reinforcement 'are independent'. Rather than considering that responding and reinforcement in this situation are made independent by another person, Miller and Seligman imply that they are intrinsically independent. Furthermore, according to this account, the subjects are exposed to 'uncontrollability', and 'inescapable' outcomes (e.g., Miller and Seligman, 1976). Seligman (1975) likens the circumstances in experiments inducing helplessness to events in life that people cannot control, such as loss of loved ones, ageing, and physical disease.

An alternative may be suggested to this interpretation of the induction procedure as a solitary person learning that events are uncontrollable. In the first case, in the experiments inducing helplessness, two parties are involved: teacher and learner. In these situations, helplessness is not only learned; it is also taught. The fact that many replications fail to induce the learning of helplessness (e.g., Costello, 1978; Rizley, 1978) suggests the irony of referring to the procedure as *learned* helplessness. In these replications something is being taught but not learned. Yet even in these instances the event is described as an exercise in 'learned' helplessness, rather than an attempt to teach helplessness.

The different terminology is not simply a case of semantic quibbling. The interpretation of the helplessness induction procedure as a teaching event has different implications from an interpretation of the procedure as a learning event. The possibility that people try to teach helplessness conflicts with the idea that the process is uncontrollable or inescapable. The procedure inducing helplessness, rather than being a situation where the outcomes are inevitable, unchangeable and uncontrollable, is one where a person (in this case the experimenter) is controlling the contingencies and outcomes and can change them at will. In describing the outcomes as uncontrollable and inescapable, the standard interpretation assigns a necessity to outcomes that are entirely changeable. In interpreting the procedure in this way, one disregards the potential flexibility of the experimenter. It could be said that the standard interpretation reifies the contingencies that surround the person in the experimental situation.

This representation of the outcomes as uncontrollable is buttressed by the analogues with genuinely uncontrollable events, such as ageing and death. But whereas processes such as ageing and death are relatively un-controllable, the outcomes in helplessness experiments are not. The idea that the changeable contingencies are immutable, coupled with the implication that helplessness results from events involving one party, suggest that the causal process in the experiments is mechanical and irreversible. In the helplessness-inducing procedure, however, the contingencies are changeable and reversible; it is a situation in which one person is controlling and manipulating the contingencies that are affecting another.

This different perspective on the induction of helplessness has practical consequences, and is not simply a theoretical matter. The different perspective placed on the induction of helplessness applies equally to the therapy for helplessness prescribed by Abramson *et al.* (1978, pp. 69–70). As the authors indicate, the basis for this therapy is implied by their theory (p. 69).

Implications for solutions to helplessness

The therapeutic proposals suggested by Abramson *et al.* (1978) include strategies which operate at both social and individual levels. The first strategy they recommend is to bring about a reduction in aversive outcomes and an increase in positive outcomes. They suggest this would involve improved welfare from social agencies, to provide facilities such as rehousing and nursing care for children (p. 69). A second strategy is to make 'highly preferred outcomes less preferred', and entails efforts to 'assist acceptance and resignation', and to 'assist renunciation and relinquishment of unattainable goals' (p. 69). Two further strategies focus on the person's perceptions and expectancies, and aim to change expectancies from uncontrollability to controllability and to change unrealistic attributions. The therapy is designed to 'force the person to criticize and perhaps change his [or her] attributional style' (p. 70), and is designed to assist the person to perceive an internal locus of control for positive events.

Like the helplessness induction procedure, the proposals clearly involve two parties and an intentional component. The therapist intentionally manipulates events so as to achieve certain effects on another. But regardless of the number of parties involved, these strategies appear to provide a solution to helplessness in recommending a reduction in aversive outcomes and in helping the person to perceive that outcomes are controllable. But the therapy does not change the actual locus of control; it is the person who controls the manipulations and the outcomes who has the actual locus of control. The actual control lies in the control of the contingencies. The recommendations put forward by Abramson *et al.* (1978) confuse control with philanthropic welfare arrangements.

Furthermore, the perceptions of controllability that therapists are to induce contradict the actual conditions of the therapy, in which the patient is given no control over the contingencies or the distribution of reinforcement. Given that the therapist (or social agency) has the control of the contingencies, it is not surprising that Abramson *et al.* propose that the perception of controllability may need to be 'forced' on the patient (p. 70). Because the therapy does not include the prospect of people controlling their own contingencies and outcomes, it is also not surprising that the therapist is to make the highly preferred outcomes less preferred, and assist acceptance and resignation (p. 69).

These aspects of the therapy are a logical consequence of the normal interpretation of helplessness, where the contingencies are construed as uncontrollable and inescapable forces affecting a single person. When the events surrounding helplessness are interpreted in less deterministic terms, and it is recognized that the contingencies, rather than being uncontrollable, are controlled by another person, it follows that a possible solution to helplessness is to place the subjects in the position of the therapist (or social agencies), and give them more control over their own lives by giving them more control over their own contingencies. This option does not follow from an interpretation of the contingencies as uncontrollable and inescapable. If a goal of therapy is to increase clients' control over their contingencies, then perceptions of controllability may change more easily than by being forced, and there will be less need to make highly preferred outcomes less preferred. This point applies equally to Weiner's (1988) comments about depressed people's aspirations: 'Perhaps the level of comparison has been set too high (e.g., attempting to join the most elite club), perhaps the individual has been engaging in social comparison with very "special" others rather than with peers of his or her background, and so on' (p. 101). The implication here is that people should lower their aspirations, forget about joining elite clubs, and restrict their social comparisons to people in similar situations to themselves. As R. Brown (1986) noted, changing comparison groups so that one makes upward comparisons with more privileged groups rather than level or downward comparisons with less privileged groups increases discontent with unfairness. But there is an alternative to lowering aspirations and restricting upward comparisons: this is to give people more control over their contingencies and thereby realize more of their aspirations.

Despite the finding that helplessness and depression frequently follow life events and circumstances, and are most dominant in groups that have less control over their conditions, interventions concentrate on changing the cognitions about circumstances, rather than the circumstances themselves (e.g., Forsterling, 1985, 1988). Even the non-cognitive components of therapy suggested by Abramson *et al.* (1978), which recommend improvement in people's conditions, if not control over those conditions, are largely disregarded in this emphasis on cognitive strategies.

This analysis has implications for several questions that have been raised in relation to depression, one of which concerns the accuracy of the perceptions of depressed people.

Accuracy of perceptions in depression

In suggesting that depressed people's perception of uncontrollability derives from conditions in which someone else is controlling their outcomes and contingencies, this analysis implies that this perception is sometimes an accurate reflection of circumstances. This position conflicts with the view in the learned helplessness model and other cognitive models (e.g., Beck, 1967) that the perceptions in depression are unrealistic or distorted and in need of therapeutic change. Yet it is the 'accuracy' position that receives more support from later research on the question. Alloy and Abramson (1979) found that depressed people are, if anything, more accurate in their perception of contingency. Abramson and Martin (1981) noted that in this experiment and others, contrary to the learned helplessness model, depressed subjects were 'surprisingly' (p. 132) accurate in judging their personal control, both in situations in which subjects' responses did control outcomes and in situations in which they did not. Non-depressed subjects, in contrast, systematically erred in judging how much control they exerted.

The finding that depressed people's perception of contingency is accurate concurs with the well-established finding that those groups, such as women and blacks (Phares, 1976), who have a high incidence of an external locus of control and depression, are those groups who have had less actual control in most societies. The present analysis shows a parallel between these findings with social groups and the helplessness induction setting, where the subject's perception of non-contingency is also accurate and hence where the actual locus of control, as much as the perception of control, becomes a target for change. Brown and Harris's (1978) survey of depression in women in Britain claimed that the idea that depressed people's perceptions are distorted or inaccurate 'is an unnecessary stipulation. Depression may also come from entirely accurate conceptualization, the "fault" lying in the environment rather than the person' (p. 83).

A possible problem with this analysis is that the perceptions of depressed people and of disadvantaged groups are not limited to uncontrollability. Abramson and Sackeim (1977) drew attention to the finding in a number of studies that the perceptions of depressed people are characterized not so much by uncontrollability as postulated by the learned helplessness model, or by self-blame as postulated by Beck (1967), but by a combinations of the two. Depressed people seem to perceive a paradoxical combination of uncontrollability and self-blame. Abramson and Sackeim (1977) noted that both perceptual constituents of the paradox are seen by therapists as distortions in the form of beliefs in impotence and omnipotence. According to Abramson and Sackeim, it is thought that 'beliefs in impotence are direct reflections of beliefs in uncontrollability' (p. 848) and that a conceptual willingness to assume responsibility and to castigate the self for events beyond personal control signifies 'a belief in omnipotence' (p. 849).

Abramson and Sackeim discussed possible ways of resolving the paradox, but offered no explanation of its origin. Yet an explanation of those paradoxical perceptions does follow from the analysis of the experiments described above. The paradox would be a logical consequence of situations in which people have little control but in which they nonetheless blame themselves for the situation, either as a result of internalizing the 'victim-blame' perceptions that others have of them or through applying some form of 'just-world' explanation of events to themselves (Lerner, 1977; cf. Tabachnik, Crocker and Alloy, 1983). Jahoda (1979) pointed out that rationalizations of this kind occurred in the depression (economic depression) of the 1930s. Many people who became unemployed as a consequence of the economic collapse at that time indulged in a large amount of self-blame. Feather and Barber (1983) found the same pattern with long-term unemployed people in a more contemporary setting.

This explanation of the paradoxical perceptions negates the idea that they are distorted representations of beliefs in impotence and omnipotence. It suggests rather that the perception of a lack of control reflects people's current circumstances and that self-blame in such circumstances derives from an internalization or self-application of the just-world motives that Lerner (1977) has proposed.

Is an internal locus beneficial?

The analysis here suggests that the paradoxical perceptions existing in depressed people and disadvantaged groups may result from situations in which people do not have actual control over events and yet are encouraged to perceive an internal locus of control or blame themselves for their circumstances. If this analysis is well-grounded, then Abramson's *et al.* (1978) proposal of shifting perception toward controllability, if applied without the recipients gaining more actual control, could exacerbate the paradoxical perceptions rather than relieve them. The same principles apply to interventions with social groups that have an external locus of control, such as deCharms' (1968) attempts to get black inner-city children to perceive an internal locus of control. Given that these children or their parents have little control over several facets of their lives, training them to perceive an internal locus of control when their conditions remain unchanged is not so much a 'training emphasis on reality perception' (deCharms and Muir, 1978) as a training course in illusion (cf. Furby, 1979; Stam, 1987).

It could be argued that encouraging perceptions of an internal locus of control is beneficial regardless of what the 'reality' is, because the perception of such control leads people to do something about their conditions, whereas the perception of an external locus leads people to do nothing because they see their lot as being in the hands of fate. Certainly, when an external locus of control is defined in terms of fatalistic perceptions and belief in chance, as in Rotter's (1966) scale, this may be so. However, as Gurin, Gurin, Lao and Beattie (1969) pointed out, if external locus of control is defined in terms of attributing the causes of events to social determinants, then people with an external locus of control rate higher on actively trying to change their conditions than do those with an internal locus of control. So it is a mistake to assume that training people to perceive an internal locus of control is necessarily beneficial.

As the previous point implies, training people to perceive an internal locus of control has important consequences. It has the effect of reducing tendencies to perceive and change social determinants of events. Although this effect may be beneficial when the source of the problem lies within the individual, it may lead to failure to solve the problem when the source of the problem lies outside the individual (cf. Caplan and Nelson, 1973; Rappaport, 1977). Furby (1979) observed that 'those in positions of power and affluence have much to gain from increasing the internality of beliefs about locus of control, and much to lose from increasing externality. If one perceives the inability to find a job as the result of one's own actions, then the result is likely to be either apathy or self-improvement' (p. 176), the latter course leading to a change in the pecking order. Furby pointed out that if one perceives unemployment to be the result of a particular economic policy, then one's actions might be less pleasing for those in power. Similarly, at an individual level the consequence of an internal perception is to try to remedy oneself internally, rather than to change or to increase control of one's conditions. Again, although the former strategy may be appropriate when the source of a problem is internal, it is likely to be misdirected or insufficient when the source of a problem lies in people's conditions.

Is giving people control already commonplace?

One might consider that the idea of giving people more control over the conditions and contingencies that affect them is so obvious and so related to the tenets of learning theory that it must already be done by researchers and therapists involved with the problem. Certainly one could suggest that at a social level, those sections of society who have a high incidence of external locus of control and depression (women and black people) have achieved several legal and social changes that to some extent lessen the 'inescapability' in the choices and control that they exercise (cf. Baucom, 1983). But at the individual level, at which change might seem to be easier to achieve, surprisingly little application of this kind has been attempted. Phares' (1976) discussion of the possibility of giving 'power to the powerless' referred only to the paper of that title by Goodstadt and Hjelle (1973). In that experiment, 'internal' and 'externals' were required to supervise a group of workers. The experimenters correctly predicted that subjects with internal perceptions would use more persuasive supervisory strategies and that subjects with external perceptions would use more coercive methods. The study provides a useful finding in showing some effects of an internal or external set on people's actions; however, it does not provide information on the effects of having more control on perceptions of control. Phares' review gave no other examples of giving power to the powerless on the individual level, yet there is no obvious reason why what has been undertaken at a social level cannot be applied with individuals.

Helplessness: conclusion

Models of helplessness would be strengthened by relinquishing the assumption that the contingencies in helplessness-inducing experiments are uncontrollable and inescapable. Such a deterministic view is not warranted by the experiments themselves and is unnecessarily fatalistic. The contingencies and outcomes in the experiments and in analogous situations in life are controllable. Therapy for helplessness should include the options of giving people more actual control over their contingencies and of encouraging people to exercise that control when it is not 'given'. This is not to suggest that control should be regarded as a universal panacea (Leiss, 1972). Rather, it is to suggest that depressed people or people with an external locus of control should not only be made to perceive an internal locus of control, to lower their expectations, and to be the recipients of improved social welfare arrangements; they should have more control over their contingencies.

The shaping of intention

Like several writers on the subject who were cited in chapter 5, deCharms (1968, 1976; deCharms and Shea, 1976) claims that attribution theories have treated self-explanations as if they were derivatives of physical causality. He counter-proposes that people act intentionally or voluntarily, and that in so doing they experience an efficacy that is quite distinct from their impressions of successive external events. DeCharms attempted to support this argument with experiments designed to help black inner-city children with an external locus of causality and intrinsic relevance, and used a 'training emphasis on reality perception' (deCharms and Muir, 1978, p. 104) to 'convert imposed to intrinsic relevance' (deCharms and Shea, 1976, p. 246). He thereby replaced an external locus of causality with perceptions of the intrinsic relevance of commodities such as school. DeCharms and Shea report that 'Both the pupils' attendance at school and their academic achievement were positively affected by the training' (p. 264).

Despite his claims to illustrate intentional behaviour in these experiments, deCharms' methods closely resemble techniques that the antithetical behavioural paradigm employs to shape an internal locus of control, methods which directly reflect behavioural conditioning models (e.g., Hiroto, 1974). This paradox follows from deCharms's identification of intention with an internal perceived locus of causality, a linkage resulting in a series of contradictions in terms: teaching agency, training origins, producing intention. The conceptual thicket underlying this paradox ensues partly from the dropping of the word 'perceived' in the relevant literature, whereby the term 'perceived locus of control' is abbreviated to 'locus of control', implying an a priori identity between the perceived and actual locus of control. But intentions are not identifiable with an (internal) perceived locus of control; people with an external perceived locus still formulate intentions.

There is a further difficulty which follows from identifying intentions with a perceived locus of control. Training children to perceive an internal locus of causality as a way of inducing intention precludes the possibility that the perception of an external locus of control found in black inner-city children may be an accurate realization of their lot. To induce the perception of an internal locus in the name of 'reality perception', while leaving unchanged the social conditions that an external locus accurately reflects, may be blindly to teach illusions. In short, identifying intention with an internal locus of control leads to several substantial problems. The studies carried out by deCharms should be seen as studies on locus of control that have little bearing on the issue of whether human action is intentional.

Seeing through illusions

In their interpretations of research examining cognitive distortions in attribution, locus of control and helplessness, many psychologists have committed the 'fundamental' attribution error, attributing illusions to causes within the person when those perceptions accurately reflect the context in which that person is situated. The factors determining perceptions of an external locus and helplessness are not always inescapable and uncontrollable, but may be controlled by other people, and can potentially be controlled by the person in the situation. From the possibility that people can control their contingencies, it follows that they need not be required to resign themselves to their present circumstances, and to change their perceptions and aspirations. Instead, they can legitimately and accurately perceive an internal locus of control, because they have a greater degree of actual control over their circumstances.

8 Phenomenological, cognitive, and linguistic therapies

This chapter continues the discussion of abnormal psychology and therapy, beginning with accounts which interpret psychopathology and therapy in terms of the phenomenological perceptions of the person in question. This section is followed by models that focus on the cognitions or language of persons suffering from psychological maladies.

Phenomenological paradigms

The behavioural models described in chapter 6 attempt to account for certain disorders in terms of the mechanical operation of efficient causes. In juxtaposition to this stance, phenomenological theorists explain psychopathology and its removal largely in terms of final (intentional) cases, and the perceptions on the person suffering the problem. As exemplars of this perspective, two major protagonists are considered: Laing and Rogers. Each author attempts to explain different aspects of psychopathology and therapy in phenomenological terms.

Laing's account of schizophrenia

Laing's analysis of schizophrenia is described by himself and others as a phenomenological account. Schizophrenia is widely considered to have a genetic basis, and some authors therefore consider that a psychological analysis is rather superfluous. But while most studies of genetic variables do imply a genetic component (e.g., D. Rosenthal, 1970), even highly favourable interpretations of such evidence do not establish that this factor is either a necessary or sufficient condition for schizophrenia. When developing an approach that focuses on psychological factors in the disorder, Laing (1960/1969) initially referred to his framework as existential phenomenology. He argued that a schizophrenic person's speech and behaviour can be understood if one rejects all causal and explanatory mechanisms and adopts that person's view of the world. The behaviour and speech can then be clearly understood as expressions and statements of the schizophrenic's feelings and desires rather than as symptoms of a disease.

Laing (1960/1969) suggested that schizophrenia can be understood if one adopts a hermeneutic approach, where one empathizes with the schizophrenic and attempts to understand the meaning that this person is placing on events. By using this method, Laing has produced an intelligible interpretation of apparently irrational and unintelligible behaviour. He argued that:

> The person whom we call 'schizoid' feels both more exposed, more vulnerable to others than we do, and more isolated. Thus a schizophrenic may say that he is made of glass, of such transparency and fragility that a look directed at him splinters him to bits and penetrates straight through him. We may suppose that precisely as such he experiences himself.
>
> (p. 37)

Laing's account suggests that schizophrenic behaviour and speech is intentional and intelligible, and he sometimes makes a persuasive case for his position. In his later work Laing refers to his theory and method as transactional phenomenology (Laing and Esterson, 1964/1970), or as social phenomenology (Laing, 1971). Laing does not suggest that this change in terminology involves a change in theory, but in fact it represents a significant development in his account of schizophrenia. With Esterson he writes: 'This is the position from which we start. Our question is: are the experiences and behaviour that psychiatrists take as symptoms and signs of schizophrenia more socially intelligible than has come to be supposed?' (Laing and Esterson, 1964/1970, p. 12). In his social phenomenology Laing implicates the schizophrenic's family in the incidence of schizophrenia. He claims that he is still using the phenomenological method and that his conclusions are derived by that method (e.g., Laing and Esterson, 1964/1970, pp. 25-6). His data are taken from interviews of the schizophrenic's family and are integrated with his interpretations of actions and statements by members of the family.

Writing of the 'social intelligibility' of schizophrenia, Laing argues that the condition becomes intelligible in the light of the behaviour and communication of the schizophrenic's family. While he retains the concept of intelligibility here, however, Laing no longer derives his understanding of the behaviour from an empathy with the schizophrenic. Schizophrenics, writes Laing, 'are deeply immobilized in a complex knot, both internal and external, of contradictory, paradoxical attributions and injunctions' (1971, p. 52). Laing's account suggests that in close relationships interpersonal attributions can be powerful contributors to schizoid self-perceptions. These interpersonal attributions are not simply descriptive communications but are functional attempts to influence the other person's perceptions: 'The attributes one ascribes to a person define him and put him in a particular position. By assigning him a particular position, attributions put him in his place and thus have in effect the force of injunctions' (Laing, 1961/1971, p. 151).

Laing argues that schizoid states of mind result from disjunctive attributions, as when one person's attribution of a second person conflicts with the latter's self-attribution. In one case study Laing cites as an example: 'A father says to his son who was being bullied at school and had pleaded to leave: "I know you don't really want to leave, because no son of mine is a coward"' (Laing, 1961/1971, pp. 154–5). Laing holds that interpersonal attributions in the context of close emotional relationships are extremely powerful, and function much like hypnosis:

> One way to get someone to *do* what one wants is, to give an order. To get someone to *be* what one wants him to be...that is, to get him to embody one's projections, is another matter. In a hypnotic context, one does not tell him what to *be*, but tells him what he *is*. Such attributions, in context, are many times more powerful than orders (or other forms of coercion or persuasion). An instruction need not be defined as an instruction. It is my lasting impression that we receive most of our earliest and most lasting instructions in the form of attribution. We are told such and such *is* the case. One is, say, told one *is* a good or a bad boy or girl, not only instructed to be a good or bad boy or girl.
>
> (Laing, 1971, p. 78)

Schizoid conditions arise in a knot of contradictory attributions, or in attributions and injunctions that contradict the person's own experience. An additional factor that empowers these attributions is the family's collusion and resistance to admitting to these goings-on. Laing reports many examples of concerted family resistance to the discovery of what is happening. There are rules against seeing the rules. The mechanism of denial produces a context of mystification.

Laing claims to have rendered schizophrenia intelligible and there is some basis for this claim. This does not guarantee, however, that Laing's account is genuinely phenomenological. We recall that Freud's account of neurosis made a number of events such as slips of the tongue and dreams intelligible. But Freud's account was not purely phenomenological. Freud employed causal explanations in addition to interpretations of the symbolic meaning of events. In Laing's social phenomenology his data are drawn from interviews of schizophrenic patients and their families, and from observing their interaction. While Laing's understanding of the schizophrenic's language and behaviour is legitimately referred to as phenomenological, his analysis of the family's language and its effects is not. Against phenomenology's principles of empathic, non-explanatory interpretation, he invokes abstract and theoretical mechanisms such as attributions and injunctions to explain the function and effect of parental language. At times Laing concedes that this is the case. For example, he claims: 'The most common situation I encounter in families is when what *I* think is going on bears almost no resemblance to what anyone in the family experiences or thinks is happening, whether or not this coincides with commonsense' (Laing, 1971, p. 77).

This is not phenomenology. Rather than being drawn from the experience of the people concerned it is completely discrepant with that experience. In fact, Laing finds that it is difficult for these people to see their experience as he sees it:

> Some people undoubtedly have a remarkable aptitude for keeping the other tied in knots. There are those who excel in tying knots and those who excel in being tied in knots. Tyer and tied are often both unconscious of how it is done, or even that it is being done at all. It is striking how difficult it is for the parties concerned to see what is happening.
>
> (Laing, 1961/1971, p. 155)

Laing also invokes the family studies of Lidz (1973), Bateson (1956), and others, who explain schizophrenia in terms of the causal operation of the family context. Yet Laing disclaims a causal account. Confusing methodology (control groups) with theory (etiology), he replies to criticisms that he uses no control groups:

> Such criticism would be justified if we had set out to test the hypothesis that the family is a pathogenic variable in the genesis of schizophrenia. But we did not set out to do this and we have not claimed to have done so. We set out to illustrate by eleven examples that if we look at some experience and behaviour without reference to family interactions they may appear comparatively socially senseless but that if we look at the same experience and behaviour in their original family context they are liable to make sense.
>
> (Laing and Esterson, 1964/1970, p. 72)

Laing's disclaimer is not convincing. The passages cited above and many others make it clear that he treats the family as a causal pathogenic variable. But this is not to suggest that Laing's is a purely deterministic account. Laing used semantic interpretations to find the meaning of schizophrenic communication just as Freud used such symbolic interpretation to find meaning in a range of neurotic actions. What distinguishes Laing's theory from Freud's account is not its phenomenology but the claim that the agents of defence are interpersonal rather than intrapersonal.

Regardless of whether this account of schizophrenia is seen as perceptive or plausible, Laing has not succeeded in constructing a phenomenological account of the etiology of the disorder. The type of explanation he uses has certain characteristics of a critical analysis: a synthesis of both interpretative and causal explanations. To provide an adequate understanding of psychological functioning, causal factors must be added to interpretations of meanings and intentions. The same point applies to Rogers' attempts to construct a phenomenological therapy.

Rogers' client-centred therapy

Laing's phenomenological analysis of schizophrenia focuses on the causes of psychological disorders, particularly schizophrenia. In Rogers' account, more emphasis is placed on therapy, although he also deals with the etiology of disorders. The aspect of Rogers' account considered here is his attempt to design a phenomenological account of therapeutic change. Rogers' model of change is based on the assumption that human behaviour is purposive rather than determined. He postulates: 'Man lives essentially in his own personal and subjective world, and even his most objective functioning in science, mathematics, and the like, is the result of subjective purpose and subjective choice' (Rogers, 1959, p. 191). To understand human behaviour, then, we must employ phenomenological methods. People can be understood only through the vantage-point of their own perceptions. Central to Rogers' account is the supposition that 'The best vantage point for understanding behaviour is from the internal frame of reference of the individual himself' (Rogers, 1951, p. 494).

Rogers developed a therapy, called client-centred therapy, that he claimed was consistent with these basic suppositions. The adoption of a phenomenological basis requires that therapy does not consist of imposing the concepts or theory of the therapist but, rather, engenders change by permitting the person's own resources to be realized. Such resources are discovered and activated in an appropriate therapeutic relationship. Rogers stresses that his therapy involves a relationship or attitude rather than a technique. In a phenomenologically based therapy, writes Rogers:

> The counsellor chooses to act consistently upon the hypothesis that the individual has a sufficient capacity to deal constructively with all those aspects of his life which can potentially come into conscious awareness. This means the creation of an interpersonal situation in which material may come into the client's awareness, and a meaningful demonstration of the counsellor's acceptance of the client as a person who is competent to direct himself.
>
> (1951, p. 24)

In specifying the characteristics of client-centred therapy, Rogers listed 'The necessary and sufficient conditions for therapeutic personality change' (1957). The client must be motivated and cooperative, and three core facilitative conditions must be present in the therapist: unconditional positive regard, empathic understanding, and genuineness. In describing the nature of effective therapeutic processes Rogers is specifying the conditions which causally invoke change in the client. Rogers is specifying a causal 'If...then' logical relationship: if certain conditions exist then certain changes will occur. Attitudes in a therapist are certainly different from physical technologies such as the shock-giving machinery used by some behavioural practitioners. But it does not follow that these attitudes are anything other than causal determinants. If specified as the conditions that lead to change, they are indeed causal determinants. An empirical buttressing of this point is Truax's (1966) research, which demonstrated that a client's verbal statements are shaped by Rogerian therapists.

This argument is not posing a criticism of Rogers' therapy. It is suggesting that there is a conflict between Rogers' description of his therapy as an event where the client's resources and purposive actions produce change, and Rogers' specification of the necessary and sufficient conditions whereby change will occur, that is, the causal conditions producing change. This tension is evident in Rogers' claim: 'The individual has within himself vast resources for self-understanding, for altering his self concept, his attitudes, and his self-directed behaviour...These resources can be tapped if only a definable climate of facilitative psychological attitudes can be provided' (Rogers, 1974, p. 116). Both the causal, 'if...then' nature of the account and the tension built into it are seen even more clearly if the 'if only' words in the passage are reversed, which does not otherwise significantly change the meaning of the passage. The contradiction between the client changing from their own resources and the client changing as a function of therapeutic conditions is made even more clear when others try to describe Rogerian principles without the mitigation of Rogers' persuasive presentation. Davison and Neale (1978) report that: 'The principal therapeutic task...is to create conditions that will allow the client to change by himself' (p. 479).

There is a second aspect of the phenomenological account which is significant and which relates to the points just referred to. It concerns the view of psychopathology and change in terms of a balance of power between psychological parties or agencies. We recall that in the Freudian account the dynamic of pathology and change was pictured as the distribution of power and energy among three parties. The id, the person's elemental desires, is at odds with the evaluating superego, who thinks those desires are completely unacceptable and must not be expressed. The ego, in serving the reality principle, has to achieve a working compromise between these forces. The phenomenological model is generally considered to have transcended this conception of pathology and change in terms of a state of politic between three cognitive agencies.

In fact, it has not convincingly done so. Psychopathology is described by Rogers as the incongruence between the experiencing organism and the self-concept, or ideal self. The organism and the ideal self correspond closely to the id and the superego of psychoanalytic theory. The ideal self incorporates the demands and evaluation of parents. In Rogerian therapy the counsellor presents unconditional positive regard, warmth and empathy. Rogers argues that the existence of these conditions, accompanied by sincerity, 'frees the client for normal growth and development'. Rogers writes as if these conditions are merely permissive or neutral, in freeing something to occur. But an alternative characterization of the situation may be suggested. Warmth and empathy are not simply permissive or neutral; they are coercive pressures. The therapist, like the parent, is still an evaluating party, but he or she is reversing the evaluation from negative to positive. It is not the case that there is no evaluator in the therapeutic context, but rather a very warm and accepting evaluator.

The aim of therapy, similarly, is to train the clients to change the values of their internal evaluator. As the counsellor has unconditional positive regard, so the client is to have positive self-regard and self-acceptance. Repression and sublimation are to be replaced, not by neutrality or an open mind, but by a gentle narcissism: 'I'm O.K.' The superego's change of mind hinges on a changed conception of human motivation and desire. While Freud believed this imperative, 'the id', to be amoral and destructive, Rogers, who reconceptualized it as 'the organism', believed it to be fundamentally positive. It is in this context that the superego or ideal self is trained to give a positive evaluation. In relation to the psychodynamic model of the psyche, then, Rogers' account does not dispose of the conflicting parties, but rather renames them and writes a new treaty.

It might appear that in this reformulation the arbitrating ego is no longer needed. Normality is no longer arbitration but congruence. But Rogers' congruence does require a form of sublimation and repression. In Freud's theory the id is repressed or is sublimated through intellectual and artistic pursuits. Rogers' theory, in turn, 'places greater stress upon the feeling aspects of the situation than upon the intellectual aspects' (Rogers, 1970). The intellect is thus repressed and must settle for getting satisfaction out of warm feelings. It may be suggested that this is not congruence, but again, sublimation: sublimation of the intellect.

Rogers' client-centred therapy has been quite effective in some instances (e.g., Di Loreto, 1971). But his account of the processes occurring is not consistently phenomenological. The 'ideal self' and 'organism' concepts are not drawn from the experience of each client, but are inferred abstractions resembling the parties of psychodynamic theories with new names and a new balance of power.

Cognitive and linguistic therapies

In the previous section it was argued that the phenomenological theories, against their own axioms and claims, used causal explanations to supplement their phenomenological interpretation of intentional actions. Causal explanations were invoked to explain both psychopathology and therapeutic change. The discussion also contested the phenomenologists' assumption that therapy involves a self-effected course of events occurring in one individual. It was argued that their therapy involved the activity of two parties. Therapy involved not only the client's action but also the causal influence of the therapist.

We now turn to cognitive and linguistic theories which share several techniques and ideas with phenomenological or positivist models, but which do not attempt to force their description into the theoretical terms of those frameworks. This section begins with Bateson's double-bind theory of schizophrenia and cognitive–semantic models of psychological disorders. The discussion then moves to models that focus on the linguistic representation of cognition and therapy. The discussion attempts to draw connections between these attempts and Habermas's (1970) proposals, described in chapter 3, concerning linguistic representations of cognitions and illusions.

Double-binds and schizophrenia

It was suggested in the previous section that Laing's account of schizophrenia, contrary to disclaimers, postulated causal mechanisms in families which result in a schizophrenic family member. Laing's model draws considerably on other family accounts of schizophrenia, all of which overtly employ both semantic interpretation and causal explanation. These theories take several forms. Some psychologists consider that the total irrational pattern of the life and relationships in schizophrenic families produces schizophrenia (e.g., Lidz, 1973). Other models are more specific in linking schizophrenia to the communications of certain families (e.g., Wynne, 1977). Even more focused is Bateson's (1956, 1972) double-bind theory. Bateson's model warrants discussion for several reasons. It is heuristic, and the moderate degree of empirical support it has received is representative for family theories of schizophrenia. It also makes very specific and, therefore, in one sense more testable predictions. Unlike Laing's account of schizophrenia, it integrates causal explanations in addition to interpretive categories.

Bateson (e.g., 1956) claims that schizophrenia results from long-term exposure to double-bind situations. He proposes that at the core of a double bind are two contradictory injunctions, each of which is accompanied by threat of punishment. These injunctions are usually on two different levels of abstraction. They are not simply contradictory, but paradoxical; they express an intrinsic contradiction. They belong to the same logical type as statements such as 'I am lying' or 'Disregard this notice'. The schizoid thinking of a schizophrenic, according to Bateson, is the product of repeated exposure to emotionally loaded injunctions of a double-bind nature, in the context of close relationships. The two contradictory injunctions are accompanied by a third class of injunction which prohibits the person from leaving the situation and prohibits them from commenting on the situation. The contradictions are thus concealed and denied.

When Bateson introduced his model, it was supported largely by clinical evidence. Subsequently there has been much research on the model, a review of which is provided by Abeles (1977). According to Abeles, research with families containing a schizophrenic member has found that double-bind communication is characteristic of such families. But research also indicates that double binds are no more predominant than other irrationalities. Furthermore, there is very little double-bind communication in a considerable proportion of families with a schizophrenic member. Furthermore, double binds are present in a number of families which do not have a schizophrenic member. Finally, a number of studies reviewed by Abeles found that patients with a number of disorders come from 'high double-bind' families. Overall, the findings contain several inconsistencies. One response to these findings has been to generalize the double bind as the universal pathogenic situation (Sluzki and Veron, 1977). Others infer that the double bind is universal but not necessarily pathogenic (Rabkin 1977; Wilden and Wilson, 1977; Wynne, 1977).

A factor which contributes to the conflicting nature of the findings is the difficulty of testing the double-bind hypothesis, in spite of its highly specific predictions. The concept of a double bind is difficult, although not impossible, to place in testable form. A further constraint is that researchers cannot know which families will produce a schizophrenic member until the disorder occurs. And once schizophrenia has occurred, any distorted communication in that person's family could be a product of schizophrenia, rather than its cause. Some of these difficulties have been overcome in more sophisticated research designs (Abeles, 1977). The outcome, however, is not clear.

Despite these problems, the double-bind notion is both intriguing and heuristic. More important for the issues here, the theory does not contain the misrepresentations or contradictions seen in the behavioural and phenomenological accounts of abnormal psychology. It cannot be said, however, that the model as yet enjoys either empirical success or failure. It is possible that this outcome is because the dialectical concept of paradox in the double bind is difficult to test in decisive empirical situations. An alternative possibility concerns the source from which Bateson's theory was drawn, in analytic logic and porpoises' signals. The model, while also drawing on observations of schizophrenics, is very much a theory of logic. There may be some changes required in making the jump to an analogue of human behaviour. Human behaviour and paradoxes are likely to be more messy, or more systematically 'irrational' than paradoxes in analytic logic. The cognitive and linguistic approaches described in the following sections draw more on clinical work with humans in modelling these aspects of cognitions.

Cognitive models: Ellis and Meichenbaum

Cognitive models treat behaviour as a function of a person's cognitions and beliefs. Therapy focuses on changing people's beliefs and the statements that verbalize and possibly sustain those beliefs. Cognitive theories are primarily concerned with the content of beliefs and cognitions (Beck, 1976; Ellis, 1976; Glasser, 1965; Meichenbaum, 1977; Raimy, 1975). Some models focus purely on beliefs and cognitions (Ellis, 1962; Glasser, 1965). More recently, emphasis has also been given to the linguistic representation of beliefs.

Possibly the most prominent of the cognitive models has been Ellis's rational-emotive therapy (e.g., Ellis, 1976). In Ellis's account, irrational thoughts are central to the origin and maintenance of psychopathology. Beliefs are not the product of anxiety but the cause; anxiety results from an illogical or irrational interpretation of events. Ellis claims that people with psychological problems ideologize themselves with irrational thoughts. Violations of these ideologies are 'catastrophized', or heavily punished.

In rational-emotive therapy the therapist first identifies the irrational beliefs of the client. Ellis (1977) has provided a list of the kinds of sentences which express irrational content, for example: 'I must be thoroughly competent in everything I do'; 'I must be loved and approved of by everyone.' The therapist points out to clients, sometimes in fairly derogatory terms, that the sentences are irrational and are not supported by available evidence. Clients are then taught to criticize their own assumptions and to systematically persist in this critique. The clients are also given graduated homework assignments requiring them to act in opposition with their irrational beliefs and then reinforce themselves when they have done so. This active component of the therapy is compatible with the interpretation placed on therapy in chapter 3.

A possible weakness in the theory is Ellis's criterion of an illusory or irrational belief. Ellis does not employ a logical criterion like Bateson's double bind or Habermas's (1970) criterion of communication that is systematically distorted or deviates from some linguistic norm. Ellis employs

134   *Explanations, accounts, and illusions*

a personal criterion of irrational beliefs. An irrational belief is whatever Ellis says is irrational. It is probable that people of most persuasions and perspectives would agree with many of Ellis's decisions as to what is an irrational belief; for example, the belief that 'I must be loved by everyone.' Along with beliefs such as these, however, Ellis categorizes as in need of therapy: extremism, religious beliefs, wishful thinking and idealism. He holds that 'extremism tends to remain as a natural human trait that takes one foolish form or another' (1977, p. 17). This notion suggests that sanity consists in mediocrity. To 'believe in the power of prayers' (p. 17) is equally irrational and thus should be 'cured'. Ellis's rational world will also purge itself of wishful thinking and insistent idealism such as the belief that 'things like justice, fairness, equality and democracy clearly have to prevail' (p. 13).

With criteria such as this, Ellis believes that he can eliminate most human disturbances: 'RET (Rational-Emotive Therapy) contends that "emotional disturbance" largely consists of devout religiosity, intolerance, whining, dogmatism, and magical thinking. Clients are taught that if they follow the logico-empirical approach and forego all forms of magic and absolutism, they can eliminate most of their disturbances' (Ellis, 1976, p. 24). In this framework, the devout religiosity is reduced by the logico-empirical one which in turn is going to eliminate magically most disturbances. Ellis's intolerance of other magic and absolutes is a consequence of making an absolute of logic-empirical dogma. A personal criterion of illusions thus lends a potentially constructive critical therapy the potential for an inquisition.

A less idiosyncratic model in the cognitive school has been formulated by Meichenbaum (e.g., 1977). Meichenbaum's model differs from that of Ellis in several ways. For example, whereas Ellis's theory explains how rational-emotive therapy achieves change, Meichenbaum attempts to clarify the common mechanisms whereby diverse and conflicting theories and therapies achieve the same end result. Meichenbaum argues that a common feature of all therapies is their provision of a new conceptualization of the patient's condition. When this new conceptualization is adopted by the patient, it produces a new cognitive structure. This new structure in turn results in new perceptions, observations, and attributions. Meichenbaum cites a passage by Lewis (1972) suggesting how psychoanalytic, behavioural and phenomenological therapists all achieve the same effect. The passage is illustrative:

> A patient's initial statement, 'I'm afraid of heights', may become
> translated in the course of therapy into various other statements
> depending upon which conceptual framework the therapist holds and
> transmits to the patient. If the therapist is a psychoanalyst, the patient
> might say much later, 'I'm not really afraid of physical heights – I know

this now – it is rather that as a child I feared another type of physical fall – that is, sexual surrender. I was afraid of a symbol...' If the therapist is a behaviourist, the translation proceeds along a different path: The patient may say 'I now realize that I am lumping all heights together, and that I can train myself to relax in a situation of slight elevation, so that I am finding that I feel more and more relaxed in higher and yet higher ones.' An existentialist translation might be 'I realize that I have been deceiving myself with this symptom – that I never before could tolerate the idea of nothingness – of nonexistence. But sharing this basic fear with my therapist has diminished my misguided fear of heights.'

(Lewis, 1972, p. 81, cited in Meichenbaum, 1977)

This conceptualization of the common mechanism activated by diverse therapies underlies the other dimensions of Meichenbaum's model. He substitutes internalized communication for Ellis's beliefs. Drawing on Luria's (1959) hypothesis that the child develops verbal control of behaviour by internalizing adult instructions, Meichenbaum argues that much adult thought consists of self-instructions. Psychopathology consists of a persisting cluster of negative self-instructions, like 'I can't do anything.' Therapy, in turn, produces a new conceptualization in which patients can address themselves with new attributions and explanations in old conditions. This inner speech alters the systems of that control attention and appraisal; it also instigates new behaviour. The new inner speech affects what the people say to themselves about the outcomes of new behaviours.

Meichenbaum (1977) describes inner speech as an inner dialogue. Dialogue, of course, as opposed to monologue, involves two parties. Meichenbaum writes that this choice of terminology is deliberate (p. 212). He postulates that humans both speak and listen to themselves. He cites research showing that when people say certain things to themselves, their responses to external conditions are affected by those self-statements.

Meichenbaum's account shares many features with the critical accounts described in chapter 3. It also explains the same phenomena as the behavioural and phenomenological paradigms without needing to contradict its own theoretical stance. The phenomenological account, to recall, tried to insist that change was generated by the resources of the client and yet specified the conditions producing desired change. These contradictions, which confound the phenomenological paradigm, are resolved in accounts which permit both phenomenal and causal explanations. Contradictions in the behavioural account arose from the attempt to argue that events like induced helplessness are mechanistic one-party events when in fact two parties and controllable factors were involved. Meichenbaum's model recognizes and then capitalizes on the role of the therapist as a second party.

Meichenbaum's model, however, has important limitations. In the first case, his analysis of language is largely restricted to its content, and not its form. It ignores the area of distortions in terms of the structure or grammar of language. Furthermore, Meichenbaum does not examine the function or etiology of contradictions in the client's cognition and language, even though contradictions are primarily a semantic phenomenon. Meichenbaum's exclusive focus on content also entails that his model lacks a clear criterion of a problematic cognition or illusion. Although the defining of illusions goes beyond simply listing certain beliefs, the criterion remains arbitrary; any statement could be deemed illusory, as in Ellis's model. This broad criterion allows for arbitrary belief conversion. Partly because of this problem, Habermas's (1970) concept of systematically distorted communication was suggested in chapter 3 as a less arbitrary criterion of illusions and cognitive distortions. Before turning to analyses that use this type of criterion, it is necessary to point out a second limitation of Meichenbaum's model.

The model pays little attention to the effect of motivational factors on a person's illusions and cognitive distortions. As a consequence, it can be applied confidently only to problems which do not reflect motivation. It is not clear how well the principles apply to cognitions that are largely an effect of some motivational factor. There is a corresponding failure to examine the relationships of power and control to cognitions and illusions. As a consequence, the possibly functional nature of illusions is not examined. In the discussion of learned helplessness in the previous chapter, it was suggested that perceptions were linked to, and reflected, the actual contingencies in the experimental situation. These factors need to be included in cognitive models. Some idea of how this might be achieved is provided by linguistic models that orient their analysis around the patient's speech, and use linguistic analyses as a basis for therapy. These models comprise the focus of the following section.

Linguistic models

The discussion of illusions and psychopathology in this and the previous chapter has argued that the events described, regardless of the accounts given thereof, are characterized by four features. First, illusions are in many cases induced by means of false information or by a concealing structure of relationships between two parties. Secondly, motivational factors play a role in some illusions that are attributed to purely deterministic causes. Thirdly, in supposedly phenomenological accounts, both causal explanations and phenomenological interpretations are commonly used, despite the theoretical pretensions of the practitioner. Finally, the change induced in therapy involves both information and action on the part of the client or therapist. These features are commensurable with critical explanations, which employ both interpretation and causal explanation, and with a critical account of cognitions, which emphasizes motivation and the context in which the cognitions occur (chapter 3). Cognitive models of psychopathology and therapy pay insufficient attention to the role of motivational factors in illusions, and to the possibility that illusions are the product of the particular relationships surrounding the person.

A final group of models emphasize the linguistic representation of cognitions and interactions. These include Bandler and Grinder's adaptation of transformational linguistics (Bandler and Grinder, 1975; Grinder and Bandler, 1976), and several recent linguistic formulations of psychodynamic analyses. These therapies are pertinent to Habermas's (1970) linguistic formulation of critical analyses, described in chapter 3. Habermas takes language as a tool of analysis, as in hermeneutic models, but he points out, in line with earlier critical theories, that there are often distortions and contradictions in language which require a causal analysis. Habermas has not spelt out these ideas in detail, but other researchers and therapists have developed analyses of linguistic form and content relating to psychopathology and therapy. These models provide a linguistic analogue and representation of perceptions and illusions, as well as the factors affecting those cognitions. The analyses reviewed here were carried out by linguists and clinicians analysing therapeutic sessions.

Labov and Fanshel (1977) present a detailed analysis of a session between a neo-psychoanalytic therapist and a patient with anorexia nervosa. Labov and Fanshel analysed the content of statements, like the cognitive therapies described in the previous section, but their work extends beyond the semantic dimension in several respects. In the first place, the content analysis was extended to include contradictions, in this case contradictions between what the patient was saying and events that were reported to occur. For example, the patient reported carrying out certain suggestions of the therapist but then later indicated that she did not do so (p. 338). The analysis also focused on contradictions between the content of what the patient was saying and the emotion she showed.

This analysis of contradictions assists the therapist in getting to the source of the problem by suggesting points of conflict and defence. Defences are inferred from the use of particular types of content. For example, the patient in this therapy concealed or blurred particular situations by using vague and ambiguous terms and words, or phrases without clear referents. The patient's language serves to mask the situation. For example, she reported that 'Jistalittle situation came up an' I tried to...use what I've learned here' (p. 116). The phrase 'jistalittle situation', it turned out, mitigated the fact that the situation she was reporting was a major confrontation. The hasty 'jistalittle' is a form of condensation, which Habermas (1970) suggests is a means of blurring and concealing aspects of a situation. As Kraut and Higgins (1984) point out, Labov and Fanshel treat the patient's language as a series of speech acts which function to shape the interaction with the therapist, as well as describing their situation.

Labov and Fanshel's analysis also provides linguistic concepts for several devices the therapist used to encourage change. The therapist interpreted the patient's statements and suggested new interpretations and perceptions of the situation. The therapist also concatenated descriptions of the situation, linking events or ideas that the patient separated. A related technique which Labov and Fanshel employed is a linguistic expansion of the dialogue between therapist and client. This expansion is based on the surface structure/deep structure distinction of transformational linguistics (e.g., Chomsky, 1965). This model suggests that the grammatical structure of a sentence comprises relationships which are not apparent in its 'surface' structure but which can be represented at an abstract level referred to as the 'deep' structure.

The use of transformational linguistics is also seen in Bandler and Grinder's (1975) account of psychopathology and change. Bandler and Grinder are not adherents of any psychoanalytic school, but their use of surface structure and deep structure can be related to the Freudian concepts of conscious and unconscious. The authors are aware of this, and concur that their model 'is an explicit representation of our unconscious, rule-governed behaviour' (1975, p. 37). Bandler and Grinder's use of structural linguistics focuses on the form of clients' language more than the Labov and Fanshel study which placed equal emphasis on its content. Bandler and Grinder claim that 'psychopathology' results from the people's faulty transformations from linguistic deep structure to surface structures.

They note three transformations which are commonly used in normal thinking, but which if over-used can produce distorted surface structures: generalization, deletion and distortion. Generalization is defined as: 'the process by which elements or pieces of a person's model become detached from their original experience and come to represent the entire category of which the experience is an example' (Bandler and Grinder, 1975, p. 14). Deletion is the process 'by which we selectively pay attention to certain dimensions of our experience and exclude others' (p. 15). Distortion results either from permutation or nominalization transformations. Permutations produce confused word orders, resulting in unclear surface structure. Nominalizations change a process word, or verb, into a noun; they turn an ongoing process into an event. 'Events are things which occur at one point in time and are finished. Once they occur, their outcomes are fixed and nothing can be done to change them' (p. 43). Bandler and Grinder's concept of nominalization is like the notion of reification, the process which makes changeable psychological or social processes appear necessary, natural or inevitable.

Much of Bandler and Grinder's *The structure of magic* (1975) consists of linguistic analyses of client–therapist communication. They use the transformational model to reveal the linguistic structure of the therapist's 'magic' in inducing change. In Bandler and Grinder's account of therapy, the therapist, who is using the same linguistic model, determines whether the client's surface structure is a complete representation of the deep structure that it derives from. The therapist, for example, may recognize that something has been deleted in the surface structure, and will aim to 'recover the "suppressed" or missing pieces' (p. 43) which have been deleted. A client may say 'I'm scared.' To which the therapist may ask 'Of what?' By challenging and expanding deletions, the therapist fills out the surface structure. Challenging generalizations has a similar effect. If the therapist perceives a nominalization, he/she will challenge it, and transform the sentence back into the process words they were derived from. If a client comments 'I really regret my decision', the therapist may ask what it is that prevents the client from reconsidering the decision. The method de-reifies the event by changing it into a process.

Like several other clinicians, Grinder and Bandler (1976) link psycho-pathology to contradictions between spoken language and 'body language'. This connection parallels analyses of distortions in critical social theories, where contradictions between words and actions articulate an underlying 'pathological' social structure. Grinder and Bandler indicate how therapists can induce change through exploring and challenging contradictions and the conflicts they reflect.

Bandler and Grinder's framework is useful in providing a clear working model of distortions in language. The model enables a non-arbitrary criterion of illusions, and a clear representation of the existence and removal of illusions. A limitation of the model is that in restricting itself to an analysis of grammatical structure, it does not explain how or why excessive deletion, distortion and generalization occur in certain persons' language. But while Bandler and Grinder do not offer such an explanation, the therapeutic process they describe can give an indication of why these transformations occur. Bandler and Grinder argue that human problems derive from people's representation of reality, not the reality itself. They report: 'When people come to us in therapy expressing pain and dissatisfaction, the limitations that they experience are typically in their representation of the world, not in the world itself' (Bandler and Grinder, 1975, p. 179). Bandler and Grinder support this conclusion with the argument that any differences between two groups in identical environments cannot derive from the environment: 'The question for us is: How is it possible for different human beings faced with the same world to have such different experiences? Our understanding is that this difference follows primarily from differences in the richness of their models' (p. 14).

This argument does not explain a great deal. It does not explain the differences in the richness of the models it refers to. Bandler and Grinder argue also that therapies achieve change, not by changing the world, but by changing the client's representation of the world (p. 156). Such an account does not explain how or why the representation itself changes. Yet the therapy they describe demonstrates quite clearly how the representation changes. The therapy is an interpersonal situation in which a therapist challenges statements made by the client. The therapist is part of the world which Bandler and Grinder deny is causing the change. Interacting with a therapist is not a representation of a process but an actual process, involving two people. To put it in their own terms, Bandler and Grinder have nominalized a process into an event wherein only representations are seen to change. If the event is transformed back into a process, it can be seen that change occurs because of linguistic interactions between two people. A reasonable inference would be that the distorted surface structure also occurred because of certain interactions between two people. However, Bandler and Grinder have not investigated this possibility.

A linguistic analysis which does investigate language in terms of an interaction between parties is that of Clippinger (1977). Clippinger's analysis of discourse represents speech as a product of interaction, but not of the interaction between the patient and therapist. He conceptualizes discourse as the outcome of relationships between conflicting parties within the patient. Clippinger designed a computer program containing modules representing these parties; the program simulates actual discourses of a patient, and generates discourse with an equivalent structure. For this task Clippinger found transformational linguistics unsuitable, because it is not able to convey intentions or motivations and conflict. Clippinger instead combines Fillmore's (1971) semantic case grammar with a cognitive problem-solving design. Clippinger writes that: 'Discourse is treated within this theory as a communication process that is motivated by a need to solve a number of cognitively posed problems. Hence the discourse itself is but a mirror of the mind and is of interest primarily for this reason' (Clippinger, 1977, p. 4).

In Clippinger's model, syntax is not an independent structure, but performs functions for cognitive processes and motivations. Clippinger designed modules which have motivational and intentional properties and which functionally represent various parties or motives. Clippinger's conception of motivation and planning correspond closely to definitions given in chapters 4 and 5 of reasons ('Why I want to do something') and intentions ('What I plan to do'). For motivation, 'discourse is initiated by the appearance of a problem that needs solving; e.g., I want some X' (p. 22). Planning processes are like intentions; they are 'groups of programs concerned with taking a given problem, as presented in the motivation concept, and finding an acceptable solution' (p. 24).

Clippinger incorporates these motivational and planning capacities into a group of modules, each of which performs a function like that of one party in the Freudian model of mind. The modules have names that symbolize their functions, such as 'Calvin' and 'Machiavelli'. Calvin, like the superego, decides what should be said, 'and like its namesake, decides on whether the concept should be thought or expressed' (p. 53). Once a concept has been declared acceptable, it is processed by the Machiavelli module, named after 'the great Florentine strategist of means' (p. 53). Machiavelli, combined with 'Cicero', performs the functions of the Freudian ego. Clippinger describes how the program generates discourse:

> Once a topic has been selected, it is passed on to a Calvin context, where it is evaluated for the appropriateness of its expression. Supplementary content is added and 'distasteful' content is deleted according to the wants of the various interrupt programs contained there. Once a concept has received Calvin's blessing and corrections, it is passed on to Machiavelli, where further work is done to make the concept suitable for expression. Here thematic markers are added and means are contrived for the expression of concepts that might have a negative audience impact... Once a concept has been given suitable preparation for expression, Machiavelli programs take charge of their realisation and pass them on to the Cicero context, where they are given lexical realisation and placed within a State format. Machiavelli then passes these State concepts back to Calvin, where they are further evaluated... If the State concepts are unacceptable, Calvin may interrupt discourse generation through his Johnsonian interrupts (er...um...ah) and decide upon a different topic of discourse or a different method of expression.
>
> (p. 63)

Clippinger argues that Freud, in implicitly regarding the mind as a problem-solving mechanism, identified many of the techniques it used to resolve cognitive conflicts. Clippinger's own model and computer program can employ and generate many of the same techniques, including displacement, projection and condensation.

And what is the significance of this? Why are the stammering splutters of unhappy patients in therapy relevant for theories of psychopathology? There are two implications to the studies outlined here, the first of which pertains to all the linguistic analyses. In these models, several distorting and emancipating processes postulated by critical theories are represented and defined in more precise terms than was previously possible. The linguistic analysis of deep structure and surface structure is a valuable tool to apply to the conscious/unconscious, illusions/reality dichotomies postulated by critical theories. The model supplies a clear framework and rules of transformation and distortion, which therapists and researchers can use to analyse distortions and the processes affecting those distortions. Barratt (1984) objects to analogues between the deep structure of language in transformational linguistics and the unconscious in psychodynamic therapies, on the grounds that unconscious processes represent dynamic factors that do not apply with ordinary language. But the use of linguistic models is applicable even where the driving force behind distortions in language is dynamic; the linguistic models can provide a mapping of the linguistic changes that occur.

At a more specific level, the nominalization group of transformations demonstrate in linguistic terms the process of reification, a concept which has previously been stipulated only in more abstract terms. Linguistic generalization can also be seen as a form of reification. Conversely, deletion corresponds to repression and concealment. Permutation transformations, wherein the deep structure is distorted during the transformation to surface structure, crystallize a process of mystification. These developments are valuable for analyses of psychopathology and therapy. They provide linguistic representations of illusions and distortions, and indicate the relationship of these representations to the interpersonal events of analysis and therapy. They illustrate Habermas's proposal, described in chapter 3, that a critical analysis of cognitive distortions and illusions should employ models that tap ordinary human language. The clearness and tangibility of the linguistic models permits critical analyses to be precise (and falsifiable).

Programs such as Clippinger's have a different significance. Conceptually, Clippinger's program represents the axioms of psychodynamic theory. Yet, while this program represents intentional phenomena such as deception, and while it is a product of Clippinger's own design and intentions, it is also operated through a machine. For decades the psychodynamic representation of cognition in terms of an ongoing politic between conflicting homunculi has been declared ridiculous, impossible and certainly unscientific. But if a machine can be programmed to generate motivations and intentions, enact conflicts between parties, and deliberately distort information, the argument that humans cannot or should not be represented in such terms, at least by science, loses some strength.

This point can be related to the history of psychology. In chapter 2 it was noted that positivism replaced the projection of teleology onto the universe with the introjection of contemporary mechanical principles, albeit from human-made machines, onto humans. As mechanical devices and theories have changed or become more complex, so apparently have humans. With the invention of the steam engine it was realized that human behaviour is all cathexis and catharsis. When the animal reflex was discovered humans were permitted to elicit and then emit a response, but no more. In time humans were allowed to believe that they functioned on cybernetic principles, and, more recently, like an information processor. And now that a machine can stimulate and generate motivations, intentions, displacements, euphemisms and illusions, it should follow that psychology's gatekeeper, or superego, will permit psychologists to conceptualize humans in such terms. The argument that these processes are mythical or pre-scientific becomes less plausible.

Social cognition and psychopathology

Several of the issues and processes discussed in research on social cognition recur in the domain of abnormal psychology. In the first case, the comments applied to various stances in social cognition are equally pertinent to analogous accounts of psychopathology and therapy. Illusions produced in behavioural paradigms are not accidental errors, but reflect motivation, which influences people through false information or other devices. The descriptions of events in phenomenological therapies, despite claims to the contrary, invoke both causal explanations and semantic interpretations.

These processes are captured to varying degrees in the cognitive models reviewed here. These theories are free of the main limitations of the positivist and phenomenological paradigms. Bateson's double-bind theory, however, lacks empirical validation; the other cognitive theories, in dealing with content only and not form, tend toward an arbitrary criterion of illusions, and do not examine the effect of motivation. Linguistic models examine cognitions as they are represented in language. They provide precise linguistic representations of processes such as reification and mystification which have previously been framed in more abstract or general terms.

For those who do not believe that a process exists till a machine can demonstrate it, Clippinger's model has a different significance. It represents the murky battle between the conflicting purposes of human interests on a machine. In a science which generally only recognizes processes that machines can simulate, such a model challenges the view that the processes postulated by some critical theories are intrinsically prescientific or unscientific. This objection is seen to be both arbitrary and unjustified.

9 Discounting and dialectics: contradictions in explanations

The discussion of explanations in previous chapters has on many issues suggested the relevance of a critical perspective. This perspective in psychology is linked to dialectical models, which emphasize the importance of contradiction and conflict in relationships and cognition (e.g., Buss, 1979a; Riegel, 1979; Rychlak, 1976). This chapter discusses conflict in explanations and cognitions, exploring dialectical perspectives but also considering a range of other approaches. The discussion revolves around the concept of discounting, which holds that people discount explanations of actions when alternative explanations are available. The chapter reviews the discounting concept, research relating to discounting, and concepts that have quite different implications concerning people's perception of alternative explanations.

The discounting principle

Numerous researchers have claimed that people discount a cause for an action when alternative causes are present (e.g., Einhorn and Hogarth, 1983; Hansen and Hall, 1985; Jones and Davis, 1965; Kruglanski, Schwartz, Maides and Hamel, 1978; Rosenfield and Stephan, 1977). Kelley (1972a) advanced the discounting concept from an isolated commonsense notion to a formal proposition that relates to other theories of social perception. The discounting principle complements Kelley's covariation model, which deals with attributions based on large amounts of causal information, and which proposes that attributions reflect the covariation in that information (Kelley, 1967). By contrast, the discounting principle applies to situations where attributors have information about only a given effect and one or more possible causes. In these conditions, Kelley (1972a) proposed that:

> The attributor does pretty much what a good scientist would do. If he is aware of several plausible causes, he attributes the effect less to any one of them than if he is aware only of one as a plausible cause. In other words, he makes his attributions according to a discounting principle: the

144

role of a given cause in producing a given effect is discounted if other
plausible causes are also present.

(p. 8)

According to Kelley (1972a), discounting is reflected either in uncertainty
as to whether a cause has contributed to an effect, or in a lower rating of
the strength of the cause. An experiment which has been presented
repeatedly as an illustration of discounting by Kelley (1972a, 1972b, 1973;
Kelley and Michela, 1980), is Thibaut and Riecken's (1955) demonstration
of the effects of differentials in status and power on attributions for
charitable actions. The participants in this study were required to attribute
a cause for the charitable actions of two persons of differing status. In the
case of the higher-status person, subjects attributed the consent to
charitability and discounted pressure, and in the case of the lower-status
person, they attributed the consent to external pressure and discounted
charitability. The discounting principle has been applied to findings
produced in relation to other prominent models, including Jones and Davis's
(1965) theory of correspondent inference and D. J. Bem's (1967, 1972)
theory of self-perception.

Kelley links the discounting principle to causal schemata, which are
cognitive preconceptions that serve to structure minimal information about
causes affecting actions and outcomes. Kelley (1972b) defines a causal
schema as 'a conception of the manner in which two more causal factors
interact in relation to a particular kind of effect' (p. 152). The theory
connects discounting particularly to the multiple sufficient schema, which
applies in situations when either of two causes is sufficient to produce an
effect. If this schema is applied, when one cause is absent, we assume the
other cause was present, but when the first cause is present, the second
cause is rendered ambiguous. Kelley's theory proposes that a second
schema, the multiple necessary schema, applies in the case of extreme
events, such as extreme delinquency or success on a difficult task. In these
cases, people consider individual causes to be insufficient and infer that
several causes must be present. When considering an outstanding
intellectual achievement, for example, the attributor infers the joint action
of causes such as ability and motivation, or perseverance and luck. In other
words, neither cause is discounted.

Kelley (1973, p. 113) cautioned that 'the discounting principle involves
many more subtle and complex points' than a simple description would
suggest, but the discounting principle is often assumed to be simple,
unproblematic and obvious to the point of being indisputable. As Hansen
and Hall (1985) note, 'the discounting and augmentation principles
proposed by Kelley (1972a) have become accepted as noncontroversial
pieces of social psychological wisdom [which] are conveyed as inferential

facts to the readers of primers on attribution theory' (p. 1482). This status given to the concept of discounting belies the state of affairs in both theory and research on the concept. In the following section we turn to a sampling of research on the question, and in subsequent sections several highly relevant theories are considered.

Research on discounting

Research relating to discounting has employed a range of techniques (McClure, 1989a). Perhaps the least ambiguous method is a paradigm designed specifically for the purpose of testing the discounting principle, and which compares two ratings: ratings of the likelihood that an isolated cause determined an outcome, and ratings of the same cause when other causes are present (Einhorn and Hogarth, 1983; Hansen and Hall, 1985; Kruglanski, Schwartz, Maides and Hamel, 1978; Rosenfield and Stephan, 1977). Kruglanski's *et al.* study used this procedure to focus on particular motives for actions, rather than the general categories of person and situation. For example, one item stated 'Frank gave a donation to charity. Frank wants to make the donation as a tax deduction. His boss is on the charity's board of directors.' Participants rated the first (focal) cause either when the second cause was not stated, or when it was stated. The study also manipulated covariation information which indicated that a cause had accompanied the outcome on previous occasions. In the absence of this information, the focal cause was rated lower in the presence of the alternative cause, indicating some discounting. The effect of covariation information differed for focal and alternative causes. Information reinforcing the focal cause increased the rating of that cause, but information reinforcing the alternative cause had no effect on ratings of the focal cause. Kruglanski *et al.* observed that this finding clashes with the discounting principle: 'The idea that a strong well-documented alternative (buttressed by covariation evidence) may not detract from one's confidence in the focal hypothesis any more than would a considerably weaker alternative...seems inconsistent with the discounting rule itself' (p. 182).

Kruglanski *et al.* questioned this implication of their data on the grounds that the discounting rule 'was well established in this and other research' (p. 182). But similar inconsistencies with the discounting principle have been found by other authors using similar procedures. Rosenfield and Stephan (1977), for example, presented participants with information about internal and external causes prior to observing an actor's (aggressive) behaviour. It was anticipated from the discounting principle that information producing stronger expectancies about one cause would lead to lower attributions to the alternative cause than information producing weaker expectancies about the first cause. But when participants had received information about both causes, an increase in the information implicating one cause did not lead to a decrease in the rating on the other cause, that is, discounting. The authors found the result 'surprising in light of the many studies cited in the introduction that have found discounting effects' (p. 100). It was only when participants received no information about one cause in a second experiment that the cause was discounted.

In Einhorn and Hogarth's (1983) studies using the same procedure, participants were given covariation information about each of the causes as it was introduced. Ratings of the first cause were lower after the introduction of alternative causes, but the decrease failed to reflect the ratings of the gross strength of the causes in isolation. This 'underadjustment' led Einhorn and Hogarth to conclude that 'a single explanation is not greatly discounted by alternatives' (p. 32), although they still considered discounting to be a well-proven phenomenon, citing Kelley's (1973) review and research by Schustack and Sternberg (1981). The studies by Schustack and Sternberg (1981) that Einhorn and Hogarth referred to were not designed to test attribution theories, but they are indeed relevant to the discounting principle, because they deal with the effects of information about target and alternative explanations on the perceived strength of the target explanations. Schustack and Sternberg found that the strength of alternative causes contributed to appropriate inferences about target causes, but the weakness of the adjustment indicated 'biases in favor of the hypothesized cause over other causes' (p. 119). Participants also ignored information about covariation between the target and alternative causes that implied 'a reduction in the responsibility of the target for the outcome' (p. 114). So their results show the same underadjustments as that obtained by Einhorn and Hogarth.

Hansen and Hall's (1985) studies similarly required participants to rate the strength of a cause in isolation and when alternative causes for the outcome were introduced. For example, they rated the strength of a person who held his/her position in a tug of war when that person was the only person on the side and when the person was supported by between one and three team-mates whose average strength was the same as the target person. They gave lower estimates of (i.e., discounted) the strength of the target person when other team-mates were present, although this reduction was limited to about 15–17 per cent per team-mate. For example, in the condition with one team-mate, where the number of forces was double that in the condition where the target person is alone, the target person's force was reduced by only 17 per cent, rather than being halved. This pattern is analogous to rating a weight as 1 kilo when it balances an object weighing 1 kilo on weighing-scales, and rating the weight as 0.83 kilo (a reduction of 17 per cent) when it is one of two equal weights balancing the same object. This finding thus demonstrates the same underadjustment in discounting that was found by Einhorn and Hogarth (1983) and Schustack and Sternberg (1981).

In summary, these experiments found that discounting did occur in some conditions, but it was limited to situations where participants received no background information either about both causes (Kruglanski *et al.*, 1978) or about alternative (second) causes (Rosenfield and Stephan, 1977). When background information accompanied both presented causes, subjects exhibited either underadjustment (Einhorn and Hogarth, 1983; Hansen and Hall, 1985; Schustack and Sternberg, 1981), or no discounting at all (Rosenfield and Stephan, 1977). This suggest that people may perceive events in terms of multiple causes, rather than discounting, and they do so if evidence suggests that multiple causes contributed to the outcome.

The experiments also suggest that discounting is limited largely to causes other than the first cause encountered. Whereas information about the strength of the initial 'focal' cause led to discounting of the alternative cause, information about the strength of the alternative cause had little or no effect on ratings of focal causes (Einhorn and Hogarth, 1983; Kruglanski *et al.*, 1978; Schustack and Sternberg, 1981). Einhorn and Hogarth (1983), Rosenfield and Stephan (1977) and Schustack and Sternberg (1981) propose that participants' failure to discount the first presented cause suggests that they anchor or focus on that cause. They consequently take little account of the strength of alternative causes, and make insufficient downward adjustments in the strength of the first 'focal' cause. Independent support for this view appears in Shaklee and Fischhoff's (1982) finding that strategies of information search followed a 'truncated search pattern'. When participants were presented with several causes for events accompanied by information implicating one of the causes, they requested further information about the implicated cause rather than checking out about other causes. People tend to anchor on the first explanation they possess, rather than following the discounting principle.

It should be noted that these studies are more consistent with other findings in the discounting literature than the authors recognize. Kruglanski *et al.* (1978), Rosenfield and Stephan (1977), and Einhorn and Hogarth (1983), whose results suggest that discounting is limited in both its strength and generality, treat their findings as exceptions to a discounting pattern that has been firmly established in other experiments. Kruglanski *et al.* refer to no experiments which might substantiate this pattern; Rosenfield and Stephan cite as evidence of discounting the experiments in the attitude attribution paradigm (e.g., Jones and Davis, 1965), but these were subsequently designated as examples of insufficient discounting by Jones (1979) and Kelley and Michela (1980). (This is because the degree of discounting was so weak given that an alternative sufficient cause was known to have contributed to the effect.) The papers cited by Einhorn and Hogarth as establishing discounting consist of Kelley's (1973) review, which is an integrative theoretical article rather than a piece of new evidence, and Schustack and Sternberg's (1981) experiment, which demonstrated similar constraints on discounting to those that Einhorn and Hogarth themselves found. It may be suggested, then, that these findings do not represent an exception to a well-established rule that people discount. Certainly the evidence that the authors cite does not establish that rule, and the results of other studies suggest that people systematically deviate from that rule, and frequently make attributions consistent with multiple causation (McClure, 1989a). Discounting has been examined in numerous other paradigms, but the findings are similar to those reviewed here. Although discounting sometimes does occur, often it does not, and when it does occur it is frequently very weak.

Extremity and moderation

The effect of opposing causes
The discounting principle incorporates the 'hydraulic' assumption that an increase in the magnitude of one cause is reflected by a decrease in the magnitude of another cause. This assumption contrasts with theories which hold that events and explanations commonly involve opposed or conflicting 'dialectical' forces (e.g., Buss, 1979a; Riegel, 1979; Rychlak, 1976). The importance of opposed causes is also recognized in knowledge structure approaches (e.g., Wilensky, 1983; see also Lalljee and Abelson, 1983). The common feature in these approaches is the inclusion of opposed or conflicting forces or energies, as, for example, in the antitheses of social and individual, subject and object, dark and light, love and hate. It is assumed that two opposed forces may coexist in any situation, so the presence of one of the opposing forces does not entail the absence or weakness of the other.

With regard to personality traits, this perspective implies that apparently opposed traits (kind/cruel) may coexist in the one personality. This viewpoint is sympathetic to recent changes in personality measurement, from the use of bipolar scales that locate opposed traits at opposite ends of a scale, to unipolar scales giving separate measures of each trait (e.g., S. L. Bem, 1974). The separate measures permit raters to indicate that they perceive a person as embodying opposed tendencies. For example, they permit raters to indicate that they perceive a person as being both tough and tender, rather than being either tough or tender. This development in personality measurement concurred with the rise in social attitudes favourable to the androgynous personality type which incorporates 'opposite' traits. Such persons are capable of being both tough and tender according to circumstances, or even in a single situation (S. L. Bem, 1974), rather than being restricted to the polarities traditionally associated with masculinity and femininity. Furby (1983) notes that people's perception of conflicting traits in others is not necessarily a confused view, but may follow logically from the conflicting behaviour patterns that people exercise. For example, a daughter may have both positive and negative feelings toward her father because he is the one who both plays with her and punishes her.

These principles also apply to causal forces. With regard to physical forces, Billig (1982) notes that when a bird rises in the air, it does so not because the force of gravity is suspended, but because gravity is complemented by an opposing force that lifts the bird. As a consequence, when a bird flies the observer does not discount gravity, or presume that gravity is absent. The bird's elevation at any time reflects the interaction between opposing physical forces. Billig proposes that these principles apply equally to the causes of people's social circumstances (their elevation, position), and to social outcomes like unemployment, wealth and poverty. Research on attributions for these outcomes has characteristically focused on the tendency for left-wing or socialist groups to attribute social circumstances to social causes (e.g., government policy) while discounting personal causes (e.g., personal responsibility), and for right-wing or conservative groups to explain the same events in terms of personal causes while discounting social causes. What is overlooked in focusing on these polarities is the nature of the explanations of people between the two extremes: the people 'in the middle'. On the political spectrum these are persons who prefer a mixed economy of attributions, which includes and 'balances' social and individual factors. These persons may explain a riot, for example, by suggesting that the persons involved must be held responsible for their actions, but that on the other hand it must be taken into account that they are socially disadvantaged. One implication of this line of conjecture is that moderate people exercise less dissonance reduction than extremists. Moderate persons tolerate the dissonance entailed by a 'balanced' explanation, whereas extremists at either end of the political spectrum eliminate dissonance by discounting social or individual factors.

This line of thought has problematic implications for the analogy between discounting and scientific inference, when one asks which of the three groups (left-wing, right-wing, moderate) is most like the scientist in the way it explains events. The answer, of course, is that none of them merits this status, because science contains the same spectrum of positions that is found in society. Scientists at one extreme maintain that traits and personal circumstances are largely genetically determined, and discount environmental factors (e.g., Eysenck, 1967), while scientists at the other extreme attribute the same phenomena to environmental variables and discount genetic factors (e.g., Kamin, 1974). Between these extremes are scientists emphasizing the influence of both genetic and environmental factors (e.g., Scarr, 1981). These persons are all scientists; if one were to accept as scientists only those who discounted one causal influence, then only the extreme geneticists and behaviourists would pass as scientists and the others would be excluded.

These instances of discounting and non-discounting concern the commonly used categories of person and environment, but theories dealing with opposed causes apply to a wider range of categories. Wilensky (1983), for example, has focused on conflicting goals. Conflicting or negative goal relationships are reflected in explanations of completed and failed actions. A person may perceive that a goal compatible with an action was present, but that a conflicting goal was also present, or that the preconditions necessary for achieving the initial goal were absent. So the person may explain their (in)action by saying 'I wanted to come to your celebration, but I also wanted to see a particular movie on TV that night', or 'I wanted to come to your barbecue, but I couldn't find a ride to get there.' Of course, in one sense only the part of the explanation that corresponds to the eventual outcome is necessary to explain the outcome. But explanations serve not merely to explain outcomes, but also to explain intentions and other factors. So explanations may include both opposing causes where the listener wishes to communicate that there are causes present that conflict with the actual outcome (Grice, 1975). In the example above, it may be important for the relationship of the communicants that the explainer indicates that there was a cause present that conflicted with the outcome ('I wanted to come to your celebration'). These functional aspects of the explanations are discussed further in the section below dealing with pragmatic influences in explanations.

There is a common structural feature to the balanced moderate explanations described by Billig (1982) and the negative goal relations described by Wilensky (1983). In both cases an adversative conjunction (such as 'but', 'however', 'although', 'nevertheless') is used as the connective which links the two opposed causes or goals. Adversative conjunctions are the grammatical connectives that link causes which in isolation have contrary implications, or are 'adversaries' (Leech and Svartvik, 1975). Children's learning of the use of adversative conjunctions has been examined in developmental psychology (e.g., Vygotsky, 1962), but the use of these conjunctions has not been examined in attribution theories, where the connectives that have been focused on are additive conjunctions and disjunctions (Kelley, 1972b, 1973). This omission of adversative conjunctions from attribution theories may result from two factors. Attribution models dealing with discounting and schemata tend to reflect the assumption that causes have a common direction or outcome rather than having opposed effects. So when two causes are considered to be present, they are categorized as an additive conjunction (A and B), rather than an adversative one (A but B). This emphasis traces back to Heider's (1958) view that the relation between causes affecting an outcome is additive, and should be represented in an additive equation (e.g., p. 82). Attribution theorists' predictions about the connectives used in explanations also reflect the assumption that people discount causes in all but extreme cases. This view underlies the prediction that causes are linked by (additive) conjunctions in the case of extreme events and by disjunctions in the case of common events.

An exception to the assumption that causes are additively related is Kelley's (1972a, 1973) concept of inhibitory causes. Kelley's main application of this concept is in relation to augmentation and completed actions. He considers the effect of an inhibitory cause on inferences about the strength of causes facilitating an outcome. When an outcome occurs in the presence of an inhibitory cause, the observer infers that the cause facilitating the event is strong, that is, the facilitatory cause is augmented (Hansen and Hall, 1985). Kelley's account recognizes that causes may stand in an inhibitory or oppositional relation to each other, but it does not consider the possibility that people may include both inhibitory and facilitatory causes when explaining actions. Kelley's model also omits the connective that connects causes in these cases (adversative conjunction).

In summary, the existence of conflicting causes affecting events suggests that when there are two opposed causes for an event, people may consider both causes to be present, rather than discounting one of the causes. In relation to extremity, opposed causes have the opposite implication to convergent causes. With opposed causes, people are more likely to infer that both causes are present for a moderate outcome than an extreme outcome, because an extreme outcome suggests that one of the opposing causes was weak or absent. Take the example of examination outcomes and the two opposed causes of high student ability and bad teaching. An extreme outcome would suggest that only one of the causes was present. With extreme success it is more likely that high ability is present and bad teaching was absent, while extreme failure would suggest the opposite. With moderate success, it is more likely that both causes are present, and that one cause has countered and moderated the influence of the other. As opposed causes are frequently connected by adversative conjunctions, the inclusion of opposed causes implies that adversative conjunctions will be used rather than additive conjunctions or disjunctions when the causes being considered are opposed to each other, for example, 'she has ability but she had poor teaching'.

This line of thinking suggests that people may see the causes affecting events as opposing rather than convergent, and in such cases people will use conjunctions of opposing causes for common events, and discount one of the causes with extreme events. Although this idea that people may use single causes more for extreme than moderate events is at odds with Kelley's theory, there are several theoretical ideas that support this notion.

Single causes for extreme events?

Several theories and conjectures suggest that people may use single causes for extreme events, rather than the conjunctions invoked by Kelley (1972b). Reeder and Brewer (1979) proposed that different types of schemata are used with different attributes. A schema with direct implications for discounting is the hierarchically restrictive schema, which applies to more judgements and achievement attributions. The schema 'assumes that dispositional classifications of the upper extreme of a unipolar continuum are not behaviorally restricted, whereas dispositions at the lower end of the continuum are behaviorally restricted' (p. 67). In relation to achievement, for example, persons who have great ability in a particular field are not behaviourally restricted, which means that they can demonstrate a full range of behaviour from extremely skilful to very unskilful. People who lack ability in that field are behaviourally restricted, and have a low ceiling to their performance. An able pianist, for example, can play both a piano sonata and a ditty, whereas the unskilled person can play only the ditty. There is an asymmetry between good performances and poor performances, such that 'a poor performance is ambiguous' (p. 68), but 'exceptionally good performance is always indicative of a correspondent disposition' (p. 68). Reeder and Brewer propose that skilled achievements in particular are 'pure' ability attributes (p. 77), and whereas people may attribute failure to a number of causes, they attribute success in skilled achievements to ability and discount other causes. They propose that 'this difference in the discounting tendency between success and failure should increase directly with the perceived skill involved in the successful behavior' (p. 77).

This cognitive schema parallels variations on intelligence measures with groups at differing points in the socio-economic scale. Standard deviations on IQ measures of intelligence show more variability in groups at the lower end of the socio-economic scale than among those at the top end of the scale (Tyler, 1965). Tyler has described these results in the following terms: 'It is not likely that a moron will ever be able to qualify as an engineer, lawyer, or accountant. However, it is quite possible for a brilliant man to be working as a lumberjack, truckdriver, or miner' (p. 337). Like Reeder and Brewer's schema, this interpretation suggests that a high socio-economic position (analogous to a skilled performance) indicates the presence of ability, while a low socio-economic position (analogous to an unskilled performance) has no definite implications for the level of ability.

Reeder and Brewer claimed that the hierarchically restrictive schema is compatible with the multiple necessary schema proposed by Kelley (1972b). But while both schemata imply that ratings of ability will be higher for extreme success than moderate success, they differ in other respects. Kelley's model proposes that extreme events invoke multiple causes, which in the case of success may not even include ability (Kelley, 1972b, p. 156), and that moderate events are attributed to single causes. Reeder and Brewer's theory, however, links extreme success to one cause, ability, whereas lesser achievements are more ambiguous and are explained by a range of causes. In regard to extreme outcomes, Reeder and Brewer's propositions reinforce dialectical theories which imply that when two causes are opposed, it is more likely that only one of the causes is present with an extreme outcome than a moderate outcome. The hierarchically restricted schema similarly points towards a single cause (ability) for extreme outcomes, and implies that causes other than ability are discounted with extreme success.

Similar ideas are suggested in Fiedler's (1982) interpretation of correspondent inference theory (Jones and Davis, 1965), which proposed that the plausibility of a given causal relationship is determined by the correspondence between the cause and the effect. Fiedler interprets this principle to imply that when people search for a cause for an effect, they search for a single cause that corresponds to the effect that is being explained. So, when attributors wish to explain a moderate event they select a moderate cause, and when they wish to explain an extreme event, they select an extreme cause. Like Reeder and Brewer (1979), Fiedler suggests that an extreme achievement is likely to be attributed to extreme ability, although Fiedler's theory would allow for any extreme cause as an explanation. Both theories, however, suggest that extreme outcomes are explained by a single extreme cause and that other causes are discounted. Both theories make different predictions to Kelley's theory as to when discounting occurs in relation to extremity.

Heider's (1958) theory of explanations also suggests that extreme actions may be explained by single causes, rather than conjunctions. Heider's conception of explanations, and more recent knowledge structure theories (e.g., Lalljee and Abelson, 1983), treat actions as being propelled by goals, rather than being derived simply from 'causes'. As interpreted by Heider, a goal-based conception suggests that people may perceive a goal as a sufficient explanation for an action, irrespective of the degree of extremity of the action. Heider proposed that for a goal-based action, the goal is in itself the single necessary and sufficient explanation of the action. Heider did not consider instances where actions have multiple goals (Leddo, Abelson and Gross, 1984; Wilensky, 1983), but focused on the relation of goals to preconditions. He accepted that the realization of a goal is contingent on the presence of preconditions, but he considered that the equifinal nature of goal-based action enables agents to manipulate preconditions to achieve their ends. Heider claimed that 'Attribution to personal causality reduces the necessary conditions essentially to one, the person with intention, who, within a wide range of environmental vicissitudes, has control over the multitude of forces required to create the specific effect' (1958, p. 102).

Heider's proposal suggests that single goals are adequate explanations of intentional actions, irrespective of the extremity of the action. His approach implies that the presence of preconditions will not be referred to in explanations, as people are assumed to be able to manipulate preconditions to achieve their goals. Two recent studies are informative in relation to Heider's claim. A study carried out by Leddo *et al.* (1984) found that conjunctions of goals and preconditions were rated as better explanations of completed actions than goals or preconditions in isolation. Whereas Heider proposed that a goal-based approach suggests simple goal-referent explanations, in which the preconditions are discounted in importance, Leddo *et al.*'s findings suggest that conjunctions of goals and preconditions will be preferred over goals in isolation. However, this conclusion is challenged by Hilton and Knott (1988), who examined perceptions of the necessity and sufficiency of goals and preconditions. They found that both goals and preconditions were perceived as necessary for an action, but only goals were perceived as sufficient explanations of the action. This finding is more favourable to Heider's claim that goals are necessary and sufficient explanations of goal-based actions. Theories of goal-based explanations, like the other theories described in this section, challenge Kelley's proposition that with extreme events, the discounting principle is waived and the effects are explained by a conjunction of causes. The theories support the contrary implication that extreme actions may be explained in terms of a single cause or goal, and that other causes are discounted.

The question of how people explain extreme and moderate events was examined in a recent series of studies which obtained explanations for moderate and extreme actions and achievement outcomes (McClure, 1987; McClure, Lalljee and Jaspars, 1988). Explanations were obtained on an open-ended questionnaire, where subjects could provide an explanation for an event in their own words, and on a structured questionnaire, where subjects were required to choose between a single cause and a conjunction in the case of extreme events, and between a single cause and a disjunction in the case of moderate events. The results support the view that people interpret some moderate events in terms of two opposing causes and some extreme events in terms of a single extreme cause. Although with certain events, such as examination outcomes and traffic offences, extreme levels of the event were explained mostly by conjunctions, with other events, such as scientific achievements and violent offences, extreme levels of the event were explained by single causes that were as extreme as the effect. For example, the participants explained a major scientific achievement by suggesting that the scientist was brilliant, and explained a grotesque murder by suggesting that the murderer was insane. The use of single extreme causes disagrees with Kelley's (1972b) proposition that extreme events are explained by a conjunction of causes, although it is consistent with the idea that an explanation corresponds to the extremity of the effect being explained. In this case, extremity is reflected in the magnitude of one cause, rather than the number of causes being invoked.

This strategy of explaining extreme events in terms of single causes is consistent with many subjects' strategy of explaining moderate events by two opposing causes linked by an adversative conjunction, rather than the disjunctive explanations predicted by Kelley (1972b). Attributing extreme success to a single cause (he is intelligent) is consistent with attributing moderate success to the same cause countered by an opposing cause (he is intelligent but he didn't work). The use of adversative conjunctions for moderate events indicates that the person perceives that there are two opposed causes present (A but B), rather than two alternative convergent causes (A or B). When two causes are perceived as opposed, it is more likely that both are present with a moderate effect, where one cause moderates the other, than with an extreme effect, where the cause that opposes that outcome is likely to be absent. It was noted above that adversative conjunctions are used to express moderate political opinions (e.g., 'the state must play a role, but you must also encourage personal initiative', Billig, 1982). The present finding shows the same pattern with moderate achievement outcomes. People perceive causes as opposing as well as convergent, and they link opposed causes by adversative conjunctions rather than disjunctions and (additive) conjunctions (cf. Billig, 1982). These results support the view that people's perceptions of the causes of the events around them have a dialectical dimension. The concept 'dialectical' is often used in support of abstruse arguments or polemical rhetoric, but the dialectical interaction of causes seen here is not mystical or particular to a political perspective, but tangible and common.

Research on explanations in social psychology has overlooked opposi-tional relationships between causes in a second respect. Studies relating to discounting in explanations of success and failure are considered to show that people discount more for failure than success. In regard to explanations of achievement outcomes, Kun and Weiner (1973) found that extreme success is explained in terms of the presence of ability and effort, whereas extreme failure is explained in terms of the absence of just one of those causes. In similar studies of explanations of action outcomes, Leddo *et al.* (1984) found that completed actions are explained in terms of a conjunction of goals and preconditions, whereas failure to carry out the actions is explained more in terms of the absence of one cause, either a goal or precondition. These results are interpreted in terms of cognitive structures; for example, Leddo *et al.* suggested that people may have cognitive frames that have slots for several causes in the case of completed actions, and a slot for a single disenabling cause in the case of failed or incompleted actions.

This type of interpretation is plausible if one considers that all the causes that relate to actions are facilitatory and contribute to the completion of that action. However, in the context of both actions and achievement outcomes, there may be causes that oppose or block the achievement of the outcome. In the case of achievements, an obstacle may counter the effect of ability and effort; in the case of actions, a conflicting goal may counter the effect of another goal, even when the conditions necessary for achieving that other goal are present. Opposing causes were entirely omitted from the studies by Kun and Weiner (1973) and by Leddo *et al.* (1984) which examined only causes whose presence contributes to success or action completion. A series of studies by McClure, Lalljee, Jaspars and Abelson (1989), which included both facilitating and opposing causes, showed that opposing causes are seen as more influential in failure than success, the opposite to the finding with facilitatory causes. Opposing causes, which have been overlooked in theories of attribution and explanation, reverse and turn upside down the effects of facilitating causes. Both the natural and the social world include opposing forces and causes; the dialectic between these forces is reflected in the explanations that people give for the events and actions that affect them.

Models and analogies: from science to magic

Do (good) scientists discount?
Kelley (1972a) claimed that when people apply the discounting principle in their explanations, they are doing 'just what the good scientist would do' (p. 8). There are a number of grounds for querying whether the discounting principle accurately characterizes the ways in which either scientists or lay persons make causal decisions. Scientific theory is certainly supposed to be elegant and parsimonious, such that if two alternative models account for a phenomenon, one should accept the simpler or more elegant of the two theories. However, this principle applies primarily to models and theories, rather than to 'causes' (Walker, 1977). Even the simpler of two theories may refer to the activity of many causes to explain an event. A scientific

account of either rare or commonplace events may include a complex network of causes. In these cases, explanatory economy consists in selecting the theory that best explains the interconnections of causes. As Walker (1977) notes, an explanation calls not for a single factor but for a single theory or system that is applicable to all cases. Scientific theories may actually include more causes than commonsense accounts, because all the relevant causal influences must be made explicit for the purposes of prediction and measurement. Causal preconditions may not be taken for granted in science to the extent that they are in common sense. So if people do not discount, this finding would not by itself validate or invalidate analogues with scientific inference.

A second issue in the analogy between discounting and scientific inference concerns the proposition that when faced with two potential models that explain an event, scientists simply discount one of the causes, without further consideration. Scientific orthodoxy stipulates that when there are two competing explanations of an event, the scientist constructs empirical tests to determine which of the two is most correct. Of course, scientists do not always adhere to this principle, but Kelley stipulated that the discounting attributor is proceeding in the manner of a 'good scientist' (1972a, p. 8), rather than a bad one. A problem with Kelley's suggestion that scientists make decisions when there is little available information is that it conflicts with the scientific axiom of reserving judgement until decisive evidence is obtained. Furthermore, when scientists do carry out research on the question, and find that one of the explanations is correct and that the other is not responsible for the effect, then the latter cause will no longer be considered a plausible cause. So this outcome, rather than being an instance of discounting one of two plausible causes for the sake of economy, would be a case of discounting an explanation because it was implausible.

In view of recent suggestions that analogies between lay attributors and lawyers may be more appropriate than analogies with scientists (e.g., Fincham and Jaspars, 1980), it should be noted that the point made here in relation to scientific inference applies equally to legal decisions about causal factors. When making the decision as to whether a killing constitutes murder or manslaughter, for example, the legal process goes to some lengths to establish whether intent, premeditation and provocation were present at the time of the offence (Hart and Honoré, 1985). Discounting in this context occurs on the basis of evidence relating to each cause, rather than in conditions where there is little evidence about the available causes, which is where the discounting analogy predicts discounting.

What follows from these considerations is that discounting, even where it does occur, may not be treated as evidence of 'scientific' inference. Indeed, if people discount causes without seeking adequate evidence, they may be said to be operating on a different basis to the scientist or the judge.

What makes causes plausible?

A second question in the analogy between discounting and scientific inference concerns Kelley's criterion for the plausibility of causes in explanations, in terms of his criterion for what makes a cause worthy of consideration in the first instance. The criterion suggested by Kelley amounts to a form of cultural consensus. A plausible cause, he suggests, is 'one that any member of the same culture and time period as the experimenter would be likely to mention as a probable cause of the behaviour if we describe it in its setting and ask "Why did it occur?"' (Kelley, 1972a, p. 10; cf. Nisbett and Wilson, 1977).

Kelley recognized that this conception of a plausible cause 'renders us too dependent on our subjects' introspections and verbal reports' (p. 10). But a no less risky hazard is that the use of cultural consensus as the criterion of the plausibility of causes renders one dependent on the beliefs and prejudices that predominate within the relevant culture. Kelley's theories do allow for 'less rational attribution tendencies' in individual and group attributions, but give little allowance to the possibility that the opinions shared within cultures may also have biases and interests, the most obvious example being the 'national interest'. These interests and biases constrain the way events are perceived and explained. If there is consensus within a culture, for example, that immigrants or Jewish persons are causing many of that culture's problems, or that the nuclear arms race is due to malevolent Soviet or American intentions, then according to the criterion of cultural consensus, that cause is a plausible cause of the event.

Now one may agree that cultural consensus is the criterion by which the plausibility of causes in the social world is determined, but this criterion of plausibility is at odds with orthodox conceptions of scientific explanation, which hold that science evaluates the plausibility of causes in terms of their empirical merit and their logical consistency. Kelley's cultural criterion of plausibility suggests that the explanations of lay attributors are evaluated on different grounds to scientific inference. The proposition that the plausibility of causes is determined by the beliefs within a culture is more compatible with Moscovici's (e.g., 1982) claim that attributions derive from social representations. These considerations suggest that the discounting principle and scientific inference have no clear implications for each other, and the issue of whether people discount must be ascertained independently of evidence about the logic of scientific endeavour.

Pragmatic functions: cooperativeness

Several psychologists have suggested recently that analogues with scientists ignore the communicative function of explanations (e.g., Slugoski, 1983). They invoke Grice's (1975) maxim of informativeness, which proposes that when people offer explanations, they do not tell the listener things that they can reasonably assume that the listener already knows. When two persons are observing a tennis match in which, say, Lendl beats Becker, neither observer will explain the victory to the other by pointing out that Lendl played the match, as the other person is already aware of the fact.

This principle has important implications in relation to discounting, because it suggests that people may omit causes from their explanations for reasons unrelated to the perceived efficacy of causes or the necessity of a cause. The maxim of informativeness suggests that people will omit causes from explanations when they assume that the perceiver already knows that the cause is present. Lendl's playing in a tennis match is a necessary condition for winning the match, but it is unlikely to be included in explanations of the victory. Observers may even omit from their explanations causes such as ability and effort when these causes are known to be present. Observers may know that Lendl trains for several hours daily, but as it is generally assumed that all professional sportspersons train regularly, this factor will be deemed uninformative and be omitted from an explanation of Lendl's success. In this case effort, which in other circumstances may not be assumed and will thus be informative, is simply assumed. Lendl himself attributed his many victories in tennis tournaments in 1985 to a change of diet (*The Times*, 4 September 1985, p. 22); all the other causes that might be assumed to be present, such as skill and effort, are omitted from the explanation, not because they are considered to be absent, but because they are uninformative in this context. It may even be suggested that when a person who is outstanding in some field does refer to ability as a factor in their success (e.g., 'I am the greatest', Mohammed Ali), the attribution has functions other than either informativeness or 'scientific' inference.

The maxim of informativeness has been discussed in relation to conversation and inference (Slugoski, 1983), but has had little application to issues relating to discounting. A single exception is Reeder and Fulks' (1980) reference to the maxim when they failed to obtain causal attributions to ability in conditions where they obtained correspondent inferences to ability. Reeder and Fulks suggested that this result might be due to the fact that ability is not an informative cause, citing Schneider, Hastorf and Ellsworth's (1979) suggestion that abilities are uninformative necessary causes. In fact, this proposal is a misapplication of Schneider *et al.*'s position, because those authors made it clear that the uninformativeness of abilities applies only to actions and not to achievements (p. 259). They suggested, for example, that we wouldn't explain Joe's yelling at the professor by saying that Joe is able to yell, but we might explain Joe's success in the professor's course by referring to Joe's ability. However, the principle has not been applied systematically to studies of discounting. Yet the principle has important implications for instances of (apparent) discounting. People's failure to include a cause in their explanation may be due to their assuming that the receiver of the explanation is aware of the presence of the cause, rather than their perception of the low strength of the cause. It follows that the omission of a cause from an explanation in itself is not sufficient evidence that a person is discounting the cause.

Pragmatic functions: uncooperativeness

Grice's (1975) maxim of communicative cooperativeness implies that a primary purpose of communication is to inform or enlighten the person receiving the communication. Most attribution theories assume similarly that a primary purpose of causal inference is to obtain answers to causal questions. At odds with this enlightenment conception of explanations are theories which suggest that explanation and communication functions as much to misinform as to inform, and as much to obscure as to clarify (e.g., Billig, 1982; Snyder and Wicklund, 1981). A prototypical but by no means exceptional illustration of this tendency would be those governments or bureaucracies that appear to follow maxims of uncooperativeness in their presentation of mis-information and non-information. The principle apparent here is to tell listeners (the public) nothing that they do not know already, and to release information that tells the listeners what they already know, or to provide information which is uninformative with regard to the question being asked.

Snyder and Wicklund (1981) note that the function of some explanations is precisely the opposite to the reductive and eliminative process of discounting. They challenge the view that people are usually 'pulled toward ruling out certain causes in favor of other causes' (p. 197), and propose alternatively that 'the attributor ... often is motivated to move *away* from the direction of attributional specificity. Rather than narrowing the range of causes to arrive at a single dominant explanation, we should at times expect efforts to break open the range of causality – to locate multiple causes and to render the end result of the "search" for causality ambiguous' (p. 198). Snyder and Wicklund observe that there are times when a sufficient cause or motive for an action is present, but because the person wishes to obscure that cause or motive, they will make their action more ambiguous. People will often 'confuse or muddy the nature of the attribution that threatens' (p. 203); they achieve this by 'inventing additional causes or ... engage in other manoeuvres in order to prevent specificity' (p. 198). Snyder and Wicklund do allow one qualification of their proposition by suggesting that their proposals apply particularly to actors' explanations of their own actions and less to observers' explanations of the same actions. But they give no theoretical rationale for this asymmetry; there is certainly no a priori reason for thinking that the first available explanations of other people's behaviour will be any less threatening than the first available explanation of one's own behaviour.

The tendency to add causal explanations in certain circumstances, rather than discounting, has also been noted in Billig's (1982) discussion of explanations of social conditions, such as unemployment. Billig suggests that when people do not like the first available explanation of an outcome like unemployment (if it threatens, in Snyder and Wicklund's terms), they will 'muddy the picture' by adding or emphasizing other factors.

An intriguing model of the ways in which people obscure a sufficient explanation by adding inaccurate or redundant factors is supplied in Kelley's (1980) description of the manipulations used by magicians to control audiences' attributions. Kelley suggests that in magic tricks there are two causal sequences: a real causal sequence that is known by the magician, and an apparent causal sequence that is constructed by the magician, and that is intended to be followed by the audience. Kelley suggests that ideas we gain about causal manipulation from magic tricks 'suggest ways in persons other than magicians – political leaders, salesmen, and others – can create false scenarios of the causes of events' (p. 34). Wilensky (1983) has offered a similar operationalization of techniques of disguise and camouflage in explanations.

Impression management operates not only to obscure the most accurate or plausible causes for actions, but for the purpose of justifying, excusing or condemning actions (Semin and Manstead, 1983). These ends may be achieved either by the addition of redundant causes when a sufficient cause is present or by discounting or augmenting causes that are already available. Such processes may apply in relation to ingroups and outgroups. In the case of negative actions by an ingroup member, personal causes will be discounted and mitigating situational factors will be augmented. Conversely, with positive actions in ingroup members, personal factors will be augmented and situational factors discounted. The pattern is inverted with outgroups (e.g., Hewstone, Jaspars and Lalljee, 1982). In this instance discounting and augmentation function to express or reinforce the prejudices of the group.

These various models of causal management predict conditions where people will discount causes, but in this case discounting is guided not by the motive to be economical (the scientist analogy) or the motive to inform (the cooperator model), but by the motive to defend or justify a particular action or to obscure a particular cause. When people's motive is to simplify or to inform, they are likely to discount, but when people's motive is to obscure an unpalatable explanation, even if that explanation comprises a sufficient cause for the effect, they are likely to add further causes, rather than discount them.

Kelley (e.g., 1972a, 1973) did acknowledge that inferential processes such as the discounting principle account for only a proportion of people's attributions. He accepted that people's judgements are sometimes an outcome of biases or personal interests, rather than logical inference. To demonstrate that explanations sometimes reflect prejudice or the motive to obscure does not necessarily invalidate inferential theories of explanation. On the other hand, Kelley (1972a, 1973) did imply that biased inferences are exceptions to the general logical rules described by the discounting and covariation models. So there is an onus on protagonists of concepts like the discounting principle to demonstrate, first, that other patterns of inferences are the exception to some more logical rule, and, secondly, that when people do follow some logical rule, the rule they follow is the discounting principle.

The economy of discounting

Attribution theories generally propose that people's explanations model the parsimonious imperatives of scientific inference, and that people discount explanations when an alternative cause is available. But alternative theories of explanation have implications that conflict with this view. Whereas Kelley's theories predict that people will discount causes with common events and invoke multiple causes with extreme events, theories focusing on opposing causes suggest that people will invoke multiple causes more with moderate than extreme actions and attitudes. This idea that extreme actions and achievements may be explained in terms of a single cause is reinforced by three models: Reeder and Brewer's (1979) hierarchically restrictive schema, Fiedler's (1982) adaptation of correspondent inference theory, and Heider's (1958) propositions about goal-based action. The available research gives some support for these views. The analogy between discounting and scientific inference is complicated by the fact that scientists themselves do not treat information in the way that the discounting principle suggests, so instances of discounting do not prove that the people are inferring in a manner similar to scientists. Other perspectives suggest that attributions and explanations are guided less by the motive to infer than by the motives to inform, impress, misinform, or defend. The implications of these theories diverge markedly from the implications of models that construe the functions of attributions as being inferential. Explanations can be legitimately modelled on the causal manipulations of the magician in addition to the inferences of the scientist or lawyer.

10 Conclusion

Theories of social cognition deal with several important issues. These include people's understanding of themselves and of others, and people's cognitions and beliefs about the events that affect them. A key issue concerns people's cognitions about the causes of their actions. Ideas on this issue are shaped by two antithetical schemes. One treats people as passive responders or information processors with no more knowledge about their actions than observers, and the other awards people the agency and self-knowing omniscience of gods. Many theorists would see their models as falling somewhere between these extremes, but their theories often share the assumptions of the more extreme stances, and lend too little or too much credence to actors' explanations of their actions, often without much in the way of theoretical justification.

Researchers in mainstream social cognition tackle the issues of consciousness, self-perception and the explanation of action in terms of a mix of information-processing and positivist (or behavioural) theories. Some claim that research vindicates the historical positivist view that people's behaviour is not propelled by their intentions, and that actors consequently have no privileged access to the causes of their actions. This stance is being challenged in two ways: by criticisms that disagree with particular aspects of the argument, and by criticisms that in more general terms object to its ideological implications. The discussion here reviews both of these lines of objection, and argues that research supports the view that action does involve an intentional component, and that people do have access to cognitions relating to their actions that an observer lacks. The discussion also suggests significant boundaries to this access.

Recent developments in social cognition have seen the emergence of concepts, such as self-schemata and person memory, that tap into cognitive aspects of people's self-concept and their perception of others. Research on these concepts provides insight into people's perception of themselves in the sense of an onlooker, focusing on people's perceptions of their own traits and distinctive characteristics. What this research doesn't capture very well are the more conative aspects of cognitions, those cognitions that relate to people's intentions and voluntary actions. This is an aspect that is addressed in several avenues of cognitive science, but hasn't yet been incorporated adequately into cognitive social psychology. An exception to this claim is action identification theory, which examines people's identification of their own and other people's actions. Of those models which could be classified within mainstream social cognition and which use more traditional methodologies, this paradigm may provide the most promising integration of cognitive and conative aspects of people's consciousness and thinking. The primary difficulty in this approach is its tendency to treat actors' identifications of their actions as valid, and to assume that actors know what they are doing when they have a high-level identification for their actions. In contrast with this view, it may be suggested that while cognitions and intentions do guide and accompany behaviour in the way that this theory suggests, people may misunderstand or misreport some or all of the causes and reasons for their actions. A critical rather than a credulous stance is warranted in relation to people's explanations.

A critical appraisal of people's accounts also differentiates critical perspectives from phenomenological models, which tend to treat such accounts as necessarily valid and sufficient. These theories have reacted to the positivist strands in social cognition by asserting the agentic nature of human action, and the corresponding validity of introspective access as a royal route to the explanation of action. Yet there are many causal influences on actions that actors are not aware of, and people may conceal from themselves or from others their motives for an action. This aspect of explanations is recognized by discourse analyses, which emphasize the pragmatic and justificatory aspects of explanations. Unlike a critical perspective, however, advocates of discourse analyses reach the conclusion that the fallibility of introspection as a source of understanding behaviour suggests that the analysis of cognitions must be eschewed. It is argued here that the arguments for this stance are questionable, and that the consequences of such a position are undesirable, not least because they remove the grounds for changing people's cognitions about themselves and about events.

The concern with changing cognitions is important in information-processing and critical theories of social cognition. It is suggested here that many instances of cognitive illusion that are commonly interpreted in terms of information-processing and behavioural models are more adequately explained in terms of motivational factors and the social context of the person(s) who holds the cognition, factors that are emphasized in critical analyses. These arguments are not merely academic, and they have implications for therapy and intervention, suggesting possibilities for change that are overlooked or precluded in other analyses. By clarifying the effect of the circumstances that underlie cognitions, a basis is provided for changing those conditions as well as working to change cognitions that reflect them.

Distortions and illusions in cognition may reflect opposition between two parties, particularly in conditions where one party conceals information or presents false information. The role of opposition in explanations is understated in models of social cognition which hold that people discount alternative and opposing causal influences in events and actions. Against this view, it may be argued that people explain some events in terms of the combined effect of two opposing causes, rather than one or more congruent causes. This is particularly likely in the case of moderate outcomes and actions. In certain contexts, analogues with the clarifying task of the scientist need to be substituted by analogues that capture the muddying, misleading function of the propagandist and magician.

Theories dealing with actions, cognitions and explanations in social psychology perpetually walk a path between two factions, two half-truths, two incomplete paradigms that reflect positivism on the one hand and phenomenology on the other. These paradigms affect the theory and research not only of those who knowingly adhere to one or other approach, but also those whose inquiry is guided by an eclectic open-mindedness, and a focus on immediate and specific concerns. An adequate account of cognition and action walks a tightrope between the methodological purity of the more positivist paradigms in the demand to meet scientific standards, and the naive and uncritical conceit of phenomenological theories in the demand to be true to its human subject-matter. There are several emerging developments in mainstream social cognition and in alternative paradigms that largely avoid the doctrinaire pedantry of these polarities. Many of these developments are compatible with and sharpened by the sort of critical perspective referred to in these chapters. An adequate understanding of people's thoughts and actions is not likely to be guaranteed by adherence to any method, whether it be experimentation, ethogeny or discourse analysis. The best methods for the task must be complemented by theories that explain people's cognitions and actions, and that show how people may counter the illusions and constraints that limit those thoughts and actions.

References

Abeles, G. 1977. Researching the unresearchable: experimentation on the double bind. In C. E. Sluzki and D. C. Ransom (eds.), *Double bind: the foundation of the communicational approach to the family.* New York: Grune & Stratton

Abramson, L. Y. and Martin, D. J. 1981. Depression and the causal inference process. In J. H. Harvey, W. Ickes and R. F. Kidd (eds.), *New directions in attribution research,* vol. III. Hillsdale, N.J.: Erlbaum

Abramson, L. Y. and Sackeim, H. A. 1977. A paradox in depression: uncontrollability and self blame. *Psychological Bulletin,* **84,** 838–51

Abramson, L. Y., Seligman, M. E. P. and Teasdale, J. A. 1978. Learned helplessness in humans: critique and reformulation. *Journal of Abnormal Psychology,* **87,** 49–74

Adler, A. 1933/1956. The meaning of life, 1933. In H. L. Ansbacher and R. R. Ansbacher (eds.). *The individual psychology of Alfred Adler.* New York: Harper

Adorno, T. W. and Horkheimer, M. 1944/1972. *Dialectic of enlightenment.* New York: Herder & Herder

Ajzen, I. 1985. From intentions to actions: a theory of planned behavior. In J. Kuhl and J. Beckmann (eds.), *Action control: from cognition to behavior.* Berlin: Springer-Verlag

Alloy, L. B. and Abramson, L. Y. 1979. Judgement of contingency in depressed and nondepressed students: sadder but wider? *Journal of Experimental Psychology,* **108,** 441–85

Antaki, C. (ed.) 1981. *The psychology of ordinary explanations of social behaviour.* London: Academic Press

Antaki, C. and Fielding, G. 1981. Research on ordinary explanations. In C. Antaki (ed.), *The psychology of ordinary explanations of social behaviour.* London: Academic Press

Austin, J. L. 1962. *How to do things with words.* London: Oxford University Press

Bandler, R. and Grinder, J. 1975. *The structure of magic,* vol. I. Palo Alto, Calif.: Science and Behaviour Books

Bargh, J. A. 1984. Automatic and conscious processing of social information. In R. S. Wyer and T. K. Srull (eds.), *Handbook of social cognition,* vol. II. Hillsdale, N.J.: Erlbaum

Baron, R. A. 1977. *Human aggression.* New York: Plenum Press

Barratt, B. B. 1984. *Psychic reality and psychoanalytic knowing.* Hillsdale, N.J.: The Analytic Press

Bateson, G. 1956. Toward a theory of schizophrenia. *Behavioural Science,* **1,** 251–64
1972. *Steps to an ecology of mind.* New York: Ballantine Books

167

Baucom, D. H. 1983. Sex role identity and the decision to regain control among women. *Journal of Personality and Social Psychology*, **44**, 334–43

Bauman, Z. 1978. *Hermeneutics and social science; approaches to understanding*. London: Hutchinson

Baumeister, R. F. 1982. A self-presentational view of social phenomena. *Psychological Bulletin*, **91**, 3–26

Beck, A. T. 1967. *Depression: clinical, experimental, and theoretical aspects*. New York: Harper & Row

1976. *Cognitive and emotional disorders*. New York: International Universities Press

Bem, D. J. 1967. Self-perception: an alternative interpretation of cognitive dissonance phenomena. *Psychological Review*, **74**, 183–200

1972. Self-perception theory. In L. Berkowitz (ed.), *Advances in experimental social psychology*, vol. VI. New York: Academic Press

Bem, S. L. 1974. The measurement of psychological androgyny. *Journal of Consulting and Clinical Psychology*, **42**, 155–62

Berger, P. L. and Luckmann, T. 1966. *The social construction of reality: a treatise in the sociology of knowledge*. London: Allen Lane

Billig, M. 1976. *Social psychology and intergroup relations*. London: Academic Press

1977. The new social psychology and 'fascism'. *European Journal of Social Psychology*, **7**, 393–431

1982. *Ideology and social psychology*. Oxford: Blackwell

Blaney, P. H. 1977. Contemporary theories of depression: critique and comparison. *Journal of Abnormal Psychology*, **86**, 203–23

Block, J. H. 1973. Conceptions of sex role: some cross-cultural and longitudinal perspectives. *American Psychologist*, **28**, 512–26

Boden, M. A. 1973. The structure of intentions. *Journal for the Theory of Social Behaviour*, **3**, 23–46

Bohm, D. 1973. Human nature as a product of our mental models. In J. Benthall (ed.), *The limits of human nature*. London: Allen Lane

Boring, E. G. 1950. *A history of experimental psychology*, 2nd edn. New York: Appleton-Century-Crofts

Bowers, J. 1988. Review essay. Discourse and social psychology: beyond attitudes and behaviour. *British Journal of Social Psychology*, **27**, 185–92

Bradley, G. W. 1978. Self-serving biases in the attribution process: a re-examination of the fact or fiction question. *Journal of Personality and Social Psychology*, **36**, 56–71

Bréhier, E. 1968. *The history of philosophy*, vol. VI. *The nineteenth century*. Translated by W. Baskin. Chicago: University of Chicago Press

Brewin, C. R. 1985. Depression and causal attributions: what is their relation? *Psychological Bulletin*, **98**, 297–309

Broughton, J. M. 1986. The psychology, history, and ideology of the self. In K. S. Larsen (ed.), *Dialectics and ideology in psychology*. Norwood, N.J.: Ablex

Brown, B. 1973. *Marx, Freud, and the critique of everyday life*. New York: Monthly Review Press

Brown, G. W. and Harris, T. 1978. *Social origins of depression*. London: Tavistock

Brown, R. 1986. *Social psychology*, 2nd edn. New York: The Free Press

Buss, A. R. 1975. The emerging field of the sociology of psychological knowledge. *American Psychologist*, **30**, 988–1002

1978. Causes and reasons in attribution theory: a conceptual critique. *Journal of Personality and Social Psychology*, **36**, 1311–21

1979a. *A dialectical psychology*. New York: Irvington Publishers

1979b. A metascience critique of attribution theory. In A. R. Buss, *A dialectical psychology*. New York: Irvington Publishers

1979c. On the relationship between reasons and causes. *Journal of Personality and Social Psychology*, **37**, 1458–61

Caplan, N. and Nelson, S. D. 1973. On being useful: the nature and consequences of psychological research on social problems. *American Psychologist*, **28**, 199–211

Carnap, R. 1937. *Logical syntax of language*. London: Kegan Paul

Carroll, J. S. and Payne, J. W. 1976. *Cognition and social behaviour*. New York: Wiley

Chomsky, N. 1959. Review of *Verbal Behavior* by B. F. Skinner. *Language*, **35**, 26–58

1965. *Aspects of a theory of syntax*. Cambridge, Mass.: MIT Press

Clippinger, J. H. 1977. *Meaning and discourse: a computer model of psychoanalytic speech and cognition*. Baltimore: Johns Hopkins University Press

Connerton, P. 1976. *Critical sociology*. Harmondsworth: Penguin Books

Copleston, F. C. 1958. *A history of philosophy*, vol. V. *Hobbes to Hume*. London: Burns, Oates & Washbourne

Costello, C. G. 1978. A critical review of Seligman's laboratory experiments on learned helplessness and depression in humans. *Journal of Abnormal Psychology*, **87**, 21–31

Coulson, C. A. 1955. *Science and Christian belief*. Oxford: Oxford University Press

Coyne, J. C. and Gotlib, I. H. 1983. The role of cognition in depression: a critical appraisal. *Psychological Bulletin*, **94**, 472–505

Cronbach, L. J. 1975. Beyond the two disciplines of social psychology. *American Psychologist*, **30**, 116–27

Davidson, D. 1963. Symposium: action: actions, reasons, and causes. *The Journal of Philosophy*, **60**, 685–700

Davison, G. C. and Neale, J. M. 1978. *Abnormal psychology: an experimental clinical approach*, 2nd edn. New York: Wiley

Davison, G. C. and Valins, S. 1969. Maintenance of self-attributed and drug-attributed behavior change. *Journal of Personality and Social Psychology*, **11**, 25–33

Deaux, K. 1976. Sex: a perspective on the attribution process. In J. H. Harvey, W. J. Ickes, and R. F. Kidd (eds.), *New directions in attribution research*, vol. I. Hillsdale, N.J.: Erlbaum

deCharms, R. 1968. *Personal causation*. New York: Academic Press

1976. *Enhancing motivation; change in the classroom*. New York: Irvington Publishers

deCharms, R. and Muir, M. S. 1978. Motivation: social approaches. *Annual Review of Psychology*, **29**, 91–113

deCharms, R. and Shea, D. S. 1976. Beyond attribution theory: the human conception of motivation and causality. In L. H. Strickland, F. E. Aboud and K. J. Gergen (eds.), *Social psychology in transition*. New York: Plenum Press

Deci, E. L. 1975. *Intrinsic motivation*. New York: Irvington Publishers

Di Loreto, A. P. 1971. *Comparative psychotherapy*. Chicago: Aldine Atherton

Dollard, J. and Miller, N. 1950. *Personality and psychotherapy: an analysis in terms of learning, thinking and culture*. New York: McGraw-Hill

Einhorn, H. and Hogarth, R. 1983. A theory of diagnostic inference: judging causality. Center for Decision Research Memorandum, University of Chicago

Ellis, A. 1962. *Reason and emotion in psychotherapy*. New York: Lyle Stuart
　　1976. Rational-emotive therapy. In V. Binder, A. Binder, and B. Rimland (eds.), *Modern therapies*. Englewood Cliffs: Prentice-Hall
　　1977. The basic clinical theory of rational-emotive therapy. In A. Ellis and R. Grieger (eds.), *Handbook of rational-emotive therapy*. New York: Springer-Verlag

Ericsson, K. A. and Simon, H. A. 1980. Verbal reports as data. *Psychological Review*, 87, 215–51

Evans, R. I. 1968. *B. F. Skinner: the man and his ideas*. New York: Putton

Eysenck, H. J. 1967. *The biological basis of personality*. London: Charles C. Thomas

Fay, B. 1975. *Social theory and political practice*. London: Allen & Unwin

Fay, B. and Moon, D. J. 1977. What would an adequate philosophy of social science look like? *Philosophy of Social Science*, 7, 209–27

Feather, N. T. and Barber, J. G. 1983. Depressive reactions and unemployment. *Journal of Abnormal Psychology*, 92, 185–95

Federoff, N. A. and Harvey, J. H. 1976. Focus of attention, self-esteem and attribution of causality. *Journal of Research in Personality*, 10, 336–45

Feuer, L. S. (ed.). 1969. *Marx and Engels: basic writings on politics and philosophy*. London: Fontana

Feyerabend, P. K. 1965. Problems of empiricism, part 1. In R. Colodny (ed.), *Beyond the edge of certainty*. Englewood Cliffs, N.J.: Prentice-Hall
　　1975. *Against method*. London: Humanities Press

Fiedler, K. 1982. Causal schemata: review and criticism of research on a popular construct. *Journal of Personality and Social Psychology*, 42, 1001–3

Fillmore, C. J. 1971. Types of lexical information. In D. D. Sternberg and L. A. Jakobivits (eds.), *Semantics*. Cambridge: Cambridge University Press

Fincham, F. D. and Jaspars, J. M. F. 1980. Attribution of responsibility: from man the scientist to man as lawyer. In L. Berkowitz (ed.), *Advances in experimental social psychology*, vol. XIII. New York: Academic Press

Fischhoff, B. 1980. For those condemned to study the past: reflections on historical judgement. *New Directions for Methodology of Social and Behavioral Sciences*, 4, 79–93

Fiske, S. T. and Taylor, S. E. 1984. *Social cognition*. Reading, Mass.: Addison-Wesley

Fletcher, G. J. D. 1983. Sex differences in causal attributions for marital separation. *New Zealand Journal of Psychology*, 12, 82–9

Flew, A. 1955. Theology and falsification. In A. Flew and A. MacIntyre (eds.), *New essays in philosophical theology*. London: SCM Press

Forsterling, F. 1985. Attributional training: a review. *Psychological Bulletin*, 98, 495–512
　　1988. *Attribution theory in clinical psychology*. New York: Wiley

Freud, S. 1895/1953. Project for a scientific psychology. In J. Strachey (ed.), *The standard edition of the complete psychological works of Sigmund Freud*, vol. I. London: Hogarth Press
　　1900/1953. The interpretation of dreams. In J. Strachey (ed.), *The standard edition of the complete psychological works of Sigmund Freud*, vol. IV. London: Hogarth Press

1909/1955. Notes upon a case of obsessional neurosis. In J. Strachey (ed.), *The standard edition of the complete psychological works of Sigmund Freud,* vol. X. London: Hogarth Press

1915/1956. Papers on metapsychology. In J. Strachey (ed.), *The standard edition of the complete psychological works of Sigmund Freud,* vol. XIV. London: Hogarth Press

1917/1957. A metapsychological supplement to the theory of dreams. In J. Strachey (ed.), *The standard edition of the complete psychological works of Sigmund Freud,* vol. XV. London: Hogarth Press

1937/1964. Analysis terminable and interminable. In J. Strachey (ed.), *The standard edition of the complete psychological works of Sigmund Freud,* vol. XXIII. London: Hogarth Press

1938/1964. The splitting of the ego in the process of defence. In J. Strachey (ed.), *The standard edition of the complete psychological works of Sigmund Freud,* vol. XXIII. London: Hogarth Press

Fromm, E. 1970. *The crisis of psychoanalysis: essays on Freud, Marx and social psychology.* Harmondsworth: Penguin Books

Furby, L. 1979. Individualistic bias in studies of locus of control. In A. R. Buss (ed.), *Psychology in social context.* New York: Irvington Publishers

1983. 'Consistency' and 'Contradiction' in the development of gender role characteristics. *New Ideas in Psychology,* 1, 285–97

Furnham, A. 1982. Why are the poor always with us? Explanations for poverty in Britain. *British Journal of Social Psychology,* 21, 311–22

Gadamer, H. G. 1975. *Truth and method.* London: Sheed & Ward Ltd

Gauld, A. and Shotter, J. 1977. *Human action and its psychological investigation.* London: Routledge & Kegan Paul

Gavanski, I. and Hoffman, C. 1987. Awareness of influences on one's own judgements: the roles of covariation detection and attention to the judgement process. *Journal of Personality and Social Psychology,* 52, 453–63

Gergen, K. J. 1973. Social psychology as history. *Journal of Personality and Social Psychology,* 26, 309–20

1977. The social construction of self-knowledge. In T. Mischel (ed.), *The self in social psychology.* London: Blackwell

1980. Toward intellectual audacity in social psychology. In R. Gilmour and S. Duck (eds.), *The development of social psychology.* London: Academic Press

1982. *Toward transformation in social knowledge.* New York: Springer-Verlag

Gergen, K. J. and Morawski, J. 1980. An alternative metatheory for social psychology. In L. Wheeler (ed.), *Review of personality and social psychology,* vol. I. Beverly Hills, Calif.: Sage

Giddens, A. 1976. *New rules of sociological method: a positive critique of interpretative sociologies.* London: Hutchinson

1977. *Studies in social and political theory.* London: Hutchinson

Ginsburg, G. B. 1979. *Emerging strategies of social psychological research.* London: Wiley

Glasser, W. 1965. *Reality therapy: a new approach to psychiatry.* New York: Harper & Row

Glover, E. 1955. The *techniques of psychoanalysis.* New York: International Universities Press

Golin, S., Sweeney, P. D. and Shaeffer, D. E. 1981. The causality of causal attributions in depression: a cross-lagged panel correlational analysis. *Journal of Abnormal Psychology*, **90**, 14–22

Goodstadt, B. E. and Hjelle, L. A. 1973. Power to the powerless: locus of control and the use of power. *Journal of Personality and Social Psychology*, **27**, 190–6

Gottlieb, A. 1977. Social psychology as history or science: an addendum. *Personality and Social Psychology Bulletin*, **3**, 207–10

Gowler, D. and Legge, K. 1981. Negation, synthesis and abomination in rhetoric. In C. Antaki (ed.), *The psychology of ordinary explanations of social behaviour*. London: Academic Press

Greenwald, A. G. and Pratkanis, A. R. 1984. The self. In R. S. Wyer and T. K. Srull (eds.), *Handbook of social cognition*, vol. III. Hillsdale, N.J.: Erlbaum

Grice, H. P. 1975. Logic and conversation. In P. Cole and J. Morgan (eds.), *Syntax and semantics 3: speech acts*. New York: Academic Press

Grinder, J. and Bandler, R. 1976. *The structure of magic*, vol. II. Palo Alto, Calif.: Science and Behavior Books

Grinker, J. 1969. Cognitive control of classical eyelid conditioning. In P. G. Zimbardo, *The cognitive control of motivation*. Glenview, Ill.: Scott, Foresman

Gurin, P., Gurin, G., Lao, R. C. and Beattie, M. 1969. Internal-external control in the motivational dynamics of Negro youth. *Journal of Social Issues*, **25**, 29–53

Habermas, J. 1970. On systematically distorted communication. *Inquiry*, **13**, 205–18

1971. *Knowledge and human interests*. Boston: Beacon Press

Hammen, C., Adrian, C. and Hiroto, D. 1988. A longitudinal test of the attributional vulnerability model in children at risk for depression. *British Journal of Clinical Psychology*, **27**, 37–46

Hansen, R. D. and Hall, C. A. 1985. Discounting and augmenting facilitatory and inhibitory causes: the winner takes almost all. *Journal of Personality and Social Psychology*, **49**, 1482–93

Hanson, N. R. 1958. *Patterns of discovery*. Cambridge: Cambridge University Press

Harré, R. 1974. Blueprint for a new science. In N. Armistead (ed.), *Reconstructing social psychology*. Harmondsworth: Penguin Books

1981a. Expressive aspects of descriptions of others. In C. Antaki (ed.), *The psychology of ordinary explanations of social behaviour*. London: Academic Press

1981b. Rituals, rhetoric and social cognition. In J. Forgas (ed.), *Social cognition: perspectives on everyday understanding*. London: Academic Press

Harré, R. and Secord, P. F. 1972. *The explanation of social behaviour*. Oxford: Basil Blackwell

Harris, B. and Harvey, J. H. 1981. Attribution theory: from phenomenal causality to the intuitive scientist and beyond. In C. Antaki (ed.), *The psychology of ordinary explanations of social behaviour*. London: Academic Press

Hart, H. L. A. and Honoré, T. 1985. *Causation in the law*, 2nd edn. Oxford: Clarenden Press

Harvey, J. H. 1981. Do we need another gloss on 'attribution theory'? *British Journal of Social Psychology*, **20**, 301–4

Harvey, J. H., Harris, B. and Barnes, R. D. 1975. Actor-observer differences in the perceptions of responsibility and freedom. *Journal of Personality and Social Psychology*, **32**, 22–8

Harvey, J. H. and Tucker, T. 1979. On problems with the cause-reason distinction in attribution theory. *Journal of Personality and Social Psychology*, **37**, 1441–6

Harvey, J. H., Yarkin, K. L., Lightner, J. M., and Town, J. P. 1980. Unsolicited interpretation and recall in interpersonal events. *Journal of Personality and Social Psychology*, **38**, 551–68

Hastie, R. and Kumar, P. A. 1979. Person memory: personality traits as organizing principles in memory for behavior. *Journal of Personality and Social Psychology*, **37**, 25–38

Hegel, G. 1966. *The phenomenology of mind*, first published 1807. New York: Allen, Unwin and Son

Heider, F. 1958. *The psychology of interpersonal relations*. New York: Wiley

Heisenberg, W. 1971. *Physics and beyond*. London: Harper & Row

Hewstone, M. and Jaspars, J. 1984. Social dimensions of attributions. In H. Tajfel (ed.), *The social dimension: European developments in social psychology*, vol. II. Cambridge: Cambridge University Press

Hewstone, M., Jaspars, J. and Lalljee, M. 1982. Social representation, social attribution and social identity: the intergroup images of 'public' and 'comprehensive' schooldays. *European Journal of Social Psychology*, **12**, 241–69

Hilton, D. J. and Knott, I. C. 1988. Personal causality and conditional reasoning: content effects in commonsense explanation. Unpublished manuscript, University of Indiana

Hiroto, D. S. 1974. Locus of control and learned helplessness. *Journal of Experimental Psychology*, **102**, 187–93

Hiroto, D. S. and Seligman, M. E. P. 1975. Generality of learned helplessness in man. *Journal of Personality and Social Psychology*, **31**, 311–27

Holroyd, K. A. 1978. Effectiveness of an 'Attribution Therapy' manipulation with test anxiety. *Behaviour Therapy*, **9**, 526–34

Jaggar, A. M. 1983. *Feminist politics and human nature*. Totowan, N.J.: Rowman & Allanheld

Jahoda, M. 1979. The impact of unemployment in the 1930s and the 1970s. *Bulletin of the British Psychological Society*, **32**, 309–14

Jay, M. 1973. *The dialectical imagination: a history of the Frankfurt School and the Institute of Social Research 1923–1950*. London: Heinemann

Jaynes, J. 1976. *The origin of consciousness in the breakdown of the bicameral mind*. Boston: Houghton Mifflin

Jensen, A. R. 1969. How much can we boost I.Q. and scholastic achievement? *Harvard Educational Review*, **39**, 1–123

Jones, E. E. 1979. The rocky road from acts to attributions. *American Psychologist*, **34**, 107–17

Jones, E. E. and Davis, K. E. 1965. From acts to dispositions: the attribution process in person perception. In L. Berkowitz (ed.), *Advances in experimental social psychology*, vol. II. New York: Academic Press

Jung, C. G. 1953. The relations between the ego and the unconscious. In *The collected works of C. G. Jung*, vol. VII. Princeton, N.J.: Princeton University Press

Kahn, A., Hottes, J. and Davis, W. L. 1971. Cooperation and optimal responding in the prisoner's dilemma game: effects of sex and physical attractiveness. *Journal of Personality and Social Psychology*, **17**, 267–79

Kamin, L. J. 1974. The science and politics of I.Q. *Social Research*, **41**, 387–425

Kant, I. 1785/1964. *The groundwork of the foundations of morals*. Translated by H. J. Paton. New York: Harper & Row

Kaufman, A., Baron, A. and Kopp, R. E. 1966. Some effects of instructions on human operant behaviour. *Psychonomic Monograph Supplements*, 1, 243–50

Kelley, H. H. 1967. Attribution theory in social psychology. In D. Levine (ed.), *Nebraska Symposium on Motivation*, vol. XV. Lincoln: University of Nebraska Press

  1972a. Attribution in social interaction. In E. E. Jones *et al.* (eds.), *Attribution: perceiving the causes of behavior*. Morristown, N.J.: General Learning Press

  1972b. Causal schemata and the attribution process. In E. E. Jones *et al.* (eds.), *Attribution: perceiving the causes of behavior*. Morristown, N.J.: General Learning Press

  1973. The process of causal attribution. *American Psychologist*, **28**, 107–28

  1980. Magic tricks: the management of causal attribution. In D. Gorlitz (ed.), *Perspectives on attribution research and theory: the Bielefeld Symposium*. Cambridge, Mass.: Ballinger

Kelley, H. H. and Michela, J. 1980. Attribution theory and research. *Annual Review of Psychology*, **31**, 457–501

Klein, D. B. 1977. *The unconscious: invention or discovery?* Santa Monica, Calif.: Goodyear

Kleinke, C. L. 1978. *Self-perception: the psychology of personal awareness*. San Francisco: Freeman

Kraut, R. E. and Higgins, E. T. 1984. Communication and social cognition. In R. S. Wyer and T. K. Srull (eds.), *Handbook of social cognition*, vol. II. Hillsdale, N.J.: Erlbaum

Kruglanski, A. W. 1979. Causal explanation, teleological explanational: on radical particularism in attribution theory. *Journal of Personality and Social Psychology*, **37**, 1447–57

Kruglanski, A. W. and Ajzen, I. 1983. Bias and error in human judgement. *European Journal of Social Psychology*, **13**, 1–44

Kruglanski, A. W., Baldwin, M. W. and Towson, S. M. J. 1983. The lay epistemic process in attribution making. In M. Hewstone (ed.), *Attribution theory: social and functional extensions*. Oxford: Blackwell

Kruglanski, A. W., Schwartz, J. M., Maides, S. and Hamel, I. Z. 1978. Covariation, discounting, and augmentation: towards a clarification of attributional principles. *Journal of Personality*, **64**, 176–89

Kuhn, T. S. 1970. *The structure of scientific revolutions*, 2nd edn. Chicago, Ill.: The University of Chicago Press

Kun, A. and Weiner, B. 1973. Necessary versus sufficient causal schemata for success and failure. *Journal of Research in Personality*, **7**, 197–207

Labov, W. and Fanshel, D. 1977. *Therapeutic discourse: psychotherapy as conversation*. New York: Academic Press

Laing, R. D. 1960/1969. *The divided self*. London: Tavistock, 1960. Penguin edition, 1969

  1961/1971. *Self and others*. London: Tavistock, 1961. Penguin edition, 1971

  1971. *The politics of the family and other essays*. London: Tavistock

Laing, R. D. and Esterson, A. 1964/1970. *Sanity, madness and the family*. London: Tavistock, 1964. Penguin edition 1970

Lakatos, I. and Musgrave, A. 1970. *Criticism and the growth of knowledge*. Cambridge: Cambridge University Press

Lalljee, M. and Abelson, R. P. 1983. The organization of explanations. In M.

Hewstone (ed.), *Attribution theory: social and functional extensions*. Oxford: Basil Blackwell

Larsen, K. S. 1986. Development of theory: the dialectic in behaviourism and humanism. In Larsen (ed.). 1986. *Dialectics and ideology in psychology*. Norwood, N.J.: Ablex

(ed.). 1986b. *Dialectics and ideology in psychology*. Norwood, N.J.: Ablex

Lasch, C. 1978. *The culture of narcissism*. New York: Norton

Latané, B. and Darley, J. M. 1970. *The unresponsive bystander: why doesn't he help?* New York: Appleton-Century-Crofts

Leddo, J., Abelson, R. P. and Gross, P. H. 1984. Conjunctive explanations: when two reasons are better than one. *Journal of Personality and Social Psychology*, 47, 933–43

Leech, G. N. and Svartvik, J. 1975. *A communicative grammar of English*. London: Longman

Lefcourt, H. M. 1976. *Locus of control*. Hillsdale, N.J.: Erlbaum

Leiss, W. 1972. *The domination of nature*. New York: George Braziller

Lerner, M. J. 1977. The justice motive: some hypotheses as to its origins and forms. *Journal of Personality*, 45, 1–52

Lewis, W. 1972. *Why people change: the psychology of influence*. New York: Holt, Rinehart & Winston

Lidz, T. 1973. *The origin and treatment of schizophrenic disorders*. New York: Basic Books

Locke, D. and Pennington, D. 1982. Reasons and causes in attribution processes. *Journal of Personality and Social Psychology*, 42, 212–33

Luria, A. R. 1959. The directive function of speech in development and dissolution. *Word*, 15, 341–52

Lynn, R. 1982. IQ in Japan and the United States shows a growing disparity. *Nature*, 297, 222–3

McClure, J. L. 1978. The socio-historical context of intercontinental discrimination in social psychology. Unpublished manuscript, University of Auckland

1983. Telling more than they can know: the positivist account of verbal reports and mental processes. *Journal for the Theory of Social Behaviour*, 13, 111–27

1984. On necessity and common sense: a discussion of central axioms in new approaches to lay explanation. *European Journal of Social Psychology*, 14, 123–49

1985. The social parameter of 'learned' helplessness: its recognition and implications. *Journal of Personality and Social Psychology*, 48, 1534–9

1987. The discounting principle in attribution theory. D.Phil. thesis. University of Oxford

1989a. Discounting causes of behaviour: two decades of research. Unpublished manuscript, Victoria University of Wellington

1989b. Explanations, discourse, and attributions: a response to Michael. *New Ideas in Psychology*, 7, 249–52

McClure, J. L., Jaspars, J. and Lalljee, M. 1989. Are explanations for intellectual and physical outcomes the same? Unpublished manuscript, Victoria University of Wellington

McClure, J. L., Lalljee, M. and Jaspars, J. 1988. Explanations for extreme and moderate events. Unpublished manuscript, Victoria University of Wellington

McClure, J. L., Lalljee, M., Jaspars, J. and Abelson, R. P. 1989. Conjunctive explanations of success and failure: the effects of different types of causes. *Journal of Personality and Social Psychology*, **56**, 19–26

MacIntyre, A. C. 1971. *Against the self-images of the age: essays on ideology and philosophy.* London: Duckworth

Malcolm, N. 1964. Behaviorism as a philosophy of psychology. In T. H. Wann (ed.), *Behaviorism and phenomenology.* Chicago, Ill.: University of Chicago Press

Marcuse, H. 1955. *Eros and civilization: a philosophical inquiry into Freud.* Boston: Beacon Press

1964. *One dimensional man.* London: Routledge & Kegan Paul, 1964

Markus, H. 1977. Self-schemata and processing information about the self. *Journal of Personality and Social Psychology*, **35**, 63–78

Marx, K. 1845/1961. Economic and philosophical manuscripts. In T. B. Bottomore and M. Rubel (eds.), *Karl Marx: selected writings in sociology and social philosophy.* Harmondsworth: Penguin

1859/1961. Preface to a contribution to the critique of political economy. In T. B. Bottomore and M. Rubel (eds.) *Karl Marx: selected writings in sociology and social philosophy.* Harmondsworth: Penguin

1867/1961. Das Kapital. In T. B. Bottomore and M. Rubel (eds.), *Karl Marx: selected writings in sociology and social philosophy.* Harmondsworth: Penguin

Maslow, A. H. 1970. *Motivation and personality*, 2nd edn. New York: Harper & Row

Meichenbaum, D. H. 1977. *Cognitive-behavior modification: an integrative approach.* New York: Plenum Press

Michael, M. 1989. Attribution and ordinary explanation: cognitivist predilections and pragmatist alternatives. *New Ideas in Psychology*, **7**, 231–43

Michotte, A. 1963. *The perception of causality.* London: Methuen

Miller, D. T. 1976. Ego involvement and attribution for success and failure. *Journal of Personality and Social Psychology*, **34**, 901–6

Miller, D. T. and Ross, M. 1975. Self-serving biases in the attribution of causality: fact or fiction? *Psychological Bulletin*, **82**, 213–25

Miller, W. R. and Seligman, M. E. P. 1976. Learned helplessness, depression and the perception of reinforcement. *Behaviour Research and Therapy*, **14**, 7–17

Mischel, W. 1968. *Personality and assessment.* New York: Wiley

Mittroff, I. I. 1974. On doing empirical philosophy of science: a case study in the social psychology of research. *Philosophy of the Social Sciences*, **4**, 183–96

Monson, T. C. and Snyder, M. 1977. Actors, observers and the attribution process: toward a reconceptualization. *Journal of Experimental Social Psychology*, **13**, 89–111

Morris, P. 1981. The cognitive psychology of self-reports. In C. Antaki (ed.), *The psychology of ordinary explanations of social behaviour.* London: Academic Press

Moscovici, S. 1976. *La psychoanalyse, son image et son public*, 2nd edn. Paris: P.U.F.

1981. On social representations. In J. P. Forgas (ed.), *Social cognition: perspectives on everyday understanding.* London: Academic Press

1982. The coming era of representations. In J.-P. Codol and J.-P. Leyens (eds.), *Cognitive analysis of social behavior.* The Hague: Martinus Nijhoff

1984. The phenomenon of social representations. In R. M. Farr and S. Moscovici (eds.), *Social representations.* Cambridge: Cambridge University Press

Mowrer, O. H. 1948. Learning theory and the neurotic paradox. *American Journal of Orthopsychiatry*, **18**, 571–610

Neisser, U. 1980. On 'social knowing'. *Personality and Social Psychology Bulletin*, **6**, 601–5

Nesselroade, J. R. and Baltes, P. B. 1974. *Adolescent personality development and historical change: 1970–1972*. Pennsylvania: Pennsylvania State University

Neu, J. 1977. *Emotion, thought and therapy*. Berkeley, Calif.: University of California Press

Nisbett, R. E. and Ross, L. 1980. *Human inference: strategies and shortcomings of social judgement*. Englewood Cliffs, N.J.: Prentice-Hall

Nisbett, R. E. and Wilson, T. D. 1977. Telling more than we can know: verbal reports on mental processes. *Psychological Review*, **84**, 231–59

Oakes, W. F. and Curtis, N. 1982. Learned helplessness: not dependent upon cognitions, attributions, or other phenomenal experiences. *Journal of Personality*, **50**, 387–408

Ostrom, T. M. 1984. The sovereignty of social cognition. In R. S. Wyer and T. K. Srull (eds.), *Handbook of social cognition*, vol. 1. Hillsdale, N.J.: Erlbaum

Parker, I. 1989. *The crisis in modern social psychology – and how to end it*. London: Routledge

Parry, G. and Brewin, C. R. 1988. Cognitive style and depression: symptom-related, event-related or independent provoking factor? *British Journal of Clinical Psychology*, **27**, 23–35

Peterson, C. and Seligman, M. E. P. 1984. Causal explanations as a risk factor for depression: theory and evidence. *Psychological Review*, **91**, 347–74

Pettigrew, J. 1979. The ultimate attribution error: extending Allport's cognitive analysis of prejudice. *Personality and Social Psychology Bulletin*, **5**, 461–76

Phares, E. J. 1957. Expectancy changes in skill and chance situations. *Journal of Abnormal and Social Psychology*, **54**, 339–42

1976. *Locus of control in personality*. Morristown, N.J.: General Learning Press

Piaget, J. 1965. *The moral judgement of the child*. New York: Free Press

Polanyi, M. 1964. *Personal knowledge*. New York: Harper

Popper, K. R. 1959. *The logic of scientific discovery*. New York: Basic Books

1972. *Conjectures and refutations: the growth of scientific knowledge*. London: Routledge & Kegan Paul

Potter, J. and Mulkay, M. 1982. Making theory useful: utility accounting in social psychologists' discourse. *Fundamenta Scientiae*, **34**, 258–78

Potter, J. and Wetherell, M. 1987. *Discourse and social psychology: beyond attitudes and behaviour*. London: Sage

Rabkin, R. 1977. Critique of the clinical use of the double bind hypothesis. In C. E. Sluzki and D. C. Ransom (eds.), *Double bind: the foundation of the communicational approach to the family*. New York: Grune & Stratton

Raimy, V. 1975. *Misunderstandings of the self*. San Francisco, Calif.: Jossey-Bass

Rappaport, J. 1977. *Community psychology: values, research, and action*. New York: Holt, Rinehart & Winston

Reeder, G. D. and Brewer, M. B. 1979. A schematic model of dispositional attribution in interpersonal perception. *Psychological Review*, **86**, 61–79

Reeder, G. D. and Fulks, J. L. 1980. When actions speak louder than words: implicational schemata and the attribution of ability. *Journal of Experimental Social Psychology*, **16**, 33–46

Reeves, R. A., Richardson, D. C. and Hendrick, C. 1979. Bibliography of journal articles in personality and social psychology: 1978. *Personality and Social Psychology Bulletin*, **5**, 524–42

Reich, W. 1934/1972. Dialectical materialism and psychoanalysis. In W. Reich, *Sex-pol: essays 1929–1934*. New York: Vintage Books

Ricoeur, P. 1970. *Freud and philosophy: an essay on interpretation*. New Haven, Conn.: Yale University Press

1974. *The conflict of interpretations: essays in hermeneutics*. Evanston, Ill.: Northwestern University Press

Riegel, K. F. 1979. *Foundations of dialectical psychology*. New York: Academic Press

Rizley, R. 1978. Depression and distortion in the attribution of causality. *Journal of Abnormal Psychology*, **87**, 32–48

Robinson, R. V. and Bell, W. 1978. Equality, success and social justice in England and the United States. *American Sociological Review*, **43**, 125–43

Rogers, C. R. 1951. *Client-centered therapy: its current practice, implications and theory.* Boston: Houghton Mifflin

1957. The necessary and sufficient conditions of therapeutic personality change. *Journal of Consulting Psychology*, **21**, 95–103

1959. A theory of therapy, personality, and interpersonal relationships, as developed in the client-centered framework. In S. Koch (ed.), *Psychology: a study of a science*, vol. III. *Formulations of the person and the social context*. New York: McGraw-Hill

1961. *On becoming a person*. Boston: Houghton Mifflin

1970. Foreword. In J. T. Hart and T. M. Tomlinson (eds.), *New directions in client-centered therapy*. Boston: Houghton Mifflin

1974. In retrospect: forty-six years. *American Psychologist*, **29**, 115–23

Rommetveit, R. 1974. *On message structure*. London: Wiley

Rorty, R. 1970. Incorrigibility as the mark of the mental. *The Journal of Philosophy*, **67**, 399–424

Rosenfield, D. and Stephan, W. G. 1977. When discounting fails: an unexpected finding. *Memory and Cognition*, **5**, 97–102

Rosenthal, D. 1970. *Genetic theory and abnormal behaviour*. New York: McGraw-Hill

Rosenthal, R. 1966. *Experimental effects in behavioural research*. New York: Appleton-Century-Crofts

Ross, L. 1977. The intuitive psychologist and his shortcomings: distortions in the attribution process. In L. Berkowitz (ed.), *Advances in experimental social psychology*, vol. X. New York: Academic Press

Ross, L., Lepper, M. R. and Hubbard, M. 1975. Perseverance in self-perception and social perception: biased attributional processes in the debriefing paradigm. *Journal of Personality and Social Psychology*, **32**, 880–92

Ross, L., Rodin, J. and Zimbardo, P. G. 1969. Toward an attribution therapy: the reduction of fear through induced cognitive-emotional misattribution. *Journal of Personality and Social Psychology*, **12**, 279–88

Roth, S. and Kubal, L. 1975. Effects of noncontingent reinforcement on tasks of differing importance: facilitation and learned helplessness. *Journal of Personality and Social Psychology*, **32**, 680–91

Rotter, J. B. 1966. Generalized expectancies for internal versus external control of reinforcement. *Psychological Monographs*, **80** (whole no. 609)

Rotter, J. B., Liverant, S. and Crowne, D. P. 1961. The growth and extinction of expectancies in chance controlled and skilled tasks. *Journal of Psychology*, **52**, 161–77

Rychlak, J. F. 1968. *A philosophy of science for personality theory*. Boston: Houghton Mifflin

1973. *Introduction to personality and psychotherapy: a theory-construction approach*. Boston: Houghton Mifflin

(ed.), 1976. *Dialectic: humanistic rationale for behavior and development*. Basle: S. Karger

1977. *The psychology of rigorous humanism*. New York: Wiley

Sampson, E. E. 1975. On justice as equality. *Journal of Social Issues*, **31**, 45–64

1983. *Justice and the critique of pure psychology*. New York: Plenum

Scarr, S. 1981. *Race, social class and individual differences in I.Q.* Hillsdale, N.J.: Erlbaum

Schachter, S. and Singer, J. 1962. Cognitive, social physiological determinants of emotional state. *Psychological Review*, **39**, 379–99

Schank, R. and Abelson, R. P. 1977. *Scripts, plans, goals and understanding: an inquiry into human knowledge structures*. Hillsdale, N.J.: Erlbaum

Schneider, D. J., Hastorf, A. H. and Ellsworth, P. C. 1979. *Person perception*, 2nd edn. Reading, Mass.: Addison-Wesley

Schneider, W. and Shiffrin, R. M. 1977. Controlled and automatic human information processing. I: detection, search and attention. *Psychological Review*, **84**, 1–66

Schustack, M. W. and Sternberg, R. J. 1981. Evaluation of evidence in causal inference. *Journal of Experimental Psychology: General*, **110**, 101–20

Scott, K. 1989. Self-perception. Unpublished manuscript, Victoria University of Wellington

Sears, D. O. 1986. College sophomores in the laboratory: influences of a narrow data base on social psychology's view of human nature. *Journal of Personality and Social Psychology*, **51**, 515–30

Seligman, M. E. P. 1974. Depression and learned helplessness. In R. J. Friedman and M. M. Katz (eds.), *The psychology of depression: contemporary theory and research*. Washington, D.C.: V. H. Winston

1975. *Helplessness: on depression, development and death*. San Francisco, Calif.: Freeman

Seligman, M. E. P. and Maier, S. F. 1967. Failure to escape traumatic shock. *Journal of Experimental Psychology*, **74**, 1–9

Semin, G. R. 1980. A gloss on attribution theory. *British Journal of Social Psychology*, **19**, 291–300

Semin, G. R. and Manstead, A. S. R. 1983. *The accountability of conduct: a social psychological analysis*. London: Academic Press

Shaklee, H. and Fischhoff, B. 1982. Strategies of information search in causal analysis. *Memory and Cognition*, **10**, 520–30

Sherif, M. 1966. *Group conflict and cooperation*. London: Routledge & Kegan Paul

Sherman, S. J. 1980. On the self-erasing nature of errors in prediction. *Journal of Personality and Social Psychology*, **39**, 211–21

Shields, S. 1975. Functionalism, Darwinism, and the psychology of women: a study in social myth. *American Psychologist*, **30**, 739–54

Shotter, J. 1980. Men the magicians: the duality of social being and the structure of social worlds. In A. J. Chapman and D. M. Jones (eds.), *Models of man.* Leicester: British Psychological Society

1981a. Telling and reporting: prospective and retrospective uses of self-ascriptions. In C. Antaki (ed.), *The psychology of ordinary explanations of social behaviour.* London: Academic Press

1981b. Are Fincham's and Schultz's findings empirical findings? *British Journal of Social Psychology,* **20,** 121–3

1984. *Social accountability and selfhood.* Oxford: Basil Blackwell

Simon, H. A. 1976. Discussion: cognition and social behaviour. In J. S. Carroll and J. W. Payne (eds.), *Cognition and social behaviour.* New York: Lawrence Erlbaum Associates

Singerman, K. J., Borkovec, T. D. and Baron, R. S. 1976. Failure of a 'misattribution therapy' manipulation with a clinically relevant target behaviour. *Behaviour Therapy,* **7,** 306–13

Skinner, B. F. 1938. *The behaviour of organisms: an experimental analysis.* New York: Appleton-Century

1953. *Science and human behaviour.* New York: The Free Press

1969. *Contingencies of reinforcement: a theoretical analysis.* New York: Meredith

1971. *Beyond freedom and dignity.* New York: Knopf

1974. *About behaviourism.* New York: Knopf

Slugoski, B. R. 1983. Attributions in conversational context. Paper presented at British Psychological Society Social Psychology Section Conference, Sheffield

Sluzki, C. E. and Ransom, D. C. (eds.). 1977. *Double bind: the foundation of the communicational approach to the family.* New York: Grune & Stratton

Sluzki, C. E. and Veron, E. 1977. The double bind as a universal pathogenic situation. In C. E. Sluzki and D. C. Ransom (eds.), *Double bind: the foundation of the communicational approach to the family.* New York: Grune & Stratton

Smart, B. 1976. *Sociology, phenomenology and Marxian analysis: a critical discussion of the theory and practice of a science of society.* London: Routledge & Kegan Paul

Smith, E. R. and Miller, F. D. 1978. Limits on perception of cognitive processes: a reply to Nisbett and Wilson. *Psychological Review,* **85,** 355–62

Smith, M. B. 1974. *Humanizing social psychology.* San Francisco, Calif.: Jossey-Bass

Snyder, M. L. and Wicklund, R. A. 1981. Attribute ambiguity. In J. H. Harvey, W. Ickes and R. F. Kidd (eds.), *New directions in attribution research,* vol. III. Hillsdale, N.J.: Erlbaum

Snyder, M. L., Stephan, W. G. and Rosenfield, D. 1976. Egotism and attribution. *Journal of Personality and Social Psychology,* **33,** 435–41

Solomon, R. C. 1972. *From rationalism to existentialism: the existentialists and their nineteenth century backgrounds.* Brighton: Harvester Press

Stam, H. J. 1987. The psychology of control: a textual critique. In H. J. Stam, T. B. Rogers and K. J. Gergen (eds.), *The analysis of psychological theory: metapsychological perspectives.* Washington: Hemisphere

Stevens, L. and Jones, E. E. 1976. Defensive attribution and the Kelley cube. *Journal of Personality and Social Psychology,* **34,** 808–20.

Stevens, S. S. 1939. Psychology and the science of science. *Psychological Bulletin,* **36,** 221–63

Storms, M. D. and Nisbett, R. E. 1970. Insomnia and the attribution process. *Journal of Personality and Social Psychology,* **2,** 319–28

Sullivan, H. S. 1953. *The interpersonal theory of psychiatry.* New York: Norton

Sweeney, P. O., Anderson, K. and Bailey, S. 1986. Attributional style in depression: a meta-analytic review. *Journal of Personality and Social Psychology,* **50,** 974–91

Tabachnik, N., Crocker, J. and Alloy, L. B. 1983. Depression, social comparison, and the false-consensus effect. *Journal of Personality and Social Psychology,* **45,** 688–99

Tajfel, H. 1974. Intergroup behaviour, social comparison and social change. Katz–Newcomb lecture, University of Michigan

(ed.) 1978. *Differentiation between social groups.* London: Academic Press

Taylor, C. 1964. *The explanation of behaviour.* London: Routledge & Kegan Paul

Taylor, S. E. 1976. Developing a cognitive social psychology. In J. S. Carroll and W. Payne (eds.), *Cognition and social behavior.* Hillsdale, N.J.: Erlbaum

Taylor, S. E. and Crocker, J. 1981. Schematic bases of social information processing. In E. T. Higgins, C. P. Herman and M. P. Zanna (eds.), *Social cognition: the Ontario Symposium,* vol. I. Hillsdale, N.J.: Erlbaum

Taylor, S. E. and Fiske, S. T. 1978. Salience, attention and attribution: top of the head phenomena. In L. Berkowitz (ed.), *Advances in experimental social psychology,* vol. XI. New York: Academic Press

1981. Getting inside the head. Methodologies for process analysis in attribution and social cognition. In J. H. Harvey, W. Ickes and R. F. Kidd (eds.), *New directions in attribution research,* vol. III. Hillsdale, N.J.: Erlbaum

Tennen, H., Drum, P. E., Gillen, R. and Stanton, A. 1982. Learned helplessness and the detection of contingency: a direct test. *Journal of Personality,* **50,** 426–42

Tennen, H., Gillen, R. and Drum, P. 1982. The debilitating effect of exposure to noncontingent escape: a test of the learned helplessness model. *Journal of Personality,* **50,** 409–25

Thibaut, J. W. and Riecken, H. W. 1955. Some determinants and consequences of the perception of social causality. *Journal of Personality,* **24,** 113–33

Thompson, J. B. 1981. *Critical hermeneutics: a study in the thought of Paul Ricoeur and Jürgen Habermas.* Cambridge: Cambridge University Press

Totman, R. 1980. The incompleteness of ethogenics. *European Journal of Social Psychology,* **10,** 17–41

Truax, C. B. 1966. Reinforcement and non-reinforcement in Rogerian psychotherapy. *Journal of Abnormal Psychology,* **71,** 1–9

Tyler, L. E. 1965. *The psychology of human differences,* 3rd edn. New York: Appleton-Century-Crofts

Valins, S. and Nisbett, R. E. 1971. *Attribution processes in the development and treatment of emotional disorders.* Morristown, N.J.: General Learning Press

Valins, S. and Ray, A. A. 1967. Effects of cognitive desensitization on avoidance behaviour. *Journal of Personality and Social Psychology,* **1,** 345–50

Vallacher, R. R. and Wegner, D. M. 1985. *A theory of action identification.* Hillsdale, N.J.: Erlbaum

1987. What do people think they're doing? Action identification and human behavior. *Psychological Review,* **94,** 3–15

Vygotsky, L. S. 1962. *Thought and language.* Cambridge, Mass.: M.I.T. Press

Walker, N. 1977. *Behaviour and misbehaviour: explanations and non-explanations.* Oxford: Basil Blackwell

Walster, E., Walster, G. W. and Berscheid, E. 1978. *Equity: theory and research.* Boston: Allyn & Bacon

Watson, J. B. 1913. Psychology as the behaviourist views it. *Psychological Review,* **20,** 158–77

Weary, G. and Harvey, J. H. 1981. Evaluation in attribution process. *Journal for the Theory of Social Behaviour,* **11,** 93–8

Wegner, D. M. and Vallacher, R. R. 1986. Action identification. In R. M. Sorrentino and E. T. Higgins (eds.), *Handbook of motivation and cognition: foundations of social behavior.* New York: Guilford

Wein, K. S., Nelson, R. O. and Odom, J. J. 1975. The relative contributions of reattribution and verbal extinction to the effectiveness of cognitive restructuring. *Behaviour Therapy,* **6,** 459–74

Weiner, B. 1988. Attribution theory and attributional therapy: some theoretical observations and suggestions. *British Journal of Clinical Psychology,* **27,** 99–104

White, P. 1980. Limitations on verbal reports of internal events: a refutation of Nisbett and Wilson and of Bem. *Psychological Review,* **87,** 105–12

Wilden, W. and Wilson, T. 1977. The double bind: logic, magic and economics. In C. E. Sluzki and D. C. Ransom (eds.), *Double bind: the foundation of the communicational approach to the family.* New York: Grune & Stratton

Wilensky, R. W. 1983. *Planning and understanding: a computational approach to human reasoning.* Reading, Mass.: Addison-Wesley

Wilson, T. D. 1985. Strangers to ourselves: The origins and accuracy of beliefs about one's own mental states. In J. H. Harvey and G. Weary (eds.), *Attribution: basic issues and applications.* Orlando: Academic Press

Wilson, T. D., Hull, J. G. and Johnson, J. 1981. Awareness and self-perception. Verbal reports on internal states. *Journal of Personality and Social Psychology,* **40,** 53–71

Wilson, T. D. and Stone, J. I. 1985. Limitations on self-knowledge: more on telling more than we can know. In P. Shaver (ed.), *Review of personality and social psychology,* vol. VI. Beverly Hills, Calif.: Sage

Winch, P. 1958. *The idea of a social science.* London: Routledge & Kegan Paul

Wittgenstein, L. 1968. *Philosophical investigations.* Oxford: Blackwell

Wollheim, R. 1971. *Freud.* London: Fontana/Collins

Wuebben, P. L. 1975. *The experiment as a social occasion.* Berkeley, Calif.: Glendessary Press

Wynne, L. C. 1976. Communication disorders and the quest for relatedness in families of schizophrenics. *American Journal of Psychosis,* **30,** 100–14

  1977. On the anguish, and creative passions, of not escaping double binds. In C. E. Sluzki and D. C. Ransom (eds.), *Double bind: the foundation of the communicational approach to the family.* New York: Grune & Stratton

Index of names

Index of subjects

Printed in the United States
48231LVS00004B/4